World of Wonders

The Lyrics and Music of Bruce Cockburn

James A. Heald

Revised and Expanded

Bruce Cockburn's Songs: Used by permission of Rotten Kiddies Music, LLC

Cover Art: Ray Gaytan, Austin, TX, "Defenders of the Forest", Pen & Ink, 1992. Used by permission.

Back Cover Photo by Lindsey Realmuto.

Published by Missing Link Records

ISBN: 1546664777
ISBN-13: 978-1546664772

Dedication

To Laura, you have always been my muse and biggest supporter.
Thank you for everything that you have done to support my
music and writing and for the joy and good times we have shared.

Streaks of Moonlight in your hair
We've got sand between our toes
And we ain't got a care
We'll be like Ginger Rogers and Fred Astaire
Tonight.

CONTENTS

Preface to the 2012 Edition

I don't know Bruce Cockburn personally, but I've been listening to his music fervently since about 1984, have heard him in concert more than half a dozen times, and exchanged awkward pleasantries with him after the last concert when he was signing his latest CD for me. I'm sure I've read dozens of reviews and interviews, subscribed to the "Humans" list-serve, and consider him a dear, if very distant, friend, with whom I feel a great kinship.

I discovered Bruce after reading a review of one of his performances in the Chicago Reader and was intrigued enough to go out and look for recordings at a local record store. All I could find was a cassette copy of **Stealing Fire**. I was hooked by the first notes of *Lovers in a Dangerous Time* and was mesmerized by the entire album. Obviously, I was drawn to the Anti-Imperialist fervor, the humanity, the poetry, and the strong music holding it all together. I picked up a copy of **Trouble with Normal** soon after and I have followed Bruce, album by album, ever since.

I did not immediately go back and get copies of everything that Bruce had ever done. Even if I had wanted to, it was not always easy to get his older records in the States (this was long before Amazon and the Internet). So, my knowledge of his earlier work was somewhat sketchy, filled in now and then by an occasional purchase such as **In the Falling Dark** or the retrospectives and re-releases, like **Waiting for a Miracle** and **Circles in the Stream**. Over the last several years, I have collected all, or almost all, of the rest and have spent many pleasurable hours listening to these songs, along with an eclectic mix of music that ranges from the Beatles to Richard Thompson and a gaggle of obscure singer-songwriters.

I have played the guitar for more than thirty years, written songs for nearly as long, and have performed and recorded with some modest measure of success. Over the years, I have performed a number of Bruce's songs, such as *Wondering Where the Lions Are, If I Had a Rocket*

Launcher, Lovers in a Dangerous Time, Don't Feel Your Touch, Last Night of the World, and *Pacing the Cage.* I have also tried, with limited success, to learn more complicated tunes such as *Train in the Rain* and *Mistress of Storms.*

During all that time I never seriously thought about writing a book, and certainly not a book about Bruce. I was an English major in college and always wanted to be a writer, but never really had the time or the opportunity or the subject to turn that fantasy into a reality. I have probably written enough poetry and songs to turn into a book, but that's another issue entirely. In any event, my creative impulses have generally had to be satisfied by writing and performing songs over the years.

A few years ago, as part of my music web site, I started occasionally blogging and started doing a few record reviews (very few). I did one for **Small Source of Comfort** and another for an acquaintance, the reclusive novelist and songwriter Junior Burke (AKA Thom Bishop), who I had known from Chicago in the late 70's. Junior is the head of the writing program at Naropa University's Kerouac School for Disembodied Poetics. Reengaging with Junior triggered some thoughts about writing a book about the Beats and the 1960's, but the research would have been daunting and it's been done so many times.

Last year [2011], I heard that theologian Bryan Walsh was writing a book about Bruce's Christianity. Given that I was thinking about the Beats, the 60's, poetry and music and writing a book, I thought that maybe Bruce might be a good subject for a book. I also thought that a book about his Christianity might not adequately present a picture of the songwriter that I had listened to and loved for so many years. Coming to Bruce's work starting in the 1980's, during his anti-Imperialist phase, and because I do not consider myself a Christian, I had tended to downplay the specifically Christian content of his work, which was easier to do given my long focus on his post-70's work.

So I did some preliminary research, started listening more intently, and started to write. I have been humbled by the task of trying to grapple with the whole of Bruce's artistic output and make sense of it, both for myself and hopefully for a wider audience. Something in this music has resonated deeply within me, from the first chords that I ever heard. I have responded on personal, political and spiritual levels to his music and the more I listen to it, the more things I find. I view this enterprise as responding to Bruce as one poet and songwriter to another. Hopefully, this has given me an interesting vantage point from which to survey his vast output.

When I started this project I had no idea whether I could finish a book. Writing 3 or 4 minute folk-pop songs is sometimes indicative of a short attention span. As this project expanded from a few days of writing to several months, I surprised myself. The commitment to finishing it actually grew stronger as time went on. And here it is. As Bruce puts it:

The gift
Keeps moving --
Never know
Where it's going to land
You must stand
Back and let it
Keep on changing hands[i]

August 15, 2012

James A. Heald

Preface to the Revised 2017 Edition

Of course, when you put a book out in the world, you get comments, both positive and negative. For this revision, I have tried to incorporate responses to some of the critiques that I have received, but much of the revision is based on further reflection on the subject as well as the publication of Bruce's memoirs *Rumours of Glory*. Songs can have more than a single meaning and quite often have personal meaning for the listeners, based on where and when we heard them, meanings that may be diametrically opposed to the literal meaning of the text. I have tried throughout this book to stick closely to the words on the page, the historical and biographical context of the songs as best as I can determine, and things that Bruce has said about them in interviews. However, I have to take responsibility for the interpretations. They are mine and you are more than welcome to disagree. My disagreement with Brian Walsh's interpretation of Bruce's songs was a significant factor in writing this book in the first place. So, I completely understand that I may be wrong about many things.

When I started this project, it was rumored that Bruce would be publishing his own book imminently, so I may have rushed my original draft into print sooner than I might have otherwise. As a result, there were some parts that I was less satisfied with than I would have liked. On the other hand, I could have fidgeted over little points for months without greatly improving the results.

While I certainly feel the need to acknowledge and respond to things that Bruce wrote about in his memoirs, I don't feel that I would change much of anything, based simply on his book. I think his reflections and stories tend for the most part to reinforce what I have written here and he has been talking about his songs, albums, political and religious views in interviews for over 40 years and those interviews were mined extensively during the writing of this book. Obviously, the personal stories about his life add a visceral dimension to his book that you will only find in glimpses in this work.. A good example of that are the stories that inspired his song *If I had a Rocket Launcher*. While the political and historical information that I provided are relevant and true, his actual experience is what gives the song its power.

Based on the memoir, I did change my analysis of some songs. *The Charity of Night* is a good example. The first vignette in the song, which is about an encounter with a sexual predator on a bridge in Scandinavia. I speculated that it was a story told to Bruce by a friend or acquaintance, mostly because it seemed implausible that Bruce would be carrying a gun in a foreign country and that he might have actually used it. Where would a relatively innocent 19 year old Canadian get a gun in Europe in 1964? Was Sweden so dangerous that his friends thought he would have needed one? In any event, it did happen to him and no shots were fired.

I had the opportunity to meet Bruce almost two years ago when he was signing autographs after a concert at the Rams Head in Annapolis, Maryland. As I was standing in line waiting, I had to work up the confidence to tell him that I had written a book about him. I had sent him a copy through Bernie Finkelstein and had also sent a copy backstage at a concert he gave at the Birchmere in Alexandria, Virginia, but I was never sure if he got it and certainly had no idea whether he had read it.

When I reached the front of the line and told him, he could not have been more gracious. He thanked me for the effort I had put in and we talked for a few moments about the difficulty of writing a book. When I told him that I really appreciated that he had played a favorite song of mine, *Planet of the Clowns*, he thought for a moment and then responded that he recalled I had quite liked the song in my book. It could have been a good guess, but it seemed from that and a couple of other comments that he actually had read the book and appreciated the effort. At least, that is how I choose to remember the encounter.

May 15, 2017

Introduction

Bruce Cockburn is, first and foremost, a visionary artist; engaging and probing songwriter, spiritual seeker, truth teller, and extraordinary guitarist. He is a songwriter's songwriter and musician's musician. If you measure success in album sales, or chart position, or merchandise sales, or mentions in People Magazine or Rolling Stone, then Bruce is not for you. While he has failed to scale the mountain of popular adoration in the United States market, he has nonetheless had an extraordinary career as a Canadian solo artist, and he's done it pretty much entirely on his terms. Given our America Centric view of the entertainment industry (and pretty much everything else), it is hard for us to realize how big a star Bruce is in Canada. It's also hard for us to realize that success outside the U.S. actually means something. We should count ourselves lucky that we have found Bruce and other kindred spirits, like South Africa's Johnny Clegg or Australia's Midnight Oil.

There are very few musicians who have recorded for more than 40 years, putting out consistently good records every couple of years, with few, if any, artistic misfires. He's sold a lot of albums and won a lot of awards. He has continued to gain in popularity and plays to packed venues across Canada, the United States, and Europe, with occasional forays to Japan, Australia and the Far East.

He has traveled to war-torn locations like Central America, Africa, Cambodia, Afghanistan and Iraq as an observer and good will ambassador. The songs that have resulted from these journeys celebrate the resilience of the human spirit, chide the powerful and greedy, and turn a spotlight on corruption and injustice.

On February 20, 2017 Bruce Cockburn received the inaugural Folk Alliance International People's Voice Award during the opening-night awards ceremony at the organization's 29th annual conference in Kansas City, Missouri. The award was created to honor "an individual who unabashedly embraces social and political commentary in their creative work and public careers."[ii] He was presented the award by legendary songwriter and performer Kris Kristofferson. Though pigeonholed early in his career as a Christian singer or the "Canadian John Denver" and later as a political singer, Bruce said that:

> the fact is though, the writing I did started from the premise that I'm supposed to distill what I encounter of the human experience into something that can be communicated, shared. I've never been interested in protest for its own sake, or in ideological polemicizing. Just f***ing tell it like you see it and feel it. If you don't see it and feel it, write about something else. Songs need to come from the heart or they don't count for much.[iii]

You may quibble with his political and personal interpretation of events, but they have been informed and grounded in having been there, from Central America to Chile to Africa and from Baghdad to Nepal and Cambodia. These aren't celebrity photo-ops. He's witnessed war and environmental devastation up close, spending time with and talking with survivors.

He also has many prominent fans and friends in the music world. In a 2001 article, it was revealed that:

> The Who's Pete Townshend, in a surprisingly smart discourse on Canadian music, once raved to me about Cockburn's "lethal intelligence" on the guitar. Bono is another longtime admirer, as is David Crosby of CSN&Y, as was the Grateful Dead's Jerry Garcia.[iv]

In addition to the great Canadian musicians that he has worked with regularly over his career, he's worked with such diverse and talented artists as T Bone Burnett, Jackson Browne, Rob Wasserman, Larry Klein, Jim Keltner, Bonnie Raitt, Sam Phillips, Emmylou Harris, Margo Timmins, Ani DiFranco, Jonatha Brooke, Booker T. Jones, Lucinda Williams, Hugh Marsh, Colin Linden, jazz pianist/composer Andy Milne, and jazz virtuoso Gary Burton. He's had songs covered by Chet Atkins, Jimmy Buffett, Dan Fogelberg, Judy Collins, k.d. lang, the

London Pro Musica Choir, and Jerry Garcia among others.

In 2001, his long-time collaborator Colin Linden:

> recalls a night, in 1992, when he and Cockburn were at a tour stop in Boulder, Colorado. "We were staying at the same hotel as (the late Windham Hill guitar star) Michael Hedges and we had a drink with him after his show. He was just so effusive on how big an influence Bruce was on him." Linden adds: "Bruce is probably the only person in the world that both Michael Hedges and Bono could consider an influence."[v]

In short, he is a musician's musician, appreciated by a large number of other artists from many different genres.

What is my approach to the music and particularly to the lyrics as I move through this world of wonders that Bruce has created over 40 years? My first instinct is to hew close to what he has written and said. Bruce has said repeatedly over the years that, "I don't make any of this shit up. People think it's imagination, but it's not. I don't have any imagination, I just report."[vi] We can take Bruce's comments about imagination with a grain of salt. There's a vast chasm between imagination and "making shit up." As Bruce himself points out in *Child of the Wind*, how you see things, "depends on what you look at obviously/but even more it depends on the way that you see." At the very least, we can consider imagination as part of "the way that you see," which in turn depends on the things that you have read, seen, and experienced. In that light, imagination is the ability to make connections between things that might not appear to be connected on the surface.

Almost without exception, the songs appear to be an attempt to describe actual experiences, thoughts, and feelings. To the extent that the language and phrasing is "poetic" or seems enhanced, I would argue that is part of the attempt to render the feelings and impact of the events as faithfully as possible in order to share them with his audience.

Obviously, Bruce is an extremely spiritual person and that outlook may make it hard for some skeptics to accept that the songs are firmly grounded in "real" experience. We can certainly argue endlessly over what is real and what is merely appearance. How does one describe things that are felt or seen "just beyond the range of normal sight"[vii]?

Most of the other writers who have approached Cockburn's work, aside from music reviewers, have approached it from a "Christian" perspective. While there is nothing inherently wrong with that approach, in practice they have disregarded signs of other obvious spiritual influences on Bruce's work and thought, such as Eastern religion, and non-mainstream Christian thinking like liberation theology.

Dealing with Bruce's spirituality is also only one aspect of this work. Over the course of his life and career, Bruce has embarked on many journeys: spiritual, personal, intellectual, political, musical and even sexual. Evidence of these journeys, with their starts and stops, detours, backtracking, and breakthroughs can be found in the songs. We have been most fortunate to tag along on these journeys and we inevitably find them intertwined with our own journeys, creating a soundtrack for our lives.

No comprehensive overview of Cockburn's musical output currently exists. This is a first stab at creating that overview. But even here, I have had to leave many things out and this book is not a review of the albums. It is about the songs and looks at larger themes in his work. I have not tried to write a biography. Bruce recently finished writing his own memoirs, which were published in November, 2014. Anything I have said on the events of his life that he has not explicitly revealed in interviews or in the memoir is likely to be more speculation than fact. He has been interviewed numerous times over the last 40 years and there is quite a bit of biographical information available, but without his approval and active participation, a biography would be out of the question. The songs, particularly in the early 1980's demand a certain amount of attention to personal issues and events. I will try to limit what I say about his life to things that I think bear directly on the songs.

As a musician, where I can shed some light on his influences, the musical compositions, and the recordings, I will attempt to provide it. I am not a historian, though I have a keen interest in current events and a strong sympathy for Bruce's point of view on issues concerning the Third World, Central America, American Imperialism, the Environment, and Aboriginal rights. To the extent that I can provide insight into some of his references to people and events I have tried to do that as well.

Especially for those not deeply familiar with Bruce's music, I might not recommend reading this book cover to cover as you might read a novel. I would suggest reading a chapter or some manageable chunk and then listening to one of Bruce's albums that relates to the material that you just read. But I have been told by many readers that they did read the book from start to finish, though I hope that during their natural breaks they took the time to listen to a healthy dose of the music. In the end, it's all about the music and the lyrics.

1 Origins

To be one more voice in the human choir
rising like smoke from the mystical fire of the heart

Bruce Cockburn, *Messenger Wind*

Bruce was born in Ottawa in May, 1945 and seems to have had, based on available sources, including his memoirs, a pretty ordinary and happy childhood. His father was a great reader and introduced his son to Greek Mythology, among other subjects. In an interview in 2006, Bruce said that he "was raised going to Sunday school, with the obligation to wear grey flannels on Sunday mornings, which was horrible."[1] His parents were agnostics, but this was the 1950's and conformity was the norm, certainly in the U.S. and Canada.

Bruce gravitated towards music at a fairly early age and as a teen studied guitar and piano and later played in bands and did folk gigs in coffeehouses. He started playing guitar because he idolized Elvis and Buddy Holly and also,

> because my grandmother happened to have one in her attic.
> When that beat-up, low-rent instrument came into my hands at
> the age of 14, I knew it would become a key component of my
> life. When I showed so much interest in it, my parents got me a
> better one. It became a refuge from the horrors of adolescence—a
> step into the world of cool for a nerdy kid with a crappy self-

image.[2]

Despite his obvious interest, his parents had their concerns, particularly about drugs and sex. As he put it: "My parents said that if you promise not to buy a leather jacket and do any of those other things then you can take guitar lessons. So I promised them and then proceeded to break all of those promises."[3]

Among other guitarists, he studied artists like Les Paul and Chet Atkins, who were very popular at the time. Later:

> Towards the end of high school I met some people that played so-called folk music, and I was fascinated. I had never finger-picked before that; I was strictly flat-pick, a little jazzy and a little of that. So, I brought something to my contact with those guys that they didn't have in their background, but here were these guys playing Leadbelly and Brownie McGee songs and finger-picking.[4]

He used to go to a club in Ottawa to listen to the folk music and eventually got a job there as a dishwasher, "to weasel his way into the scene."[5] As he got into folk music and finger-picking, he gravitated towards the old blues players. He mentions several in a 2009 interview in *Acoustic Guitar Magazine*:

> The model for me in terms of adding the finger things was Mississippi John Hurt, who had a style based on an alternating bass and playing a melody on top. It's a beautiful, effective way of making the guitar work with a song, which will translate into almost any kind of music.[6]

Bruce has also listed Bill Broonzy, Lightning Hopkins[7], and Mance Lipscomb[8] as early influences on his guitar style. After finishing high school in 1963, he spent three months in Europe, including playing guitar on the streets of Paris. After that he went to the Berklee School of

Music in Boston for three semesters, where he studied jazz composition and musical theory.[9]

While his class work didn't necessarily leave that much of an imprint on his recorded music, particularly in the early years, the experience was useful and he seems to have absorbed a lot. As he said much later:

> At that time, the jazz guys were starting to explore the music of other cultures. There were people experimenting with Arabic scales. That was exciting to me because it felt fresh. The school was on Newbury Street then. You'd walk up and down the alleys in the Back Bay, and from the apartment windows you'd hear people practicing. It was so rich and had a huge effect on me that hasn't gone away. Also, the Jazz Workshop [legendary jazz club] was around the corner, and I got to hear John Coltrane, Roland Kirk, and a host of people who were incredible players. The technical things that I learned at Berklee have not been a big part of what I do, but the process of learning them put me on a good track.[10]

After his time at Berklee, Bruce played in moderately successful bands in and around Ottawa and Toronto for about three years. In addition to playing the local clubs, they also opened "for The Lovin' Spoonful, Cream, Wilson Pickett, and Jimi Hendrix in Toronto, Ottawa, and Montreal."[11] Bruce officially went solo in 1968, after tiring of the rock scene. Bruce said later that he was "trying to leave behind the years of bad rock bands, trying to clear out psychedelic decadence that was itself a reaction to institutional decadence. Looking for purity in nature. Looking for connections behind things."[12] As he said later, those years also "left me with a little body of songs that I liked better when I played alone"[13] so he ended up going solo.

Bruce was hardly alone in going solo or acoustic. After the Summer of Love and the British Invasions, folk music and singer-songwriters were making a big comeback in 1969 and 1970. The Beatles were breaking up and going their separate ways. Crosby, Stills and Nash had released their first album. John Sebastian went solo at Woodstock. Joni Mitchell had released a couple of albums. The Band was playing their mostly acoustic, country tunes. Jorma and Jack formed Hot Tuna to play old blues and folk tunes. James Taylor burst on the scene. Dylan had reappeared after his seclusion and unplugged again and then went Country with **Nashville Skyline**. And, of course, Gordon Lightfoot was recording *If You Could Read My Mind*, while Glenn Campbell and Johnny Cash were on TV. I could name lots of other folkies who enjoyed some level of fame and notoriety in the waning years of the 60's.[14]

I mention these, not to necessarily draw specific comparisons between Bruce and any of these artists. But at the same time that loud rock & roll was reaching a crescendo, there was a resurgence of more introspective, acoustic-based music. These artists were fellow travelers on the path that Bruce was embarking on.

Bruce had very good fortune in getting his entre into the music business, which is often a black hole for young artists, fraught with bad contracts and bad faith. In 1969, Bruce hooked up with Bernie Finkelstein, who had managed some bands in the Toronto area. Eugene Martynec, who was a guitarist and vocalist for one of these bands, wound up as the producer. Gene had no previous producing experience. Bernie had hardly any money at the time, but was determined to do his own thing by creating an acoustic record label, and True North Records was born. Gene brought Bruce to Bernie's attention and after hearing Bruce perform at the Pornographic Onion in 1969 and a deal was quickly struck. Bruce was more concerned about artistic control than almost anything else. Bernie recalled their negotiations in a 2006 article:

> I remember him saying to me: 'Bernie, I'll only sign with you if you can guarantee to me that I can do the album solo.' I thought, well, this is paradise. I was doing all this with less than $5,000 and I had to book a studio and make album jackets, find distribution, and here was a guy begging me to make a cheap record. Well, okay, let's do it.[15]

4

Despite the explosion of music in the late 50's and 60's, recording was still a very expensive proposition, leaving little opportunity for the do-it-yourselfer. Truly portable tape recording equipment was not available until the late 1970's. In order to do any serious recording in 1969, particularly with a band, you almost had to have a record contract or a rich patron.

Bernie expands upon this version of the story in his recent memoir, including revealing some of his misgivings. Certainly, the financial pressures made it impossible to do a full band recording and Bruce was adamant about doing it solo, but Bernie also thought that they were missing the opportunity to capitalize on the commercial potential of songs like *Going to the Country* and *Musical Friends*. Bernie's memoir gives great insight into the mind of a promoter. He realized that they could sell these acoustic records, despite the lack of a hit, because of the new markets in FM and College Radio combined with strategic touring (good gigs at the right time and place).[16]

In any event, the creation of True North Records, almost accidentally as a vehicle for recording and promoting Bruce's music, gave him a level of artistic control that few novices at the time could have dreamed of. This was both a good and a bad thing. In the short run, it may have inhibited Bruce's commercial success and development.

The fact that all three of them were essentially learning the business, the nuances of recording, and producing at the same time may have had some impacts on the quality, and certainly the distribution reach, of the initial products. The financial constraints that prohibited exploiting the commercial potential of some of Bruce's material and Bruce's resistance to exploiting that same potential contributed to a lower key introduction of his music to a broader public. But who's to say if he wouldn't have been over-exposed and burned out by a more "conventional" path to stardom.

If turning from Rock & Roll to folk and acoustic music was not that unique a career choice, there was one specific area where Bruce and Bernie were definitely swimming against the stream. In the late 60's there really wasn't a Canadian Music Industry. The list of Canadian artists who made it big in the U.S. at that time is staggering and includes such iconic figures as Joni Mitchell, Neil Young, and the Band. Other Canadian exports during that period included Paul Anka, Gordon Lightfoot, the Guess Who, Leonard Cohen, Steppenwolf, and David Clayton-Thomas of Blood, Sweat, and Tears. That fertile cultural exchange has continued to today with the USA probably being the prime beneficiary.

Apprenticeship and Mastery

Bruce's first three albums (**Bruce Cockburn**, **High Winds, White Sky,** and **Sunwheel Dance**) considered together could be seen as part of his apprenticeship and growing mastery in his trade. From the start, his music is imbued with spiritual overtones drawing from a variety of religious traditions. He mixes blues, folk, country, some jazz and even Middle Eastern and Oriental sounds. The first three albums only have two instrumentals, but one is the short, but magnificent *Sunwheel Dance*.

The songs in his first collection, released in 1970, reveal many of the elements that appear throughout his work, although the lyrical content doesn't have, in my opinion, the emotional depth and clarity of his later works. The guitar playing and the musical composition are sure-handed and mature. His characteristically fluid fingerpicking is evident throughout, as is his humor and thoughtfulness. Thematically, he has already begun to play with contrasting symbolism of light and darkness, and contrasting the sometimes dreary urban environment ("Toronto don't take my song away") with the natural environment (*Going to the Country* is all sunshine and happiness).

The songs are introspective and dreamlike. The world that they explore is a small, local world: a trip to the country; a rainy afternoon; a surreal and childlike bicycle trip; drinking and smoking and playing music with his musical friends; contemplating the changing seasons; being "together alone" with a lover; contemplating the sea, and the ice and rock in "Thirteenth Mountain". Solitude predominates and the cast of characters is small and they are little more than ciphers. Even the musical friends are barely described. The most distinct and memorable characters are the cows in *Going to the Country*.

The picture of Bruce that emerges from the first album is that of an intense loner, often lost in thought and preoccupied with spiritual questions and searching. At the same time, he doesn't really belong to a spiritual community. He doesn't see anyone out there who can be his spiritual guide or mentor. He feels like he has to go it alone. The song *Musical Friends* is the only song in the collection where he unequivocally has a companion. His musical friends are great for hanging out with and drinking, singing songs and crashing on a sofa, but the portrait he draws of them is superficial at best. You wouldn't be able to pick them out of a lineup. Even the one true love song in the collection is called *Together Alone*, and he may be daydreaming about his girl rather than actually being with her as the song unfolds. Finally, he keeps his emotions fully in check.

I must admit that prior to starting this project I had only listened to the entire album once or twice. The only song that I have listened to more than a few times over the years is *Going to the Country*, which was collected on **Waiting for a Miracle** in 1987. As I look at these songs, I am looking at them more than 40 years after the fact, through the lens of all of Bruce's subsequent work, and 50 years or so of listening to and sometimes playing the music of his contemporaries in folk, jazz, rock, blues and country.

According to Bruce, the album was recorded in three days.[17] That may have some impact on how listeners might react to the record today and also to its minimal splash in the U.S. market, where it was also hampered by poor distribution. But it seems to have had little impact on how people perceived it at the time in Canada. With a little help from Bernie Finkelstein and a willingness to load his wife and earthly possessions in a camper he started to criss-cross the country and establish himself as a Canadian icon.

Cockburn's second album, **High Winds, White Sky** was released in 1971 and is immediately a much more buoyant and joyful album and a step forward both musically and lyrically. The songs are lyrically more self-assured and the music feels less fragile, the arrangements more complex.

Bruce switches gears to country-folk on *One Day I Walk,* and is supported by an ensemble, including mandolin, banjo and bass with harmony vocals on the chorus. Here, Bruce seems to be in no hurry at all, taking in the good and the bad that life has and will throw his way. He seems to be saying that it's all good and sooner or later he'll get home. He'll stop and smell the roses when he can, and he'll appreciate the stones. The second verse suggests busking on a corner for change, where he's sitting watching the world go by and singing other people's songs ("cried out glad and cried out sad/with every voice but mine").

Let Us Go Laughing starts out as a quiet meditation on nature, with Bruce canoeing at sunset watching the sun slip away and the stars and moon rise. As distant lightning "stirs the cauldron of the sky" he turns the canoe towards the shore. The mood changes during an instrumental interlude and the pace of the music picks up. The music turns into an Irish fiddle tune or jig. Bruce meditates on life and death and in the chorus suggests that we get on with it and "let us go laughing". He hopes the "holy hermit" will "guide you to the shortest path." Solitary meditation is all well and good, he seems to be saying, but we need to move and we need to be with others and "go laughing."

An autumn walk by the sea is the subject of *You Point to the Sky*. He and his lover are enjoying the scenery, talking of how their lives have changed and speculating about the future; they "construct a tapestry of what will come." She "point[s] to the sea" and Bruce "see[s]/what seems to be so free/bound by/ empty sky." In the context of this song that might be a throwaway image or random observation. However, the sea as a symbol of freedom crops up in many other songs, such as *Man of a Thousand Faces* from the first album and most importantly in *All the Diamonds*. At the end of the song, they "tumble down the path" towards home. The final line is a very self-effacing comment about how they are just "comic beggars trading laughs for scraps from the tables of the wise."

As a lyrical statement, the song seems very slight, like a sketch that an artist might make for a later painting. They go for a walk, talk about the past and future and "climb toward the melting point of time" and then go home. And yet it feels like much more than that. Bruce has a way sometimes of making something out of almost nothing, hinting at something much deeper with a few well-place brush strokes. One of the elements of his spirituality and artistry is a very strong sense that there is more to this world than meets the eye and this song seems to capture that perfectly.

The song *Shining Mountain* describes an actual hike or camping trip in the mountains east of Vancouver on a summer day. The mountain is shining in the late afternoon sun. Bruce watches the sun "sink into the sea" and "drown in golden fire." After night falls, the "fireflies danced" and trees and crags "began to sing/above the black forest."

The opening musical phrase picks up from the previous song, the instrumental *Ting/The Cauldron*, and there's a hint of the oriental mood of that piece, but then the song transforms into a slow, medieval folk song, almost chanted rather than sung, about a quest of sorts. Bruce climbs the mountain "to see what I could see" and "to see what I could be." In the final verse, he changes those lines to "to know what I did know" and "to know whence I did know." In other words, Bruce has tested and validated his sense of himself with this journey into the Mountains. Bruce's dense dulcimer picking and steady rhythm frame the lyrics and a gong sounds like a church bell chiming as the song fades out at the end. There was some criticism obliquely directed at Bruce about dropping his performing periodically in the early years to go on long road trips across Canada with his wife. He responds to this criticism in his memoirs as follows:

> Our explorations of the numinous Canadian landscape *fed* the songs, and our souls. We caught the west in the last of its wild state. Many of the songs I wrote in the seventies reflect our

travels through the great expanse of the Canadian prairies, across the Rocky Mountains, to the moisture-rich West Coast. Space was everywhere, and there is *space* in the songs.[18]

There are many songs that one could point to where this is especially true and vivid. The western songs on *Dancing in the Dragons Jaw* or *Celestial Horses,* come immediately to mind.

For me, **Sunwheel Dance,** which was released at the end of 1971, is the first fully realized Bruce Cockburn album. There is still a little roughness around the edges, but the elements are all there. The album has a much fuller sound than the previous albums, but it is still primarily acoustic. Bruce and his producer flesh out the sound with drums, bass, cello, violin, and a sparing use of electric guitar, piano and some electronics. Bruce expands his instrumental contributions to include dulcimer, mandolin, bottleneck guitar, harmonica, piano, and electric guitar.

The album contains several bluesy songs, meditations on nature, a Christian parable, a vision of a conversation with the Devil, his first instrumental masterpiece in the title song, and his first recorded political commentary. While I am discussing most of these songs in the context of his later work, I'd like to comment on a couple of the songs here.

Fall starts out as a minor key folk song/lullaby with a simple strummed accompaniment. Martynec fills in with piano and electronics starting at the second verse and a violin also joins in. Bruce takes a little Django inflected solo after the second verse and the sound gets fuller as the song goes along. Harvest is done, the trees are shedding their leaves, and the season is changing from autumn to winter. Bruce sings to his companion: "Don't cry/we'll walk down the meadow with sunrise inside/so dry your eyes."

When the Sun Falls is a stately violin and dulcimer duet. There's an air of mournfulness in the melody, far more sorrowful than the words would suggest. At sunset, "the bird of paradise spreads his wings" and flies. When the "rain shines/the earth...spreads her hues bright." In the final verse, "You come to me/bringing the sun and rain/bringing my song." I would think that these things would be making him jump for joy. "You" could refer to either a physical being, such as his wife, or to the spirit. But we can only ask, what has made him so sad? Why is he almost mourning while singing this?

For the Birds is pure celebration of nature. The song is comprised of an intricate guitar part and a short, simple verse repeated over and over. It picks up steam and a growing choir and a jaw-harp accompaniment as it goes on. In the simple lyric, "every day/ flashes like a spray of blue jays" while the sun seems to transform them into golden eagles. It is uplifting and joyful, filled with child-like wonder at God's creation.

2 *On the Road*

Feet fall on the road
Bound to motion
Though chains be of gold
They are chains all the same

Bruce Cockburn, *Feet Fall on the Road*

Like many musicians, Bruce Cockburn has spent a lot of time on the road, going from town to town with his guitar in hand and telling his stories to people near and far. Just out of high school he took a boat to Norway and made his way to Paris, busking on the street before heading home. In the early 70's, he drove back and forth across Canada in a camper with his wife and his dog, singing his songs to all who would listen, while soaking up the beauty of the Western landscape and the Maritime coastal regions.

Later his touring expanded to Europe, Japan and South America. He visited Central America, Africa, Nepal, Baghdad, Afghanistan and Southeast Asia as part of Humanitarian missions. In one sense, he was just a kid from Ottawa who'd read Jack Kerouac and thought he might get out and see the world.

The song *Going to the Country*[1], which leads off his debut album, is the first of many songs where the road plays a prominent role. It is simple and direct, one of the most playful and joyful pieces that Bruce has ever written and stands up well to repeated listening. He's looking out the car window and sees "Cows hangin' out under spreading trees." He hits the gas and "zoom! They're gone behind the sign." The wind in his hair "tells me how it feels." He passes a farm house with "silver roof flashing by" and a "tractor-trailer truck says goodbye with a sigh." The birds sing and Bruce echoes them, "singing in my bones." He doesn't care where he's going. He says he'll "get it when I get there is what I'll do" and "if I get enough I'll give some to you."

There is perfect harmony between Bruce and the world expressed through this simple tune. The rhythm is infectious and Bruce deftly mixes finger picking, intricate single note runs and rhythmic strumming. This is one of the best examples of his guitar playing on the album and stands up against almost any of his later works.

Recently, Bruce talked about his inspiration for the song and how the music came to be. Originally,

> he says he was thinking of writing a classic blues shuffle along the lines of "Going to Chicago Blues." "But when I actually tried to put that music to the lyrics I'd written, it sounded stupid," he says. "Then there was this other thing that came along—a folkier, more melodic idea—that worked much better for those lyrics. That's happened so many times over the years. I might imagine the lyrics one way while I'm writing them, but they end up being very different in the end. Knowing that leaves a certain openness with respect to where the lyrics can go.[2]

If you play the song as a standard 12-bar blues (which I did to see for myself), I'm not sure it sounds stupid, but it doesn't really convey the sunshiny temperament of the song nearly as well as the actual music does. Bruce mixes in major 7th, minor and 6th chords and doesn't use the dominant 7th, which is key to the blues.[3] He does use a diminished 7th chord, which is mostly what gives the song a bit of a blues tone.

Interestingly, for all of Bruce's acknowledged indebtedness to

Mississippi John Hurt and other blues players, he rarely uses the unvarnished blues structures in his songs. At most, as with this song, you can hear a little bit of a blues echo in the songs.

It takes a few years before we get to another explicit road song, though a number of his meditative nature songs from the first few albums could loosely be considered songs of the road. *Silver Wheels*[4] is a high octane blast that starts out with just two acoustic guitars, finger-picked with more or less the same rhythm and the same part with enough of a delay, or just separated in the mix so that you can clearly tell them apart. There are also drums and bass in the mix. A trumpet solo picks up in the first break and does some fills through the remaining verses and picks up again as the song winds down at the end. This is a stream of consciousness song, piling up the images that he sees and the sounds he hears as he travel cross country on a highway. In an interview in 1995, Bruce said that the song was:

> basically a list of things unfolding as they unfolded, which is a thing that you encounter in the poetry of [Allen] Ginsberg, for instance, and also in the poetry of a French poet named Blaise Cendrars who, I think, probably influenced Ginsberg as well. He's got marvelous travel poems that span the globe and have a kind of mythic quality. Ginsberg, of course, goes less for the myth and more for the gritty reality...and this is kind of in between, I think.[5]

Bruce specifically mentions Ginsberg's book *The Fall of America* as an influence in his songbook that covers the period.[6] Helen Vendler wrote of that book in the *NY Times* when it came out in 1973, that:

> Ginsberg has it in mind to write a long "poem of these states" (incorporating earlier poems like "Wichita Vortex Sutra") which will finally sum up the physical and spiritual map of America - its natural rivers, mountains and coastlines, its man-made cities, superhighways, and dams, its media (radio, TV, magazines,

newspapers, movies), its social life (bars, universities, dancehalls), its political activity (especially its isolationism, suspicion, and hatred of foreigners), its poets and musicians (including rock and pop), its mythology (comics and S.F.), its graffiti, its religion (a poisonous fundamentalism), its banks, its wars, its violence, its secret police, its history, its seasons - in short, the whole of our common life.[7]

Bruce does not attempt to burden this song with all of that baggage, preferring to chronicle a single road trip or perhaps conflating images from several trips across the continent. But he manages to pack a great deal into seven verses. He starts his song on a prairie road, where his "hot tires sing like a string being bowed." A "sudden town rears up and explodes" and in a flash, before he can even recognize anything, the "fragments resolve into white line code."

After the town, there is "black earth" undulating under "grey skies." His wheels "outrun a river colour brick red mud," that cuts through "hills soil rich as blood." Then construction slows him down to a "stop caution hard hat yellow insect machines." The images pile up and explode into your consciousness with pure adrenalin.

"100 miles later the sky has changed," and he's coming up to a city and the road widens to four lanes, it's sunset and the "red orange furnace sphere notches down," which "throws up silhouette skyline in brown." The glare of the sun makes it hard to see out the windshield and they suddenly come upon an "iron horse overpass," where he sees someone walking, the only significant character in the song; "a man walking like the man in the moon/walking like his head is full of Irish fiddle tunes." Who knows what that would really look like, but what an image. Presumably he's got a smile on his face and he's lost in thought, but we'll never know.

There's another verse describing the urban detritus on "the skin around every city." Then in the final verse, we are inside the car listening to the radio "gargle top 40 trash," which is the "Muzak soundtrack to slow collapse," presumably the collapse of civilization or the fall of America, to borrow a phrase from Ginsberg. In addition to the muzak, there's the sound of the car and also "the whine" as the "planet engines pulsate in sidereal time," that you can hear "if you listen close." Sidereal is an astronomical term that relates to measuring time in terms of the movement of the stars. Even in our petty world we are connected with the entirety of the universe. This connects the song thematically to *Lord of the Starfields* on the same album, creating a sharp contrast, but also a bridge between the boundless universe of the Creator and this seemingly disconnected and chaotic world of man.

One might consider *Northern Lights*[8] to be a clear-cut road song, but then Bruce takes a left turn and it becomes something else. It starts out as a folkie acoustic tune. The band kicks in on the second verse with bass and drums. Keyboards come in during the fourth verse. There's a brief wordless chanted chorus after the fourth verse and at the end.

This is an easygoing song. Each verse is a line repeated three times and a fourth line that resolves the thought. Bruce is leaving town at "half past nine" on a Sunday night. His car "mirrors are showing the day's last light," as he's leaving Calgary driving east for Medicine Hat, Alberta.[9] Stars are shining ahead of him like a "shimmering curtain of light." The stars or perhaps wisps of cloud form "rippling cliffs and chasms/that shine like signs on the road to heaven."

The chorus chant follows, marking a break in the song. The first four verses are primarily descriptive. In the fifth verse, the earthly journey to Medicine Hat is transformed into a journey towards heaven. Bruce tells us that he's "been cut by the beauty of jagged mountains," expressing his feelings of wonder in the face of the magnificence of nature. And then, the following line says that he's been "cut by the love that flows like a fountain from God." These cuts have left scars, which he considers both "precious and rare."

Bruce is clearly referring to the phenomenon known as the "stigmata", which are sores, pain or other bodily markings "corresponding to the crucifixion of Jesus."[10] He's saying that he's been touched very deeply by God's love and carries the marks of that love. In the final line before the chanted chorus, he "feel[s] like he's made of air."

Despite the specific, but fairly low-key, references to Christianity, non-Christians can easily relate to this song. It's deeply personal and it's fun. It's infused, rhythmically, with a light hearted energy. Bruce is, in this moment, high on beauty and love and being on the open road. And it serves to change the perspective of the album from external visions to a more internal focus, while maintaining the metaphysical and mystical themes.

Life Short Call Now[11] is a much more recent road song. He's in his car driving and reading the billboards; a random barrage of information including promises of "paradise and tattoos." They hint at a multitude of "possible futures" and are "all laid out/on the sweeping curve of the interstate."

Bruce is alone in his car, with "no city", "no land", "no lover", and "no wife." He wonders about all the "ways to say goodbye" that he's used in his "nomad life." Later, he's in a motel room looking out the window. A "lone car" approaches and drives on, "leaving only voices in the hall." Next door "the bed is banging on the wall." He wishes there was someone to call him.

He's as lonely as he's been in years and we've got "no idea how I long/for even one loving caress." We've got no idea how he longs "for you to step into his heart." We hear his plea that "life [is] short," so please "call now." Most of the images are tawdry. This is certainly not the glamorous life of a pop star. Bruce is kind of an everyman in this song, the traveling salesman like Willie Loman.

Bruce plays the resonator guitar over drums, percussion and bass. There are some distant keyboards in the background. After the last chorus there are lovely swelling, ethereal vocals and a trumpet solo.

Musically, the song *Iris of the World*[12] reminds me a little of the acoustic version of his song *World of Wonders* on **Slice of Life,** though more driven. The violin is played as somewhat of an annoying background presence. There's a monotone harmony vocal on the chorus. It starts out with the mundane indignities and uncertainties of crossing a border in these post 9/11 days and how the minutiae that border guards check miss the bigger picture.

That is followed by snapshot images from the road and the feelings that they spark. There's the message of love painted on a boulder by the side of the road. Because of the irony that "all things are growing colder" in "the age of Global Warming" he commends the painter for opening his heart to his lover.

The third verse is kind of self-assessment, the kind of mental chatter that I can imagine myself getting into on a long solitary drive. He's not a very practical guy. He's "good at catching rainbows/not so good at catching trout." He's "got a way with time and space/but numbers freak me out." Our laundry lists might be different, but we're no strangers to this kind of dialog.

Night begins to fall and he sees "the road under half moon sky" as it "rolls out in shades of blue." He's "raw anticipation" for his lover and their impending "rhythmic rendezvous." Despite the indignities suffered in the passage, what comes through and what lasts is love. Driving is the source of many of the images that fuel the songs on the entire collection. The song is in EADGAD tuning (the two high strings tuned down from B and E) and has a nice, descending melody line in the verses.

Other Modes of Transportation

One thing that becomes apparent very quickly when you try to divide Bruce's songs into discrete categories is that it is very hard to do. His songs are rarely about just one thing. He really doesn't have any classic road songs, like Bruce Springsteen's *Thunder Road*, *Born to be Wild*, or Jackson Browne's *Running on Empty*. His mind is always as restless as his feet, and his mind connects seemingly off hand observations to a myriad of historical, spiritual, and cultural thoughts.

January in the Halifax Airport[13] is a good example of Bruce as journalist, observing the mundane events going on around him while he is stuck in a distant airport waiting for a plane. There's an air of "why am I here?" in the first verse. He muses on "distant times in distant lands" and "worthless money changing hands." His thoughts are gloomy and he misses his wife like "the flowers in bloom."

In the second verse, he reports that something is going on in Cyprus and "some Winnipeg boys" are on their way. He hopes they make it back alive. He hopes that he and his wife "live to touch, if just once more" because he "need[s] you like the river needs the shore." This seems a little melodramatic for being stuck in an airport in winter, but the longing feels very real.

In the final verse, Bruce generalizes about what he's learned from these thoughts triggered by moments that most of us wouldn't even give a second thought to. Life is "delicate and strange," without leading to understanding. "We stumble through familiar scenes/never thinking what it means." As the long day has turned to night, he needs his wife, "like I need the stars above."

This kind of journalism, and the way that he uses it in this song, becomes a more important element of his songwriting going forward, particularly in the 1980's. Prior to this, and even through the next several albums, he tends to use his observational skills to illuminate and express his own emotional and spiritual conflicts. Here he introduces the conflicts in the outer world and expresses a greater connection and understanding of what other people are thinking and feeling. The style is more conversational and the images are less obviously "poetic." This truly is more journalistic in tone and structure.

Skipping forward to the mid-90's, Bruce has said that *Night Train*[14] was part of an experiment in writing under the influence of Absinthe, which is an alcoholic beverage with mild psychotropic properties. It was also one of the drinks of choice of poets and painters in 19th Century France. We can assume it is the "dark drink" mentioned in the second verse. He says in his memoirs that he drank the liquid and was not feeling anything. He was worried that the experiment was going to be a failure, but then his "eyes fell on Juan Felipe Herrera's *Night Train to Tuxtla*. Suddenly everything was there. The song unfolded like a dream."[15] He then also describes a video treatment for the song which came to him at the same time, but which was unfortunately never made.

The drums, percussion and the rhythm guitar mimic the chugging rhythm of a train. Rob Wasserman's bass plays over the top almost like a lead guitar. There's a very distinct sound in the drumming on this album that I would call trashcan drumming, for lack of a better word. The drum sound is a little bit hollow like the sound you get from beating a trashcan, and the drummer uses very little high hat and cymbals.

As the song opens, Bruce hears "the night train passing" and it makes him think of someone "getting away." They are leaving future judgment "far behind them," leaving themselves as a "prisoner only of the choices they've made."

In the second verse, the "ice cube" in his drink "shines like starlight." He sees the moon out the window "floating somewhere out at sea." He feels like he's "an island in the blur of noise and color/Alcatraz, St. Helena, Patmos and the Chateau D'If." Three of the four tiny islands mentioned by Bruce were either prisons or places of exile. Napoleon was exiled on the remote island of St. Helena. Patmos is a small Greek island, where John had a vision from Christ recorded in the Book of Revelation. The Chateau D'If was a prison for political and religious persons in the Bay of Marseille. It was also famously a setting used by Alexander Dumas in his book *The Count of Monte Cristo*.[16]

In the bridge part, "everyone's an island edged with sand/a temporary refuge." But "the sea that binds us" will eventually "wear it down – dissolve it – recombine it." We are isolated and alone. We can try to get together and take refuge in that, but the things that bind us together also slowly tear us apart.

In the following verse, Bruce talks about death and how "it doesn't take much effort." In the darkness, "violence/sweeps the landscape like a headlight on a train," but it is soon gone and we don't remember it.

He sees the ice cube again in his "dark drink" and "starlight shines like glass shards in dark hair." He imagines or hallucinates that his "mind's eye tumbles out along the steel track," becoming one with the train.

In the second bridge part he notes that "in the absence of a vision there are nightmares/and in the absence of compassion there is cancer." This cancer and this nightmare rules our "palaces and mean streets" and the soundtrack or "mantra" of our lives is the "rhythm of the night train." This is a dark and dystopian vision of modern life. The song ends with a screeching, discordant electric guitar solo, a little like a train braking.

Foreign Assignments

How I Spent My Fall Vacation[17] is a travelogue which contains several different scenes. It starts out somewhere in Italy, as the "sun went down looking like the eye of God." Bruce and a friend, "two guys in leather jackets," are in a "dim empty cinema" shivering. Looking:

> Out the window… you can see old walled monastery
> Now become a barracks for the paramilitary police

Something formerly sacred has been turned into something sinister. You can't hide anything from either the eye of God or the paramilitary police. You can feel the tension in the air.

In the second verse, Bruce recalls an old couple that he saw "on a Japanese train." Her face was "half lit, rich with soft luminosity" as she dozed. He remembers the clanking of the wheels "in 9/8 time" and her husband's "friendly face suddenly folded up in a sneeze." Across the water, he sees a volcano flying "a white smoke flag of surrender."

In the third verse, he remembers "a full moon night," walking with friends to a "great restaurant in a funny old part of Rome with twisting streets that were hard to identify one from another."[18] They come upon a young cop at a street corner, carrying a "machine pistol." The cop was nervous and "snapped the safety off…and slid a trembling finger to the trigger." Bruce wants to say something calming, but thinks better of it. They keep moving and disappear into the night.

In the final verse, he wonders if he'll "end up like Bernie in his dream,"[19] displaced "in some foreign border town" and "waiting for a train part hope part myth." Or will he just wind up "sitting at home growing tenser with the times." Then they are back at the cinema and he thinks about "that guy in 'The Seventh Seal'/watching the newly dead dance across the hills." They are shivering and watching "the eye of God blaze at us like the sun."

Bruce was introduced to foreign film, "Fellini, Bergman and the more cutting edge people of the day" when he was in high school.[20] I can just picture him and his friend watching this film in Italy, in Swedish with Italian subtitles. In any event, Bruce loves movies and considers them a big influence on his songwriting, "as big an influence on what I do as poetry or old blues guys."[21] Starting fairly early in his career, images and movement have played a big part in Cockburn's songs, and as he adopted a more journalistic style for reporting on events in the outside world, that cinematic eye for detail becomes even more important in his work.

Tokyo[22] was written in 1979 at the end of his second tour of Japan. This is one of Bruce's great travel songs about one of the largest cities in the world. It's also one of his most straight ahead rock songs, with an insistent caffeinated beat. It's a city of snarled traffic, concrete, and bright, flashing neon. The "noise and smoke and concrete seem to be going on forever."

The plot of the song revolves around seeing an "accident scene." It's mentioned casually in the first line of the song, where "they're getting prepared to haul a car out of the river." He follows that with two lines of description about the concrete landscape, the traffic jams and the "drivers getting high on exhaust." But he comes back to the crash in the last line, "thinking about the water down below and what got lost."

In the second verse he feels like he's in a video game with its "pachinko jingle and space torpedo beams" and "comic book violence." He sees "grey suited business men pissing against a wall." In the final line, like a movie, he cuts back "to crumbling guardrail, slow motion car fall."

In the chorus, he tells us he can't sleep in Tokyo, as his "mind keeps

22

ringing like a fire alarm" and he feels like "dice bouncing around in a cup." He suffers from jetlag and flashing lights and the foreignness of a place where you can't speak the language or even understand the street signs.

In the last verse, he's getting out of this crazy scene where the "dragon of good fortune struggles with the trickster fox," by "flying headlong/to meet the dark red edge of dawn." But he's been badly shaken by the accident scene and is thinking about the victims; how "somebody will be crying/and somebody will be gone." The chorus repeats and the song ends.

Berlin Tonight[23] captures the uneasiness of the two Germanys in the time before the fall of the Berlin Wall. Bruce toured Germany in February 1985. The song talks about being there for weeks and the weather being mostly overcast or rainy. It was "only once – gap-glimpsed moon over that anal-retentive border wall" as they "laughed through some midnight checkpoint under yellow urban cloud."

The picture of Germany is dreary and oppressive with its "scratchy acid-bitten transparent trees" and "brown haze." Bruce is "rushing after some ever-receding destination."

In the chorus, he's in a bar or beer-hall and there is someone "table-dancing in black tights/waving a silver crutch in the blue lights." He feels like he's "on the front line of the last gasp." Does he feel here that the Cold War is ending? Or that it can't last much longer like this? While often in Bruce's work, a "crutch" is just a crutch, here it seems to also be symbolic. Even though Communism has spiritually crippled the population, they can still dance and they still perhaps have the strength to triumph. He has an exquisite eye for detail.

In the final verses, he sees a field with "green shoots of winter wheat and patches of snow" and a Russian walking a dog. A "hawk follows traffic on the autobahn" and there is a convoy of tanks. "A turret gunner laughs" as Bruce says he "throws up my hands…all glasses and grin to him under my 'commie' fur hat." A brief moment of humor lingers in the tense air.

Radium Rain[24] is a song about being in Europe at the time of the

Chernobyl nuclear accident. "They're hosing down trucks at the border" and "raindrops falling on my head burn into my mind."[25] In the papers and on TV officials are saying that everything is fine, but "in the meantime don't eat anything that grows and don't breathe when the cars go by."

People try to get on with their lives, but there's added tension in the air. People are losing their grip and there's "a man on a roof with a blindfold on and a hand grenade in his fist." Even Bruce succumbs to it; "I walk stiff, with teeth clenched tight, filled with nostalgia for a clean wind's kiss." In the final verse, he sees some birds in the sky, writing something "in a language I can't understand." It's "God's graffiti," but there's no answer to the question of "why so much evil seems to land on man."

I like the song, but at almost 9:26, sometimes I think it drags on too long, with a plodding rhythm. Still, there's some nice blues piano and there's an almost 4 minute instrumental break at the end of the song. The interplay between piano and guitar in the break is reminiscent of the blues and jazz of **Night Vision** from a decade earlier.

Islands and Beaches

Being on the water or near the water is a prevalent image in Bruce's songs. Whether canoeing on a lake, sailing on the ocean, or walking on a beach, it is a potent metaphor in his work for freedom and meditative calm. It is also an environment where wonder turns to spiritual insight.

Never So Free[26] is a seaside song, filled with vivid images of a sunny day in Devon or Cornwall in the southwest of England.[27] This is one of many impressionist paintings in his early work. There are only two guitar parts, one is mostly a combination of bass notes and strums. The verse phrases start off with a slow run of three bass notes and a single strum, followed by two bass notes, a strum, and a rest. The last line of each verse is a more complex and "lighter" melody. The acoustic lead guitar part comes in at the very end of the first verse.

The seagulls are "wheeling" and "white as whale bone" and "bright as a bottle, sunlight skips wave to wave." A "dog and a black man work on the deck" of a fishing boat.

After the third verse there is an instrumental bridge, which is much brighter melodically and rhythmically. This is a modernized bit of Django-infused jazz playing, making use of harmonics and arpeggios, along with bursts of notes and color. It resolves into the lazy signature pattern and then slides into the final verse.

Bruce feels the strong urge to move on as "part of a map of somewhere/teases my foot like a haunting dream." Finally, he feels like he has never been "so free, lost in the seagulls flight."

Coming almost a decade later, the song *Waiting for the Moon*[28] is another beautiful little acoustic guitar piece. It's one of two songs written on vacation in the Canary Islands in September of 1981. It's not about much of anything at all, yet it captures a moment in time so perfectly, with such vivid language, that you feel like you are there. Bruce is by the waterfront on a hot afternoon. His head is filled with "thoughts buzzing like flies around meat" which "land here – land there" turning "quick circles in the air."

The band joins in on the second verse with bass, drums and keyboards. He sees the "leather-faced old men by the café wall" and "kids in the surf." He has his camera and gazes out to sea "trying to identify the sky's end." Instead of the sky's end, he sees "little spots on the horizon" that turn into gunboats as they draw nearer.

There's an instrumental break after the second verse, with a short, fluid electric guitar solo. In the third verse, he wonders whether the sailors will be friendly or hostile. There's no real hint of worry in his words. He shrugs it off, as "speculation is a waste of time" and asks a companion if they "want to go have a glass of wine."

The song *Dancing in Paradise*[29] was written in Jamaica at Easter time. Bruce plays the charango and there's a slow, halting Caribbean rhythm to the music. The words of the song, except the chorus are spoken by Bruce in a near monotone. The spoken words tell a tale of poverty and murder and the price of fish and flour "going up up up almost by the hour."

That is contrasted with the "sentimental world" of the tourists and beach bars "where they're playing reggae versions of Jim Reeve's Greatest Hits" and where the government and businesses "throw away money on spectacular shows." Jim Reeves was a popular country singer and songwriter who died in a plane crash in 1964.[30] This song is another example of how First World money doesn't mix well with Third World reality.

Bruce also gets into a long digression about how:

> the jungle's always trying to reclaim the right of way
> And the mangoes cacao turmeric goats soursop
> Mushrooms cane plantains limes
> Horses crayfish long-legged birds donkeys
> Curved horns of cattle above dense grass
> Ganja sensitive plant ackee
> And some thorn whose prick brings lockjaw

In the tropics, civilization is in a constant battle with the forces of nature and the fecundity of the natural world can overwhelm any of the advances that people make towards taming it for our purposes. Soursop is a Tropical fruit with medicinal properties, apparently including aiding in the "quest of the perpetual stiff bamboo." Ackee is a flowering tree, and the flower is used in Jamaican cooking.

Down Here Tonight[31] makes use of a compelling marimba rhythm.

> I was in Tobago, on the beach, thinking about the coast of Nicaragua, and people's resiliency in the face of setbacks - The Big Universe was present, as it sometimes is, and everything was touching everything else...[32]

There's a "sweet wind blowing off the bay/sweeping the heat of the day away." The last fishing boats are coming in, "stars dust the sky," and the night "will be filled with song." In the chorus, "talking drums say everything's alright" and the pounding of the surf "sends a message/to the far starlight" that "we're doing okay down here tonight."

War Zones and Third World Encounters

Tibetan Side of Town[33] is one of Bruce's greatest travel songs, bringing us so close to the experience that we can almost taste the "hot millet beer" and, just like Bruce, we're "sucked into this scene like this liquor up/this bamboo straw." The words of the verses are spoken. Bruce is riding "through rutted winding streets of Katmandu" on the back of Tom Kelly's motorbike. The song is:

> an attempt to capture the flavour of Kathmandu. China has been
> bulldozing Tibet and its culture since the 50's. This has produced a
> lot of refugees, many of whom live in Nepal. One of the aspects of
> Tibetan tradition which was immediately accessible to me was the
> consumption of Tungba (spelled various ways by various
> Westerners). This is a kind of flat ale made from fermented millet,
> drunk hot. An acquired taste, but not that hard to acquire. The
> search for Tungba came to occupy a fair amount of what leisure
> time I had on that trip. Tom Kelly is an American photographer
> who at the time had lived in Kathmandu for 9 years, and who had
> the largest motorcycle I saw in Nepal. The guitar style here, as in
> 'Rocket Launcher', is modified Bill Broonzy - everything
> happening over a bass drone.[34]

The studio arrangement for the song (it's also been released in several live versions), which is densely orchestrated with cymbals, bass, drums, keyboards and electric guitar, somewhat obscures the acoustic guitar part. After I had heard him play the song in concert without any accompaniment, I went back and listened to the song and was able to separate out all the extra parts and see that it was pretty much the same as he was playing live.

This song is filled with smells, sounds and tastes. Everything "moves like slow fluid in this atmosphere/thick as dreams." As they drive through the streets, he sees a "beggar with withered legs [who] sits sideways on skateboard, grinning" and comments that "there's a joke going on somewhere but we'll never know." It's a simple, somewhat comical image, but there's a depth of compassion in this little portrait. Then he tells us of the young mother, who "covers her baby's face against diesel fumes." Later we hear "the rustle of bare feet and slapping sandals/And the baritone moan of long bronze trumpets/muffled by monastery walls."

As he sums it up in the chorus, there are "hard bargains going down, when you're living on the Tibetan side of town." The song is a good example of how he pulls sharp observations together to make a compelling story out of a motorcycle ride through city streets to a bar. And not just a compelling story, but a commentary on poverty and the uncertainty of life.

Dust and Diesel[35] chronicles part of his first Central American trip. It also falls into that category of journalistic songs, like *Nicaragua*. They are very cinematic; giving you the feeling that you are right there watching it unfold. This is a delightful song. Bruce had this to say about the song in a 1992 interview:

> the songs from Nicaragua were written after the fact, but with notes; they were almost complete in the notebook in Nicaragua. 'Dust and Diesel' is one of those, so is the song 'Nicaragua', although it's got a bit more editorial content. 'Dust and Diesel' is straight reportage, really. All I did was make a list of things that happened and put it to music.[36]

While it might be a simple list of what he saw during a drive through the country, what a list. There's the woman directing traffic ".45 strapped over cotton print dress" whose beauty gives him "a moment of loneliness." Then there's the farmer sleeping on a truck with "feet trailing over like he's trolling for dreams." Who can forget the "lone tarantula standing guard" over the corn spilled on the road? These are details filtered through a highly charged imagination.

The Coming Rains[37] is both travelogue and love song that simply catalogs the images accumulated during a long day on the road. The beat of the song is relaxed and rolling. It's a loose jam with a trashcan drumbeat, Wasserman's languid jazz bass, vibes, tambourine, and Bruce on dobro and electric guitars. The first verse is a beautiful description of a road trip in an alien landscape.

> All day the mountains rose behind a veil of smoke
> from burning fields
> And road dust dyeing black skin bronze and the road
> rolling like a rough sea
> It's quiet now, just crickets and a dog fight somewhere
> in the far away

Bruce holds the image of his lover in his heart and "the thought of you comes on like the feel of the coming rains." The descriptions throughout the song are vivid and self-explanatory. In the second verse they come to a village and get treated to a meal of "cassava and a luckless hen." And since he looks like a wealthy foreigner, the villagers ask him for an outrageous gift of "one well three lanterns and 200 litres of fuel." Of course he can't give it to them, and he lived to tell the tale, so I guess it all worked out.

Night comes on and they reach the town, where "neon flickers in the ruins" and "seven crows swoop past the luscious moon." Bruce imagines what he would do if he was a shaman and "had wings like those there'd be no waiting/I'd come panting to your door and slide like smoke into your room." As with many of Cockburn's not quite love songs, love is a natural part of life. When he's away from his lover or wife, which has seemed to happen quite frequently in his "nomad life," they are a constant presence, but not all consuming. He still lives his life and keeps his eyes open to what is going on around him.

The Mines of Mozambique[38] starts with a short, discordant violin intro by Hugh Marsh. The song tells the story of the aftermath of war in

Mozambique. Civil war and unrest had marked the country from its independence in the 1960's until it was finally resolved in the early 1990's. But even after the fighting ended, landmines littered the landscape.

Interestingly, according to the album notes, this song and *The Coming Rains* were both written on the same day. They share similar instrumentation and general sound, although *Mines of Mozambique* is harder edged, with more prominent electric guitar, matching the more intense subject matter. The ruins that are only hinted at in *The Coming Rains*, are more fully described here:

> Rusted husks of blown up trucks
> Line the roadway north of town
> Like passing through a sculpture gallery
> War is the artist
> But he's sleeping now

In an interview in 1995, he had this to say about his experience in Mozambique:

> When you step on a land mine -- it depends on which kind it is -- it either rips you to shreds or it takes your legs off." [There are an estimated two million land mines in the countryside of Mozambique, many of them unmapped, even since the democratic elections of October 1994. As 4.5 million refugees return from inside and outside Mozambique, they are attempting to go back to farmland that may still be deadly, though the war is over.] "Now you can travel around the country, but you have to watch where you put your feet. The cities are still full of displaced people and many of them have missing parts. [Finding mines] is so slow. They have to find everything by hand. It's very dangerous work and very costly work."[39]

Postcards from Cambodia[40] came out of a trip to Vietnam and Cambodia in 1999, sponsored by the Vietnam Veterans of America Foundation.[41] It's mostly a spoken word piece over exotic rhythms and beats, the keyboard percussion sounds like a marimba. Hugh Marsh's violin adds texture and depth to the choruses.

Death hangs in the air, from the opening quote from Abe Lincoln, to "the three tiny death heads carved out of mammoth tusk/on the ledge in my bathroom," to the "glass-paneled" tower outside Phnom Penh "filled with skulls from the killing fields." Here, Bruce is witnessing the aftermath of something even more terrible than 9/11. He sees "18,000 empty eyeholes peering out at the four directions."

In the shadow of this monument, life goes on. A "Brahma bull grazes…in hollow of mass grave" and "young boys play soccer." The "water-filled bomb craters" and "seven million landmines in terraced grass, in paddy, in bush" all the way "west toward the far hills of Thailand." This is the "macro analog of …intricate bas-relief of thousand-year-old-battles pitted with AK rounds." The bas-relief is on the magnificent temples of Angkor Wat.

We humans have done great violence to a beautiful, small country, and with the landmines the pain and suffering will continue indefinitely. We Americans have the stain of this blood and horror on our hands too. We have not been blameless, but as Bruce sings in the chorus, "this is too big for anger/it's too big for blame." And we can thank Bruce for his simple prayer "that we don't fear the spirit when it comes to call." Bruce comments at length about this song in his memoirs. The line about not fearing the spirit came from a dream and he calls it, "a plea that we remain open to the touch of the Divine, a reality that is so much bigger than our day-to-day selves…absence of a relationship with spirit allows us do things like murder each other by the hundreds of thousands."[42]

Santiago Dawn[43] presents a vision of hope for the future growing out of a bloody past. Bruce visited Chile in 1983, about a decade after the overthrow of Savador Allende by the CIA and the Military. The song starts with Andean pipes (or possibly synthesizer mimicking the pipes) and a sparse drum beat, just once every fourth beat. Then Bruce joins in on the charango, a high pitched stringed instrument traditionally made from an armadillo shell[44]. After the first verse the drums join in with more beats, but still sparse and the bass starts up mostly on the beats. Bruce attempts to recreate scenes of the coup in the first six verses. There's the "quiet clash of metal and boots" of the "bullies in drab green suits." The "thugs with their dogs and clubs" are "hunting whoever still has a voice." Doors are "snapped off a makeshift frame" and the "barricades burst into flames."

In the second half of the song, he begins with "bells of rage – bells of hope/as the ten year night wears down." He has a vision of the dead "sisters and brothers... coming home/to see the Santiago dawn." He sees "them marching...rising like grass through cement." It is natural and inevitable that these spirits should return. They can't be paved over and forgotten in their unmarked graves.

Cockburn's travel writing in these distant war zones tends to reflect his instinctive longing for peace and reconciliation. He's as much a realist as an idealist and looks on these places with a discerning eye. Over his decades on the planet, he's seen a lot of the bad things that people do to one another, but he remains hopeful, despite these walks along "rifled roads and landmined loam."[45] But his hopefulness and spirituality have been severely tested. As he notes in his memoirs, "Where was God in all of this? That nagging question came up in Chile, as it has in many times and places since the 1970s, as I've hovered around the bizarre cruelties of man."[46]

3 Spirituality in the Early Works

Two roads diverged in a yellow wood,
And sorry I could not travel both
And be one traveler...

Robert Frost, *The Road Not Taken*

In order to understand Bruce's Religious or spiritual views, you have to look both inside and outside the songs. As a poet, Bruce has pulled imagery and ideas from numerous sources including, most importantly, his own observations. With regard to religion, he fuses images from various religious traditions, particularly from Christianity, Eastern Religions and Shamanism.

Brian J. Walsh, in his book *Kicking at the Darkness: Bruce Cockburn and the Christian Imagination*, argues that "while Cockburn's work employs an incredibly rich array of metaphors, narratives, and images, it seems to me that we do well to interpret his work as a whole through the symbolic horizon of a broadly Christian worldview. Cockburn is indeed on a journey, but that journey has an unmistakably Christian shape and direction."[1] If we change the word "Christian" to "spiritual" I would have little argument with these ideas. I do not contest that Bruce is, or has been, a Christian; he has said as much on numerous occasions, though in some recent interviews he has backed off from even asserting that. I would argue that to pigeonhole him as a Christian is to limit our understanding of the breadth and depth of his work. I would also argue that Bruce is far more interested in seeking the truth than in attaching labels to his experiences.

Walsh continues to elucidate his purpose as follows:

> I do not presume to have definitively uncovered Bruce Cockburn's worldview. In an important sense, Cockburn is not really the subject of this study. What I'm really striving for is the renewal of a Christian imagination. And I invite you to enter in to the imaginary world that Cockburn constructs for us in his songs, precisely because I find that entering this world is so helpful in the shaping of such a Christian imagination.[2]

Whether any of us could "definitively uncover Cockburn's worldview," it is clear that simply taking Cockburn's work on its own terms is not really part of Walsh's purpose. Bruce would probably recoil at the notion that what he has created is an "imaginary world." To be fair to Walsh, I assume he really means that it is a product of the imagination, rather than "imaginary".

If you remove a handful of songs from his canon (out of about 300 known songs), I don't think that we would even be having a discussion about Bruce's Christianity. *Lord of the Starfields* is the most obvious of these songs. Without them, Bruce becomes no more a Christian artist than U2 is a "Christian" band. Bob Dylan and Paul Simon have had "Christian" phases that are arguably more overt than Bruce. T Bone Burnett, who produced two of Bruce's albums in the 1990's, has perhaps equally strong Christian views, but hardly anyone talks about his work in a Christian context, though perhaps songs like *Zombieland*, *Humans from Earth*, and *Primitives* throw people off his trail. And even the other Bruce has shown some religious fervor, in songs like *Rocky Ground* from his recent album **Wreaking Ball**. My point is not to deny or diminish Bruce's Christian faith, but to place it in a larger context by looking at the range of his religious and spiritual influences.

Non-Christian Influences

Going back to his youth, Bruce was exposed to "various aspects of Buddhist teaching, first through the Beat writers, then Merton, Chogyam Trungpa, the Sutras themselves, etc."[3] As he says, Bruce got some of his spiritual insights from the works of Beat Writers, such as Kerouac's *Dharma Bums*, and some of Allen Ginsberg and perhaps Gary Snyder, the thinly veiled hero of *Dharma Bums*. Snyder's combination of Zen Buddhism, shamanism, natural imagery, and ecological vision has a strong sympathetic resonance with Bruce's writing and thinking. I would be surprised if he were not familiar with Snyder's work in addition to Ginsberg and Kerouac.

Thomas Merton was a Trappist Monk, poet and writer. His most famous work is probably his autobiography *The Seven Storey Mountain* published in 1948. But Merton wrote many books, "mostly on spirituality, social justice, and a quiet pacifism."[4] All of those elements find expression in Bruce's work. Although a Christian, Merton was deeply interested in Eastern religions and mysticism in general. Merton may also have had as great an influence on Bruce's Christian perspective as he had on his understanding of Eastern religions.

Chogyam Trungpa was a Tibetan Buddhist, who among other things developed the Shambala Meditation Centers and other retreats and centers and founded Naropa University in Boulder Colorado.[5] Coincidentally, he hired Allen Ginsberg and William Burroughs to teach poetry and literature there and had a long association with the Beats.

Some of Bruce's imagery and some of his underlying view of the world may have come from the *Diamond Sutra*. In Chapter 32 of that work, the Buddha says that:

> This is how to contemplate our conditioned existence in this fleeting world:
> Like a tiny drop of dew, or a bubble floating in a stream;
> Like a flash of lightning in a summer cloud,
> Or a flickering lamp, an illusion, a phantom, or a dream. [6]

If you read the whole sutra, you will find many parallels with the way Bruce describes his experiences, particularly in the early albums. Lightning is a potent image in a number of songs, as is sunlight flashing on the water. This is often associated in Bruce's songs with a flash of insight. A good example comes from the song *To Raise the Morning Star*, from the album **Stealing Fire**:

> Rising like lightning in the pregnant air
> It's electric -- I can feel its might
> I can feel it crackling in my nails and hair --
> Makes me feel like I'm dancing on feet of light[7]

In a 1992 interview he says that people have called him a mystic, but he doesn't really know what that means and that it's kind of a catch-all term for things that people can't quite put their finger on. However, he then says:

> I certainly have a sense of the presence of the spiritual in things. I value that sense quite a lot, too. It's kind of a sense of interconnectedness that goes beyond anything that you could easily put into words or define in any way, but that is nonetheless very present and real and comforting, in a way, because it's so much deeper and bigger than the things that humans normally do to each other and all the rest of it." [8]

This "sense of the presence of the spiritual" and "sense of interconnectedness that goes beyond...words," is the essence of the mystical to me. From the songs, it appears to me that Bruce comes to the spirit and very often experiences it directly and viscerally, not through the written words of the Bible and other spiritual teaching, especially literal interpretations of those words. Certainly, as a voracious reader, words were part of Cockburn's experience, but my guess is that he also had very visceral reactions to things that he read, flashes of deep insight and emotional resonance. Of course, this is just speculation on my part.

This is similar to Shamanism and Zen Buddhism and other experiential spiritual practices, which Bruce also references frequently in his works. What is striking about his work in this regard is precisely his ability to find a way to articulate the ineffable.

His deep connection to nature and strong sense of the spiritual presence that exists in many sacred places around the globe is a clear component of his worldview. It also seems that he values that "cosmic" connection far more than he values the dogmas and trappings of religion. During a convocation speech at Queen's University in May 2007, Bruce:

> talked about an earlier trip to Nepal. He said he was hiking in the foothills around Mount Everest when he came across an elderly American former seminary teacher who had come to Nepal 25 years earlier to preach the Gospel and was returning to the U.S. "He was bitter and seemed diminished," Cockburn said. "He said that in 25 years he had not made a single convert. His words were, 'These people don't want to know about God.'
>
> "I felt terrible for him, as he appeared so oblivious to the spiritual surroundings. He'd spent a quarter of a century not learning what he might have about God!"[9]

This preacher could not really see or feel God, and was therefore unable to appreciate the spirituality of this distant place and its people.

In Bruce's early works, the mystical sense of the interconnectedness of all things is often the main form of religious expression. *Feet Fall on the Road* is a fascinating and enigmatic little tune that has sonic roots in late 60's folk pop. The song starts out as a deliberate and stately folk tune. At the beginning Bruce just has to get away from where he is; he has to move. It's not that there's anything wrong with his life or where he is, but his feet are "bound to motion" and "though chains be of gold/they are chains all the same."

In the second verse, an unnamed traveler:

> Awakens to find
> It's not the river that flows
> But the bridge that moves o'er

This is a little bit of Buddhist or Taoist relativism. Rivers give the illusion of flowing and bridges give the illusion of being still. This verse is like a haiku and so is the verse that follows. "In the hand of the cloud/liquid as time" again contrasts appearances and reality. The cloud appears solid as a hand, perhaps even holding up the heron in flight, but clouds are just water vapor. The heron is really free and in motion where it "know[s] the grace of space."

The song then breaks free of the "chains" of the folk tune and is transformed into a jazz fusion jam buoyed by Eugene Martynec's fluid electric guitar, bass and drums. The music demonstrates the meaning of the words and bridges the perceived divisions between folk, pop, and jazz.

Life will Open is a lovely, introspective tune, with a plaintive 12 string guitar, dulcimer and cello accompaniment. The lyrics meditate on the impermanence and contradictions of the world and the illusion of our lives. Waves break, dissolving the rocks they strike. "Eden is a state of rhythm like the sea" and "timeless change;" always the same, but always changing.

We are all dreamers, "busy dreaming ourselves and each other into being," but he cautions that "dreaming is a state of death." I think that he means here that dreams are like death because they are not real life and we can get lost in them. The song suggests that somehow we have to become real. The chorus hints at a way to become real, although it's not exactly an easy task that he proposes:

> If we can sing with the wind song
> Chant with thunder

Play upon the lightning
Melodies of wonder
Into wonder life will open

The chorus gets loud, almost symphonic, like the storm that Bruce is describing. For Bruce at least, music is a path to translate "melodies of wonder" into a life of wonder. We have to follow the things that are real, like wind and thunder and lightning, but they are also impermanent and ever-changing.

In the final verse, Bruce states that we are all "children of the river we have named existence." In this river, "undercurrent and surface pass in the same tense." This suggests that what we see and what we can't see, the physical and spiritual dimensions as it were, are really the same substance. He follows that idea with the idea that "nothing is confined except what's in your mind," and "every footstep must be true." The paradoxes and contradictions pile up.

Basically, our minds can't contain or comprehend the actual world. It's just too immense. It is truly boundless, to borrow a concept from a much later song. Still, we have to be sure footed as we make our way forward and our only hope, as the chorus repeats, is to be fully attuned to the "natural" forces like wind, thunder, and lightning. While there seems to be some elements of Buddhist thought at play here, much of what Bruce is expressing seems to be more primitive and instinctive.

Nanzen Ji[10] is a deeply personal, meditative and improvisational song, combining Eastern and Western mysticism. The temple of the title (which means "Southern Mountain Temple") is "considered the most famous and important Zen temple in the world."[11] The three short verses are like haikus, little bursts of images floating on top of the acoustic guitar. He sees the temple and feels a "cooling wind" and his "mind [is] swept clean like arctic sand." There's a "white stone lake/crystal clear" and he walks "on the voices of nightingales." He is surrounded by pine trees and he sees or imagines a "tiger leap[ing]," while he sips "emerald tea" which "reflects the Lord."

The music is mostly acoustic avant-garde jazz, similar to things that you might hear from Michael Hedges or John McLaughlin, with little flurries and bursts of notes and some staccato percussive sounds, and lots of bends to add a little dissonance and give it an oriental feel. The song has a distinct melody and structure, but has lots of space in the arrangement for improvisation. It's easy to imagine that if Bruce did perform it, it would be a little different every time.

This song closes the album **Further Adventures of** after two very Christian songs; the apocalyptic song *Feast of Fools* and *Can I Go With You*, which appears to be about the Rapture. If Bruce ended the album on these two songs, he would have been making a pretty definitive Christian statement. To take us to a Zen monastery in Japan completely shifts that perspective. It is as if Bruce felt the need to balance his Western apocalyptic thoughts and pull back from the abyss and rapture.

Bright Sky is an interesting acoustic guitar piece, with some light percussion that has a mix of Christian and Native American influences. Bruce said of this song in notes to his *All The Diamonds* songbook, that he:

> wrote these words on the way south from Faro, Yukon after my one experience of the Farrago festival - lots of communal spirit (and spirits). The guitar part was inspired by a record I heard of traditional Swedish fiddle duets.[12]

There are ten "verses," each of a single line, followed by the single line chorus, which goes "In the bright sky, bright sky." If you put the verse lines together, they form two related little stories.[13] The first story is about watching a flock of geese coming overhead and flying away "on a river of wind" honking their song as they go. They go higher and higher out of range of hunters. As they disappear, Bruce feels like they are "taking part of my soul," with them. He hopes that "maybe together we can touch down whole."

In the second story, we see things from the perspective of Bruce's soul, flying with the geese. He says that he's never seen the northern lights, but now "there were all those people floating like Noah's Ark" and "we all rush away on a river of wind." This vision of many souls flying away with the geese is exhilarating. The last line echoes the last line of the first part of the story. He still hopes to "touch down whole," but this time he adds a bit of a caveat, that "if I live I'll be coming back again." Bruce has said elsewhere that he believes in reincarnation and this could be a vision of death and reincarnation. Or it could be interpreted as a shamanic vision where he takes flight with the geese and gains some insight into the larger spirit world that we are all part of. Bruce may also have been aware the wild goose is a symbol of the Holy Spirit in Celtic tradition.[14]

Mystery[15] is a sing-along style folk song that disputes the notion that "there is no mystery". As Bruce notes at the end of the first verse, "it's everywhere I turn." The most arresting image in the song comes from the verse where he says he "stood before the shaman, I saw star strewn space/behind the eyeholes in his face." Bruce had this to say in response to an interview question regarding whether this verse was about a peyote vision:

> I was totally straight, in the middle of an afternoon. The shaman in question was the guy who painted the painting that we used on the cover of *Dancing In the Dragons Jaws*. He was the first native painter to come out and actually paint their myths...
>
> We went to his apartment; well, at least to an apartment that he was temporarily staying in, in Toronto. At one point during the conversation with him I had this vivid...I was looking at his face and we were talking about tea or something totally inconsequential, and I'm looking in his face and I had that experience of where his eyes were windows into space and it freaked me right out and I didn't say anything, but he saw me react or something. He saw a look come over my face I guess, and he kind of smiled and didn't say anything. He kind of smiled a knowing smile and that was the extent of it, but it was shocking. I had to assume it was something real because I wasn't stoned. At that point it had been a long time since I did anything like that. I gave up on all that kind of stuff really at the end of the

sixties, even before that. So it had been at least ten years since I'd done any of that kind of stuff and there he was.[16]

This incident would have happened in 1979 or 1980, around the time that **Dancing in the Dragon's Jaw** came out. The song was written or finished and recorded more than two decades later, which shows you how long it takes sometimes for ideas to find their way into an appropriate song. It's safe to say that the late 70's was one of Bruce's most active periods for mystical experiences.

The song starts out with Bruce on the resonator guitar. For the first two verses, it is just Bruce on guitar and singing. Drums, keyboards and background vocals come in on the third verse. There is an instrumental break on acoustic guitar after the fourth verse. Piano comes in on the fifth verse. There's another guitar solo between the seventh and eighth verses. Horns and more layered keyboards come in with the eighth verse. In the last verse, Bruce calls on "all you stumblers who believe in love" to "stand up and let it shine."

Journey to Christ

Although Bruce's parents were agnostics and he was raised an agnostic, he attended Sunday school as a child and young adult. This most likely gave him a reasonably good grounding in the basic stories of the Old and New Testament. Of course, as a teenager, he and his friends, "used to look in the Bible for the juicy bits, ya know? The guy stabbing his dagger into the king's belly until the fat closed over his fist – that was a good one."[17]

Bruce and his family outwardly conformed to a rudimentary Christian faith to fit in with the 50's ethos. He grew up in a very Christian-centered world. In the 50's and early 60's, not being a Christian or even a Jew was a pretty radical thing, especially if you talked about it. Even today, as secular and profane as the Western world has become, an openly agnostic or atheist candidate would probably not be electable to a major office in the United States. We are steeped in the

Judeo-Christian worldview and its stories from birth, especially people from Bruce's and my generation.

Bruce said of his early albums that, "I wasn't a Christian yet when I made those records although I was heading (being dragged by the nose might be better) that way."[18] Leaving aside who or what may have been dragging him by the nose, it is clear in the early albums that philosophical and spiritual concerns were uppermost in his mind. Almost all the early songs show a far greater interest in what's going on inside his mind than in the outside world.

Man of a Thousand Faces is a very curious metaphysical song from his debut album. It opens with some deliberate strumming with the sound of waves underneath. The title may come from Joseph Campbell's book *Hero with a Thousand Faces*, which is an exploration of mythology, heavily influenced by Jung's ideas about archetypes and universal consciousness. Campbell uses the term to show the similarities between the stories of different traditions. Some of the images are consistent with a mythological connection, such as "the glass eye of the idol", "things forbidden," and "jewels on the Serpent's crown." Bruce calls himself a "man of a thousand faces," which may mean that he either doesn't know who he is, or that he doesn't show his true face or feelings. Rather than embracing this multiplicity (or the commonality that Jung and Campbell see at the core of it), Bruce is genuinely troubled by it in this song. As he says in his memoirs,

> In his novel *A Perfect Spy*, John Le Carré tells the story of a boy brought up by a con artist father. He grows up to be a chameleon, blending in with whomever he's with, so much so that his genuine self disappears under all the quick-change facades, leaving the guise of the moment to be the truth.[19]

One of the many interesting images in the song is the opening image. In the opening line, Bruce says that he is "looking to be by a window/that looks out on the sea." This is followed a couple of lines later, by this thought:

Surf of golden sunlight
Breaking over me
Man of a thousand faces

There are a couple of curious things about this extended passage. The first is that rather than simply being at the ocean, he wants to be behind a window, looking at the ocean. Metaphysically, this would suggest a separation from the object of his desire. And yet, as he imagines the sunlight as surf, the sunlight penetrates the window and breaks over him. The images and the way they are presented here have a dreamlike quality that continues throughout the song. The thousand faces may also be suggestive of dreams where objects seem to change appearance and shape from moment to moment.

In the following verse, it appears that he is looking out a window at a garden. "In the Garden paths take form," but a hailstorm obscures the way. There are "things forbidden, things unknown" and Bruce "must travel on alone." Capitalizing garden suggests that Bruce is referring to the Garden of Eden. Eating the apple brought death into the world and forced the expulsion of Adam and Eve from the Garden. So Bruce, like our Biblical forebears, must leave.

In the next verse, he says that, "In memorium friends come round/but the hard ground holds its own" which suggests something or someone has died. "Time for pulling, time to ride" suggests to me the familiar Pete Seeger song *Turn, Turn, Turn* which comes from Ecclesiastes, where everything has a season and "a time to plant, a time to sow". Bruce says in the following line that it is "my turn, but where's the guide?" But as he said in the previous verse, he must travel alone. There is no guide. There is no one who knows the way.

Still he longs for the sea, "the jetty...and the gulls", where "truth is hid." He asks a second time: "anybody here know/where such a place is?" Having left the Garden, he's stuck in a city whose towers are "jewels on the Serpent's crown" and the space between them is twisted "till every eye is blinded." There is no help for him in this place, because everyone is blinded to the true reality. Given the image of the serpent, it also suggests the inhabitants have been tempted and blinded by false knowledge.

Finally, he asks God to make a deal to end his agony and confusion:

> Lord will you trade your sunlit ocean
> With its writhing filigree
> For any one of my thousand faces?

Bruce is enmeshed in a spiritual or existential dilemma. He has a vision of where he needs to be, but he has no tools to help him get there. Getting there truly would be a "hero's journey" in Campbell's parlance. The question is whether God would make such a trade for one of his faces, particularly if they are simply false masks? Or is there even a God to make that trade?

The image of "sunlit ocean/with its writhing filigree," or more prosaically, the intricate, shimmering pattern of the sunlight sparkling on the water is something that will reappear in a number of songs, like a thread connecting them together.

Thomas Merton has some very pertinent things to say on the subject of masks that have a bearing on this song. He says in New Seeds of Contemplation that,

> The problem of sanctity and salvation is in fact the problem of finding out who I am and of discovering my true self... God leaves us free to be whatever we like. We can be ourselves or not, as we please. We are at liberty to be real, or to be unreal. We may be true or false, the choice is ours. We may wear now one mask and now another, and never, if we so desire, appear with our own true face.[20]

In this light, Bruce's dilemma is connecting with his true self. The sea, the light, and truth are always with him. They are hidden in plain sight in the illusions and falsehood of the exterior world.

Dialogue with the Devil, from **Sunwheel Dance**, starts off with a distinctive strummed suspended chord riff with bass notes. Bruce is "standing on a rock in a river/staring at the splintered sun." The splintered sun would most likely be the sun seen through tree branches, but it carries an overtone of disintegration. He is distraught, has the blues and even thoughts of suicide. "You could drown yourself in jewels/like a thousand other fools" appears to have a double meaning. One obvious meaning is that you could drown your sorrows with material wealth. But in the last verse, he sees the river "on the surface flashing diamonds," so the line could also literally mean throwing himself in the river and drowning.

In the second verse, Bruce is "sitting on a mountain of ash/face to face with past regret," and he thinks that he could "roll down to the canyon," throw himself off a cliff, and "piss away this incarnation." His thoughts have turned to suicide again. The final line of the verse, "remember that you pay for what you get," suggests that killing yourself may not be as easy or clean a "solution" to his problems as it seems. After the second verse, the devil speaks and echoes the sentiment of the last line, by saying cryptically, "don't you know/how hard it is/to hit the ground and mean it."

In the next verse, Bruce finds himself in the city. "Walk the jangling streets of the city" recalls Dylan's line from *Mister Tambourine Man*: "in the jingle, jangle morning I'll come following you." Bruce is trying to find the "buried sun" in the city, in a sense wasting his time looking for something that isn't there. He repeats the lines about "drowning yourself in jewels." Here it does seem to mean following material wealth as he "wanders, waiting for it to be done". "It" could be life or it could just be finding what he's looking for.

Then the devil speaks again, exhorting him to celebrate. He says:

> Why don't we celebrate?
> Love can make you sad.
> Come on, let's drive ourselves mad.

So, as we might have guessed, love is the cause of Bruce's agony and the devil suggests celebrating and driving themselves mad. Rather than "losing your mind," I believe he is talking about spiritual madness or ecstasy, like the Sufi mystics (whirling dervishes) or the Taoist masters drinking themselves to spiritual insight in the sacred grove. But Bruce comments to himself that the devil is "aware/how hard it is/to kiss the sun and mean it."

The devil is frustrated at this point and screams his lines again about celebrating. This is followed by an intricate solo mixing Django Reinhart-inspired picking with one of Bruce's characteristic thumb thumping bass lines.

The final verse repeats the images of the first two verses. He is back on the rock in the river, "staring at the rain" and "the surface flashing diamonds" as the river rolls "down the twilight canyon." He ends the verse with a sly tweak at the devil, saying that "we shall kiss the sun in spite of him." Then Bruce muses in his own chorus, with a more light-hearted melody, "why don't we celebrate?"

Bruce manages to turn what could have been a fairly simple love song, into a powerful expression of an ecstatic spiritual experience. We can debate whether Bruce really had an encounter with "the" devil and what that might mean from a religious perspective. I would point out that this devil doesn't actually give Bruce any bad advice or tempt him to do anything bad, other than to celebrate, which Bruce decides to take him up on at the end of the song, though not in the same spirit as the devil intended.

The devil also teaches Bruce something when he asks, "don't you know/how hard it is /to hit the ground and mean it." Bruce echoes that later, when he observes that the devil knows how hard it is "to kiss the sun and mean it." It appears he's talking here about intention and commitment being a necessary part of true experience.

What is crystal clear, after the encounter with the devil, is that Bruce has altered his state or mood dramatically. He has purged himself of the negativity that plagues him at the beginning of the song.

The guitar work on this song is very interesting and sounds very different from most of his other early work. The signature riff and the strumming on the verse as well as the cadence and the interspersed lead parts sound eerily like Neil Young. The lead work is more complex and "cleaner" than most of what Neil has recorded, but I can imagine something similar coming from Neil. Structurally, there is also some passing similarity to the suite structure that Stephen Stills used in songs like *Bluebird* and *Judy Blue Eyes* as opposed to a more standard song structure. With regard to his own song catalogue, there is also some similarity to his later song *Gavin's Woodpile* and perhaps *Loner*.

Salt, Sun, and Time, released in 1974, opens with one of Bruce's most striking Christian songs, *All the Diamonds*. It is a deeply personal song, with the simplicity almost of myth. Bruce has said "this is a song I wrote the day after I actually took a look at myself and realized that I was a Christian in fact."[21] However, the first verse doesn't even hint at any overt religious content. What he values is not real diamonds, but the vision of sunlight flashing on the sea:

> All the diamonds in this world
> That mean anything to me
> Are conjured up by wind and sunlight
> Sparkling on the sea

Notice that Bruce uses the verb "conjure" here. Conjure evokes connections to magic and shamanism rather than Christianity. The interplay of wind, sunlight and the sea contrasted with diamonds also reflects a Buddhist view of the transitory nature of our world and that any solidity in that world is just an illusion. All of the molecules and atoms that make up a diamond are constantly in motion and mostly empty space. Bruce evokes primitive religious urges, by giving human or god-like powers to the wind and sun. They "conjure up" the diamonds. As we have seen in many of his earlier works about nature, he has a strong tendency to use anthropomorphic imagery. Whether or not this is simply a "poetic" convention, it is interesting that in one of his most famous "Christian" songs, he does not invoke God in his description of nature.

In this verse, Bruce repeats an image that first appeared in *Man of a Thousand Faces* when he referred to the "sunlit ocean/with its writhing filigree" and then again in *Dialogue with the Devil* of the water's surface "flashing diamonds." As I noted earlier, the image of diamonds may also have been inspired by a reading of the *Diamond Sutra*. The key line is worth repeating here. In chapter 13, the Buddha says, "This Sutra is hard and sharp, like a diamond that will cut away all arbitrary conceptions and bring one to the other shore of Enlightenment." [22] But in Buddhism, the hardness and sharpness of the diamond is also ephemeral and an illusion, like the sunlight on the waves. I don't think it's an accident that the image appears in two other deeply personal and spiritual songs.

In the second verse, he contrasts this image with his past life, again not really making an overt religious statement. Even the "Thank God" could almost be taken as a secular statement, if the song went no further. As for his life, he "ran aground in a Harbor town, [and] lost my taste for being free." He is stuck on land, in the world of men, within sight what he values most, until God sends a "gull-chased ship" to carry him to sea again, where he can be free, or possibly pass over "to the other shore of Enlightenment." Brian Walsh points out ships were sometimes used as a metaphor for the church in early Christian iconography.[23] Metaphorically, a ship "is the Church tossed on the sea of disbelief, worldliness, and persecution but finally reaching safe harbor with its cargo of human souls."[24] What's interesting here is that Bruce reverses the typical direction, to be carried away from the safe harbor, out to sea where he can be free.

The bridge part contains the most overt Christian reference, as he sings, "two thousand years and half a world away, /dying trees still grow greener as you pray." The power of faith in Christ reaches across both time and space to give life, even to dying trees.

The final verse goes back to piling up images of the ship and the sea to conjure up an almost blinding light.

> Like a pearl in a sea of liquid jade

His ship comes shining
Like a crystal swan in a sky of suns
His ship comes shining.

Merton has many passages which could shed additional light on this song. In <u>Conjectures of a Guilty Bystander</u>, he says that "at the center of our being is a point of nothingness which is untouched by sin and by illusion, a point of pure truth, a point or spark which belongs entirely to God."[25] This point,

> Is like a pure diamond, blazing with the invisible light of heaven. It is in everybody, and if we could see it we would see these billions of points of light coming together in the blaze of a sun that would make all the darkness and cruelty of life vanish completely."[26]

Many things are striking about this song. One is that the Christian references are subtle, and not particularly biblical. He also tells a very simple story to convey a complex message. And finally, what is most striking about the song is the visceral and sharp visual imagery used to convey his experience.

As expressed in this song, Bruce tends towards a mystical, rather than a doctrinal vision of Christianity. The song was also inspired by "a boat ride through the Stockholm archipelago,"[27] and some of the sharp imagery was no doubt drawn from that real life experience. Bruce described the album later as "Matthew, Mark, Luke and John meet Django Reinhardt,"[28] although other than *All the Diamonds*, you need to strain to find reference to God or Christ in any of the songs.

C.S. Lewis and Charles Williams

Bruce described the closing song on **Night Vision**, *God Bless the Children*, in 1986 as "C.S. Lewis meets the surrealists."[29] The song has Bruce playing a contemporary folk melody on acoustic guitar. Subtle electric guitar adds some depth in the second verse, but then fades away.

The song presents a sharp contrast of images of sunrise with night coming on. As night is falling, the world of time and the senses is dissolving and coming apart. Everything is shades of gray as the moon rises. The world is a "mask" and "illusion is queen". The morning sun reveals a starkly different world with stunning images of nature.

> Day comes
> The hawk of gold
> Springs forth in flame from a highway paved with diamonds
> Lion rampant on a green field
> Ramparts cracked into the sky
> While the Christ stands by
>
> With pain the world paves us over
> Lord let us not betray
> God bless the children with visions of the Day

Nature is a strong, active and even violent presence; the hawk "springing forth in flame", the lion "rampant" and a "highway paved with diamonds". The images associated with man are "cracked" and "the world paves us over" with pain.

A talking lion is a major character in Lewis' *Chronicles of Narnia* and it is likely that other images in this song were inspired by those books. Curiously, the Christ is a passive presence. What is he waiting for? Is he just watching the scene unfold? Is he indifferent? We don't know.

Bruce was significantly influenced by his reading of C.S. Lewis and Charles Williams. Lewis was probably most famous for his children's series, *The Chronicles of Narnia*, and also his space trilogy, but after his conversion to Christianity he also wrote the influential book *Mere Christianity*. A girlfriend of mine who was trying to save me asked me to read it in 1975, apparently thinking that I would be overwhelmed by its wisdom and convert on the spot. Lewis attempts to make a logical case for Christianity in the book, but to me all the logical points seemed to lead to cliffs and dead ends where you have to make a gigantic leap of faith, a leap I was not prepared to make.

In terms of his "spiritual" writing, my sense of Lewis, and this is also true of my interpretation of Cockburn, is that he is most effective when the spiritual point arises spontaneously or organically out of experience, rather than by referring to scripture.

The song *Wondering where the Lions Are* is a wonderful bit of mystical songwriting over a bouncing folk tune with a sing along chorus. It is also a good example of a song where the spiritual message arises out of the experience. As the song begins, Bruce is waking up to a new day, happy to be alive and happy that the world is still here.

> Sun's up, uh huh, looks okay
> The world survives into another day
> And I'm thinking about eternity
> Some kind of ecstasy got a hold on me

When you hear the lines, you may figure that this is just riffing on the anxiety and perils of modern life and growing up in the Cold War era. I remember growing up with the air raid drills, as if crawling under our meager school desks or crouching in the halls would have actually saved us from anything. There were nights when I was a child when the sound of planes brought a little rush of anxiety.[30]

Bruce is tapping into that collective anxiety, but there's more of a back story to it. In an interview in 1994, Bruce told writer Paul Zollo that he had a relative who had a classified job in the government involved with monitoring transmissions and breaking coded messages. This relative told him one night at dinner, quite seriously, that "we could wake up tomorrow to a nuclear war" between China and the Soviet Union. Instead it was a beautiful day and he had the dream that he mentions in the second verse.[31]

> I had another dream about lions at the door
> They weren't half as frightening as they were before.

Bruce suggests that he was "partially inspired by Charles Williams' book *In the Place of the Lion*."[32] This is a fascinating book, and well worth a read for Cockburn enthusiasts, despite being weighed down by wooden characters and sometimes stilted dialog. The novel begins with two men seated by the side of the road in the countryside in the dark. They had been walking all day and were resting, waiting for a bus to take them home. While they talk, they are approached by a group of men carrying lanterns, pitchforks, rifles and large sticks. They warn the two to get off the road as there's a lioness on the loose from a circus. They walk on to find some shelter in a house nearby. As they get to the porch, they look back over the garden and see the lioness and then a man approaching it. They see,

> Forms and shadows twisted and mingled for two or three seconds in the middle of the garden, a tearing human cry began and ceased as if choked into silence, a snarl broke out and died swiftly into similar stillness, and as if in answer to both sounds there came the roar of a lion — not very loud, but as if subdued by distance rather than by mildness. [33]

The next day Anthony is recalling the incident, but also a dream that he had previously, where

> he had seen stalking over hills and hills and hills, covering continents of unending mountains and great oceans between them, with a stealthy yet dominating stride. In that dream the sky had fallen away before the lion's thrusting shoulders, the sky that somehow changed into the lion, and yet formed a background to its movement: and the sun had sometimes been rolling round and round it, as if it were a yellow ball, and sometimes had been fixed millions of miles away, but fixed as if it had been left like a lump of meat for the great beast... [34]

As the novel unfolds, creatures representing Platonic ideals begin to break through from their world into our material world, causing considerable destruction and fear in a tiny town outside London. By the end of the novel, Anthony is able to repair the breach between the two planes of existence and the creatures return from whence they came.

The lions may also have been inspired by C.S. Lewis' *Chronicles of Narnia,* which Bruce was familiar with and had inspired some lines in his song *God Bless the Children* from several years earlier. Lewis wrote about how he came to write the books in the essay *It All Began with a Picture*:

> At first I had very little idea how the story would go. But then suddenly Aslan came bounding into it. I think I had been having a good many dreams of lions about that time.[35]

It's not that likely that Bruce was aware of this essay when he wrote the song, but it is an interesting coincidence that Lewis talks about his many dreams of lions, leading up to writing the Narnia books. Then again, Bruce may have just been dreaming of lions.

Throughout the song, Bruce repeats variations on the lines that he's "thinking about eternity" and in an ecstatic state. In the third verse, he has a vision of the interconnectedness of all things:

> Walls windows trees, waves coming through
> You be in me and I'll be in you
> Together in eternity

In the following verse he remembers being "up among the firs where it smells so sweet." In his ecstatic state, the chorus then kicks in and he's "wondering where the lions are."

The chorus is followed by two verses that are more concrete and physical than mystical. A "huge orange flying boat rises off a lake," while a "thousand year old petroglyph" is "doing a double take." Bruce has said that, "the lake is Sproat Lake (on Vancouver Island, BC) and the flying boats are, Mars Water Bombers, used for fighting fires. The petroglyphs are on Vancouver Island too."[36] Since Bruce wrote the song in Ottawa, these are memories or journal notes that he has woven into the song.

The next verse is about "young men marching" with their "helmets shining in the sun." They are "polished and precise like the brain behind the gun /(should be!)" This could be a memory that Bruce is connecting to the anxiety about nuclear war that starts off the song.

The chorus kicks in again and we're back to "wondering where the lions are." In the final verse, Bruce pictures some freighters "on the nod on the surface of the bay," perhaps thinking back to Vancouver Island in his memory. He says that "one of these days we're going to sail away/sail into eternity." With this we are back to other songs where Bruce uses the sea and sailing as a symbol of spiritual and physical freedom.

Lewis, Williams, and their friend J.R.R. Tolkien were all very much interested in myth and legend. Tolkien and Lewis were scholars of Medieval Languages and Literature and this is reflected in their fantasy writing. Williams was an editor at Oxford University Press as well as a novelist, poet and non-fiction writer.[37] His novels, unlike Tolkien and Lewis, are set in the contemporary world but with an occult twist.

The three share a dualistic view of the universe, with strong demarcation of right and wrong and good and evil. Their works make use of images of light and darkness to emphasize this duality. A lot of this worldview and the language and metaphor used to describe it come straight out of their medieval and mythic source material.

They also tend to portray the natural world of small villages as beautiful and good and the world of cities and industry as corrupt and decaying. This is best illustrated in the *Lord of the Rings* with the Shire and Rivendell representing the good, light and natural and Mordor representing an almost nuclear wasteland or a hellish vision of William Blake's "Dark Satanic Mills." The Orcs are right out of a Hieronymus Bosch or Brueghel painting. Charles Williams is more subtle, and is perhaps more comfortable with the darkness, allowing more shades of gray into his cosmology.

There are definite parallels here to Bruce's work, particularly in the 1970's, and he has commented on these influences. But this is not rocket science. As children, we tend to like playing in the sunshine, and some of us are scared of the dark. It's not a great leap stimulated by a little childhood reading or bedtime stories to begin associating light with good and dark with bad, or at least with the unknown.

Bruce's reference to the Bible and specific Christian stories is most pronounced in songs on three albums: **Joy Will Find a Way**, **In the Falling Dark**, and **Further Adventures of**. This open use of Christian images and biblical references can be illustrated by looking at several songs; *A Life Story*, *Lord of the Starfields*, *In the Falling Dark* and *Feast of Fools*.

A Life Story starts out with a modern jazz storm; swirls of percussive guitar echoed by keyboards and odd bits of percussion, including shakers, cymbals, bells, and finger tapping on the guitar body. There's lots of space in the music, a mixture of sound and silence. After about two minutes this resolves into some mid-70's jazz fusion and the vocals begin. This is one of Bruce's most overtly Christian lyrics. There are three verses, each ending with a statement about Christ. These statements emerge from impressionist naturalistic imagery, reminiscent of a J.M.W. Turner painting.[38] It is as if Bruce has created a whole life story out of a few simple brush strokes.

In the first verse, a storm is brewing. There's a distant cry and a bird's "wings-slash-free". This is followed by the statement that "Christ is born for you and me." In the second verse, the storm intensifies: "wind rush/reed bend/storm tossed sea." This is followed by the line: "Christ is nailed upon a tree." In the final verse the storm has ended. The "mists part" at sunrise. He sees a "shining key", perhaps symbolic of opening his heart and consciousness to Christ, and sings that "Christ is risen to lead us free." This is a very simple and beautiful statement of Christ's Birth, Death, and Resurrection.

I was reminded of Turner when reading these lyrics because of the contrast between the storm and the light at the end. Turner somewhat famously had himself lashed to the mast of a sailing ship in a storm, so that he could see and feel the storm up close and personal. His early work included a period where he did scenes from mythology and possibly some biblical scenes.

Later in his career, he did wonderful watercolors which are almost abstract and almost always filled with amazing light and color that presages the Impressionists. That kind of commitment to veracity and visceral experience is shared with Bruce. The other connection that I see is in the combination of modernist and traditional elements, with Bruce's use of modernist jazz and then jazz fusion with what might be construed as a fairly "traditional" lyric.

Lord of the Starfields is another overtly Christian song and contains at least one very important statement of Bruce's beliefs. He says that he was trying to write something like a psalm. For me, the best lines of the song are from the chorus: "O love that fires the sun/Keep me burning." This seems to sum up Bruce's true spirituality, which at its best is about intense personal experience of the divine. Calling God the "love that fires the sun" is a very interesting image and puts the verses of the song to shame. Love is the fuel for a full, spiritual life. It is also a fundamental part of the fabric of the universe in Bruce's view. As he said in a recent interview with Brian Walsh, "they're going to find a particle, that's the love particle one of these days, that's so sub-atomic that it just sticks everything together...I really feel that love is a force in the universe as physical as gravity."[39] The song came to Bruce, "one clear summer night, walking on a gravel road... lined with dark walls of dense spruce and cedar. Deep space overhead, far from urban light spill, blazed with millions of distant nuclear furnaces. All the way to the edge of everything, love resounded."[40]

In the Falling Dark is a darker, brooding, minor key meditation. Bruce is sitting on the roof of a friend's house as the sun goes down and the stars are coming out. It is another of the journalistic songs, with Bruce transcribing the things that he sees and feels and the thoughts that arise in the process. The lights of the city "lie tumbled out like gems." The moon "is nothing but a toothless grin/floating on the evening wind." The "sweat and lube oil" from the auto shop below "pervades the night" and he feels "the rush of life" moving by "at the speed of light."

He hears footsteps, guitars, and "voices sing." "Far in the east a yellow cloudbank climbs" and the clouds are "stretching away" into "tomorrow's time."

The universe is expanding, like the clouds or the rush of life. But here on the ground things are moving like:

> So many grains of sand
> Slipping from hand to hand
> Catching the light and falling into dark

Anticlimactically, "the world fades out like an overheard remark/in the falling dark." In our limited minds, we're missing the real things that are going on all around us.

In the last verse he expands on that thought. We're all radiant beings of light, even the "kids and dogs and the hard-shelled husbands and wives." There's "all that glory shining around and we're caught taking a dive." Even "the beasts of the hills" are shouting at us that "we're all one in the gift of grace." But we can't see it and don't get it.

Feast of Fools is an apocalyptic song, and also the closest thing to a rock song on **Further Adventures of**. The inspiration for the song is from the Middle Ages feast day, where the "social order was allowed to be reversed, at least for a day. The village idiot…was paraded around with a fake crown on his head, and pelted with cabbages and less edible projectiles [the interviewers "polite rephrasing of Bruce's actual noun"]."[41] This was essentially a way for the peasantry to blow off steam and allow the aristocracy to protect the social order. Bruce goes on to suggest that the song continues to be relevant, since "we are going from this age of 'neo-liberalism' to this age of 'neo-feudalism' with respect to the world economic order."[42]

The lyrics suggest that there's a need right now to overturn the hierarchy and "under certain conditions/you have to forget the rules." Rather than just a day, Bruce seems to be implying with the song that we really need to just clear the slate and start over again.

One of the characteristics of this particular feast of fools is that it is democratic and individuals have control of their destiny, at least for a day: "everybody has a voice" and "nobody goes to the bottom/except by their own choice." This is the time for the lonely and unloved "to be held in love." Outlaws "can all come home." Perhaps the only beauty in the song lyrics is the following passage:

> People's hands weave light
> There is a diamond wind
> Flowering in the darkest night

Bruce reuses the image of a "diamond wind" in his song *Child of the Wind*, but it also connects this song to *All the Diamonds* and the trilogy of songs discussed earlier. Light and beauty are emerging, even from darkness and chaos. But beauty is also seen here as something fleeting, that we get a brief glimpse of and then it is gone.

Even as there is gain for those at the bottom of the ladder, the festival is a time of reckoning for others. It's time for the gravediggers to "get that final shove." The "faceless kings of corporations" will glimpse "the horizons of the universe." Does that mean that they will see that there is a limit to their greed? Or like the fate of the gravediggers, is this premonition of their death? And "it's time for chaos to win," but the prize turns out to be nothing.

In the final chorus, he changes all the lines. We can look at these statements as a summing up of all the things that we have seen and heard in the song. He tells us:

> It's time for the singers of songs without hope to take a hard look
> and start from scratch again
> It's time for these headlights racing against inescapable dark
> to be just forgotten
> It's time for Harlequin to leap out of the future into the midst
> of a world of dancers
> It's time for us all to stand hushed in the cathedral of silence
> waiting at the river's end.

First, he tells "the singers of songs without hope" to go back to the drawing board. If the social order is turned upside down, hopelessness must, at least for a moment, turn to hope. This also reminds me of the lyric from *Last Night of the World*: "I've seen the flame of hope among the hopeless/and that was truly the biggest heartbreak of all," and it was also the "straw that broke me open." When you reach the bottom, it can radically change your perspective. The "headlights racing against inescapable dark" suggests the futility of much of our earthly striving for wealth and power.

In the next line, he says "it's time for Harlequin to leap out of the future." Harlequin is a clown or joker, but also a nimble dancer. The image suggests that the future could or should be more uncertain and unpredictable. It is also likely that this Harlequin is Christ. Bruce says in a recent interview that he may have got the idea of associating Christ with the harlequin or joker from the theologian Harvey Cox.[43] It's also a hopeful line, since he sees the world transformed into "a world of dancers" with Christ intervening in our lives. In the final line, Bruce tells us that we should "stand hushed in the cathedral of silence waiting at the river's end." In the song *Life Will Open*, Bruce sang that "we are children of the river we have named 'existence'." Here, he may be suggesting that at the end of our lives there's a "cathedral of silence waiting." The silence is a welcome relief from the chaos of the Feast, the chaos of life. Rivers end or empty out into the ocean, which Bruce has used as a symbol of freedom and enlightenment.

Rather than a logical argument or well defined story, the song is something of a collage. Bruce is using the medieval festival image to represent our lives in this world, not to simply talk about a discrete event. It is a vision of a chaotic and uncertain world, but also a world of possibilities. We have "a voice" and we make "our own choice," even if it often seems that things are stacked against us. Amidst all the chaos and pain, we manage to "weave light" and find the "diamond wind…in the darkest night."

Bruce thanks Michael Moorcock, the English science fiction writer and author of *The Cornelius Chronicles*, for inspiration in the album notes. These books, offering a dystopian and absurdist vision of Europe dissolving into chaos, may have been a source for some of the images and thoughts in this song. I found the books, which admittedly have their rabid admirers, to be almost unreadable. The main character, Jerry Cornelius, is an assassin and rock and roll guitarist in a through the looking glass version of the psychedelic 60's, where the U.S. military is bombing London in the second novel. Jerry seems to be killed and reborn in each of the books. As the books proceed, the narrative gets more and more difficult to follow on any logical level. Bruce also thanked the American theologian Harvey Cox for his book *The Secular City* and particularly noted some impact on this song.

Creation Dreams

Dancing in the Dragons Jaw, released in 1979, is one of Bruce's most cohesive albums, sonically and thematically. I think of it as an album of Western landscapes, with endless blue skies, sunshine, badlands, desert, mountains and canyons. It is a magical landscape of Medicine men and shamans. This is still an acoustic guitar-based album. One of the major sonic differences between this and the previous albums is the heavy use of marimba.

We've already discussed a few places where C.S. Lewis has influenced Bruce's songs and there are others. Bruce talked about his experience reading Charles Williams in detail in a radio interview in 1986 with Phil Catalfo:

> Generally that whole album [Dancing in the Dragon's Jaw] reflects probably the closest I've been able to come to expressing that particular kind of spirituality. The album was influenced partly by the fact that during the period that songs were being written I read all of the works of Charles Williams, who is an English writer with a particularly pronounced ability to describe spiritual things in very vivid terms. Most of his books are novels. They're sort of mystery novels almost, that deal with different

elements of the occult, but bringing it around to a Christian point of view. And his own particular experience seems very strange. There's a sense of depth of being in those novels that is really both disturbing and thrilling at the same time. [44]

A passage from the book *The Place of the Lion,* which we have discussed previously, provides a vivid example of the power that Bruce is describing in this interview. The main character, Anthony is leaving the bedroom of a villager who has fallen into a coma after his confrontation with the Lion. The house, as becomes evident in this passage is at the intersection of the material world and the world of ideas.

> Anthony followed, shutting the door after him, and as he turned to step along the landing, found that he stood on a landing indeed but no more that of the simple house into which he had so recently come. It was a ledge rather than a landing, and though below him he saw the shadowy forms of staircase and hall, yet below him and below these there fell great cliffs, bottomless, or having the bottom hidden by flooding darkness. He was standing above a vast pit, the walls of which swept away from him on either side till they closed again opposite him, and some sort of huge circle was complete. He looked down with — he was vaguely aware — a surprising freedom from fear; and presently he turned his eyes upward; half-expecting to see that same great wall extending incalculably high above his head. So indeed it did, but there was a difference, for above it leaned outward, and far away he saw a cloudy white circle of what seemed the sky. He would have known it for the sky only that it was in motion; it was continually passing into the wall of the abyss, so that a pale vibration was forever surging in and around and down those cliffs, as if a steady landside slipped ever downwards in waves of movement, which at last were lost to sight somewhere in the darkness below....[45]

This experience goes on for a number of pages and is the critical center of the book.

Bruce has commented that *Creation Dream,* the opening song on the album, is a vision of Christ singing and dancing the world into creation.[46]

The most specific the imagery gets is "angel voices mixed with seabird cries." Of course angels are not exclusively associated with Christianity and could evoke many religious traditions and mythologies. The singer/dancer is also not identified as male or female. But the dance is very beautiful:

> I saw you dancing
> Throwing your arms toward the sky
> Fingers opening
> Like flares
> Stars were shooting everywhere
> Lines of power
> Bursting outward
> Along the channels of your song

This could just as easily be Shiva in the Hindu tradition or Venus emerging from the sea on a seashell in Botticelli's famous painting, or Native American spirits. Whatever your beliefs, this is marvelous, mystical imagery. Musically, there's a lightness and buoyancy to the song. It has a strong acoustic guitar part, but is supplemented by a full band: marimba, jazz bass, drums and percussion.

Hills of Morning begins on an overcast day, the sky filled with yellow haze. The "sulphur sky" suggests that the devil is lurking nearby. Bruce is with a group of people "busy waiting" and "watching the people looking ill-at-ease." People are going about their business, moving "back and forth/in between effect and cause." While watching and participating in this mundane scene, Bruce sees something;

> just beyond the range of normal sight
> This glittering joker was dancing in the dragon's jaws

What are we to make of this vision? The "glittering joker" dancing "in the dragon's jaws" is a stunning image. I think immediately of Coyote in Native American mythology, which is sometimes the Creator, but is also a trickster and sometimes a fool.[47] One of the reasons my mind goes there is that the vision is "just beyond the range of normal sight." This is very much how shamans describe their visions, or at least how writers like Carlos Castenada have described them. It could also be Christ, as Bruce has previously associated Christ with the Harlequin or joker.

What is the dragon's jaw? It certainly doesn't sound like something you'd want to be dancing in. Bruce suggests in the same interview that the dragon is a metaphor for the terror that exists around us in the world. In the 70's, that terror was most explicitly the terror of nuclear annihilation. But dragons are fairy tale creatures. And he beautifully says in a recent interview with Brian Walsh that, "kids don't need fairy tales to know that there are monsters. What fairy tales do is tell them they can kill them."[48]

Bruce's vision becomes clearer in the first two lines of the chorus; "Let me be a little of your breath/moving over the face of the deep." The "face of the deep" comes from Genesis: "And the earth was without form, and void; and darkness was upon the face of the deep. And the Spirit of God moved upon the face of the waters."[49] Here, Bruce is fusing creation stories from the Judeo-Christian and Native American traditions. This kind of syncretism is common in Bruce's songs. In the final two lines, Bruce wants "to be a particle of your light/flowing over the hills of morning," which is a wonderful image of awakening spirit.

In the third verse, Bruce addresses the Joker, telling him that "the only sign you gave of who you were" was "the way the dust motes danced around/your feet in a cloud of gold." Though we can assume that Bruce is also thinking of Christ here, I'm not aware of any Biblical origin for this image.

In the final verse, Bruce seems to be addressing people who either don't believe in the spiritual dimension of the universe, or who only put their faith in what they can see. It's also possible that it could be the Joker addressing Bruce. He sings that "everything you see's not the way it seems" and "tears can sing and joy shed tears." Then in the final two lines, he finishes his argument that, "You can take the wisdom of this world/and give it to the ones who think it all ends here." Again, he is arguing that there is more to life than meets the eye, including a rich spiritual dimension. And he's also making the claim that death is not the end. Bruce is suggesting that we should gather up all the empty wisdom "of this world", the cut and dried wisdom of the empiricists and business and commerce, and give it back to the doubters.

Badlands Flashback is one of a handful of his songs in French and another mystical vision. Bruce is standing in the desert. He stoops down and picks up "a fragment of white seashell."[50] He imagines 'the ancient sea" and its "moving diamond-shapes," which is really just the "grasses flowing." Here we have another use of diamonds to describe a vision of the sea sparkling in the sunshine. He also sees a herd of antelope with their hooves flashing like "glass." Finally, he hears a laugh, which "rings like crystal in the empty sky" and sees someone "dancing like a flame." This is intended to be Christ, as the song was written on Easter in 1979, but the setting of the song again suggests a Native American twist.

He calls this song a "flashback," so we're meant to see this as something of a déjà vu experience. He's been here before. And we've just listened to three mystical songs in a row, which have similar, but slightly different views of the same creation mythology. They also have different musical settings and one is in a different language.

After a short acoustic guitar and marimba intro, the verses kick in with bass, congas and a light touch of marimba. After the third verse, there is an almost three minute instrumental break with guitar solo, followed by a piano interlude, a more intense guitar solo with occasional chimes, and then swirling piano comes back into the mix. After the last verse, there is more piano and guitar interplay which resolves in the repetition of the first verse.

Incandescent Blue is a New York City song, gritty and urban. At the start of the song he has "sneaked across the border" and he's "in this tunnel, waiting for the roaring train;" watching "black kids working out kung fu moves." He has a little anxiety about getting beaten up and he wants to get away. To describe this he uses a great Western image, "if you don't want to be the horse's hoof prints you got be the hooves." And he gets on the train and rides up out of the tunnel into the urban canyons.

The chorus kicks in and he's transported by the sound of a "lonesome violin." As the train comes out of the tunnel, he "see[s] the notes float up into the overcast sky/and change to white birds as they fly." The bird/notes "soar away free into incandescent blue." The birds and the incandescent blue sky conjure up a vision of the West and the Big Sky Country. White doves also happen to be a symbol of the Holy Spirit.

It's evening coming on and he sees the lights in all the buildings. He thinks about people "getting ready" for "steppin' out tonight." But it's a daily grind, and it's beating them down. There's an almost imperceptible "sound, like hammers" in their heads from beating them "against the walls." Perhaps he was also hearing the distant sound of a jackhammer on a construction site.

And then Bruce is transported again by the sound of the violin soaring like a bird into the "incandescent blue." The song is a constant tension between being caught in the "concrete vortex" that "sucks down the wind" and howls "like a blinded violin" and the pure freedom that he glimpses and hears in the other violin. He longs for the "tongues of fire" to "come and kiss my brow." He needs God's help to liberate him from this increasingly oppressive urban landscape. Bruce comments in one of his songbooks, that he was also anxious because he didn't have a work visa for a gig.[51] Did he play illegally, get the visa at the last minute, or did the gig fall through?

In the song *No Footprints,* Bruce returns to the Western landscape around Banff. I spent a couple of very lovely sunny days there and in Jasper in the summer of 1977, cycling around the mountain lakes and hiking in the woods. It's an incredibly beautiful area that's well worth a visit. For much of the seventies, Bruce traveled back and forth across Canada with his wife and dog in a camper and this song perfectly describes a morning campsite scene.

In the first verse, Bruce paints a picture of the mountains floating over the mist, like a Chinese painting over a very loose and unhurried acoustic guitar and jazz piano composition. The sky is hanging above the mountain like "a net." Then there's a crack of bird wings that "rip the net." The net is no less an illusion than the clouds holding up the heron in his earlier song *Feet Fall on the Road.*

The chorus announces the arrival of the sun. "The dance flows on," and "everything flows toward the rim of that shining cup." Based on all the songs that have preceded this, the dance is life, energy, Maya, and creation. In the second verse, Bruce contemplates the sticks of a campfire and a "pile of ash." The "crossed sticks lie on earth/between crossed sticks" like some sign from the I Ching. A dog, perhaps his own dog, runs by and the chorus repeats.

Then the song changes gears and the melody and feel of the piece changes. Bruce is addressing his lover directly and the words get more intimate and they flow more quickly. He's no longer describing a scene from nature, but telling her what he feels:

> Through these channels/words
> I want to touch you
> Touch you deep down
> Where you live
> Not for power but
> Because I love you
> So

And he tells her to "love the Lord/and in him love me too," and if she goes her way with Him, Bruce will "be right there with" her. A new chorus tells us that they'll be "leaving no footprints when we go." The very last line says that "where we've been, a faint and fading glow." They'll be treading lightly on the planet as part of the eternal dance.

The album begins and ends with the dance of creation and is shot through and through with movement and light. Even in the darkness of the NY subway, Bruce's spirit soars up into the incandescent blue on the notes of a violin. This is an album of bright sunlight, forests, rivers, petroglyphs, canyon walls and visions.

Brian Walsh devotes an entire chapter of his book primarily to this album, but also including other songs and images of the dance in Bruce's work. As he puts it,

> The stars, the seasons, all of creation are taken up in the "cyclic ballet" of the cosmos. And since Jesus is the creation-calling Word made flesh, the "dust motes dance" around his feet, rejoicing in the appearance of the Lord of the dance.[52]

Since Bruce has explicitly said that the song *Creation Dream* is a vision of Christ, I won't quibble with this general assessment. What is interesting to me, however, is that the notion of Christ as Lord of the dance, and the dance of creation, is not biblical. Indeed if you peruse Walsh's notes to the chapter, he does not refer to any biblical precedent for the images of the dance in these songs. He also doesn't speculate about the origins of the images. However the word picture that Bruce draws of Christ in *Creation Dream* is, consciously or not, the image of the Indian god Shiva.

> One of the most eloquent and expository of Shiva's manifestations depicts him as *Nataraja,* Dance-King or the Lord of the Dance, whose cosmic *lila,* or "play," forms the very nature and reason of reality. Shiva fills the whole cosmos with his joyful dance called *tandava,* which represents his five activities: *shrishti,* or creation; *sthiti,* or preservation; *samhara,* or destruction; *tirobhava,* or illusion; and *anugraha,* or salvation.[53]

I can easily imagine the many armed Shiva dancing on the waters in the song, as the universe explodes from his fingertips. Bruce has appropriated the iconography from one religion and applied it to Christ. This is also another example of his openness to and respect for other religious traditions.

4 Earthly and Spiritual Love

Tu me touche comme la pression
Des etoiles sur les tenebres[1]

Bruce Cockburn, *Loner*

Love songs make up a large percentage of popular music, perhaps the largest percentage. This is equally true for singer-songwriters, though perhaps the permutations of love songs have become more complex in recent years. There are songs of falling in and out of love, songs of perfect love, maternal or paternal love, songs of sex and desire, and songs of the memory of love. But if you are looking for love songs like the Beatles' *And I Love Her* or *I Will* you will not find many in Bruce's catalog. Even with an expansive definition of what a love song is, I was surprised at how few love songs Cockburn recorded in the 1970's.

More than any other category, the love songs seem to be the most autobiographical, especially starting in the 1980's. The songs become increasingly confessional and have an unflinching honesty and lack of sentimentality. As love songs, they are unusual and quirky, containing the same attention to observed detail that characterizes all of his best songs. He mixes in the political and the spiritual and even mundane and seemingly trivial observations, giving them the feel of life happening in real time. In that sense, they are often very cinematic.

Together Alone is a sweet and dreamy little love song, and the only real love song on Bruce's debut album. It's an upbeat, and intricate, finger-picked ballad. The opening lines pretty much tell you all you need to know: "So many things to see in this old world/but all I can see is you." He catalogues all the places that he sees her and hears her. Even though we are alone in this world, as the philosophers and cynics might say, he "just want[s] to be with you/together alone."

After listening to the song, though, we don't really learn much about her and what makes her so special; not even the tiniest physical description of her hair, her eyes, or her smile. The only distinctive thing he has to say about her is that he knows she "won't be pleased/by all that I do." Then he follows that with, "surely we can find a way/to overlook what you don't like." This is not exactly the most flattering thing to put into a song. But it also suggests that he's not really going to change whatever it was that she didn't like.

Love Song[2], from his second album, is filled with a child-like innocence and is permeated with a sense of discovery and surprise. Bruce uses an interesting mix of long and short phrases to create that sense of surprise. Musically, the verse phrase appears to be eight quarter notes, followed by a whole note, followed by two eighth notes and a quarter note, with each note being a syllable. It seems a little like a jack in the box, where it winds up slowly, stops, and then releases. The interplay between two guitars gives the music depth and adds to the joyful bounce of the lyrics. The first verse is quite beautiful:

> In the place my wonder comes from
> There I find you
> Your face shines in my sky

The second verse, switches the focus to her. The "world comes from" inside her heart. And if she looks in her heart "where the world comes from", she "will find me." If she comes with him, "they will sail on the wind" and "sway among the yellow grass." The chorus finishes with the thought that when she is beside him, he is "real."

This is a song about an intense and joyful relationship, a communion of two beings deeply intertwined emotionally and spiritually. Even if he was blinded, his eyes "closed forever", he would find her because "you shine across my time." The song *No Footprints*, that we discussed previously, is also a great expression of the interweaving of the spiritual and physical dimensions of love.

Ambiguity is at the heart of the song *High Winds White Sky*[3]. The dreamlike, fragmented imagery conveys his loneliness. He is looking out at the world from a high vantage point. He describes the woman in question as a princess. He may have given her a "glittering ring" and she's the "daughter of the stars/you are/life beginning." But then "the wind's travelers' tales tease" the treetops and "the ships have all sailed to the mouth of the sea," suggesting a bitter end to the courtship. It was all just talk, and then she went away. The last verse suggests emptiness and time moving on as the "wheel turns" and "the spider spins" his web. The song ends on the unsentimental and unromantic line, "falsehood lies panting like a fish in the palm."

Bruce reported much later that he "had a major crush on somebody when I wrote this, but it never amounted to anything."[4] Given that he was married at the time, perhaps the "falsehood" in the last line is an admonition to himself, for possibly betraying his wife.[5] It's interesting that these two songs are on the same album and presumably from the same time period.

The song *Stained Glass*[6] was written in London and is one of the purest example of Django Reinhardt's influence on Bruce.[7] If you took away the words, you might think that you had been transported back to 1930's Paris and were listening to Django himself or a devoted disciple. Think of a song like Reinhardt's *Nuages*, which Bruce has covered.[8] You have the simple strummed rhythm guitar part overlaid with the distinctive single note melody part; all arpeggios, pull-offs, hammer-ons, and trills.

The lyrics illustrate the theme of the evanescence of our reality. Bruce is inside a café, overlooking the Thames River, sipping a glass of wine. Through the stained-glass window he sees a "sequined sky." The "breezes on oiled water paint a pointillist façade" on this "ceaselessly shifting world." The view of the river is like a Seurat painting. It is also very much like the Imagist poetry of Ezra Pound and William Carlos Williams.

Bruce continues, thinking distractedly that "like today I'm far away." And he imagines that he sees his wife's face (presumably) "behind the time-blurred pane." Bruce is awakened from his daydream by the vibration of strings and the "Music leaps out," but "words unsaid whirl away like dust," perhaps lost forever. However, the song ends with a beautiful thought: "Across a fold in space you touch my hand." Quite possibly, they'd spent the day apart. Maybe she was shopping and now she surprises him with her touch at their rendezvous.

If you're not that familiar with Django Reinhardt, the following story might help. Recently my wife and I were listening to music, and I had my iPod on shuffle and a Django tune came up. She asked me what it was and I told her. She said that she thought it was from a Woody Allen soundtrack. That was quite a good guess, since Woody is also a big fan of Django and has used his music on a number of his later soundtracks. His film *Sweet and Lowdown* is about a fictional Depression era guitarist, played by Sean Penn, who is obsessed with Django.

A Long-time Love Song[9] is one of Bruce's most tender compositions. The first verse has a touch of sadness for things that end. The conversation trails off into nothing and "through shimmering spaces a single thrush calls." The thrush is often used to symbolize death. Bruce finishes his lament, by singing "A song when it's over is no song at all."

He tells the story that:

> There was an old people's home near where I used to live in Toronto - sometimes walking the dog late at night I'd come upon them loading a body in a long black hearse. Only at night. In the light of afternoon, you could see them enjoying the large garden. One wizened gray couple was always holding hands and looking at each other so romantically that it had to be a song."[10]

Given the emotional resonance, it's pretty clear that Bruce is really putting himself into the song, imagining himself and his wife growing old together. This one has a gentle island beat and light rolling piano in the chorus as he sings:

> And you know I long to feel that sail
> Leaping in the wind
> And I long to see what lies beyond that rim

With Bruce, the freedom of being on the water isn't just about religion or spirituality. Here, he imagines growing old with his "ever-new lover and friend" as a journey into the unknown. As in *All the Diamonds*, the boat is carrying them away from the comfortable harbor towns. And when life is over, their "translucent life-span evaporates away/to bead on the cool grass in a cyclic ballet." The cycle of life, death, and rebirth continues endlessly. It's an interesting thought that we might end up as dew on the grass.

Little Seahorse[11] is a lighthearted love song to his unborn daughter. The flute joins with acoustic guitar, bass and congas. His daughter is the seahorse, "swimming in a primal sea," in the womb. When he hears the tiny "heartbeat like a leaf quaking in the breeze/I feel magic as coyote in the middle of the moon-wild night." The coyote has a great many avatars in Native culture, but is generally associated with magic and trickery. He feels like he's "watching the curtain/rising on a whole new set of dreams." He's filled with anticipation at this new chapter in his life.

Outside, "the world is waiting" to "sweep you away" like "a locomotive" or "a Lake Superior gale," but Bruce and his wife will be there. She'll never be alone. As the song makes abundantly clear, he "already loves" her, despite not knowing her.

After the Rain[12] is probably the most purely jazz song on **Dancing in the Dragon's Jaw**, with a very prominent jazz bass line, acoustic guitar, piano, and drums. Bruce said of this song, in concert, that:

> What it's about to me is sort of the destruction of the personality
> by love; personality and ego and all the things involved in that.
> It's also about driving through the city streets on a rainy night. [13]

Underneath all the jazz layering and the rush of images piled up in the verses and spit out in places almost like rap or hiphop, this is a very powerful song about love.   He's "blown like smoke and blind as wind/except for when your love breaks in," and "it's like a big fist breaking down my door." He's "never felt such a love before," and quite possibly never expressed this kind of emotional depth before either.

In the first chorus, he expands on this idea powerfully:

> Maybe to those who love is given sight
> To pierce the wall of seeming night
> And know it pure beyond all imagining

This is clearly the good stuff. Like the mystical songs that precede it on the album, this is an almost mystical evocation of love. This is spiritual and otherworldly, "beyond all imagining." And at the end of the song, he notes, perhaps wistfully, that it's "music too high for the human ear."

This is far and away the most passionate love song that Bruce had written and recorded to this point in his career. But then, it is also arguable that **Dancing in the Dragon's Jaw** is his most emotionally and spiritually intense studio album to that point. And it is also one of his most unequivocally positive albums. What little darkness there is in his mood and lyrics is overwhelmed by the deep spiritual connections and electricity that charges through the music.

The transition from **Dancing in the Dragons Jaw** to **Humans** is one of the most dramatic in Cockburn's entire catalogue. Bruce is wrestling with an entirely different set of demons on this record. It's about crisscrossing the globe and close, sometimes uncomfortable, human contact rather than solitary contemplation and mystical union with all things in wide open spaces. It takes the urban grittiness of *Incandescent*

Blue, the final song on the earlier album, and strips away the mystical transformation that occurs when the violin plays. The love songs on **Humans** take a tour through the stages of loss and grief: denial, anger, bargaining, and depression.[14] There is a glimmer of acceptance in the final song on the album, but true resolution doesn't really start until more time has passed.

Bruce adds reggae to his musical palette on songs like *Rumours of Glory* and *What About the Bond.* Then there's a more confessional tone to most of the songs that deal with his separation from his wife. The entire album is about uncertainty, doubt, and loss. There are only a few small victories to report on, and even those tend to be somewhat equivocal. The events leading up to his divorce definitely took him out of his comfort zone. He has said that it made him realize how much he needed other people.[15] He had always felt a deep connection to all living things, but in some ways it might have been abstract before this and didn't always apply to people.

More Not More[16] feels and sounds like 70's rock, another departure from his folky and jazz oriented music of the previous decade. Bruce is hanging out with his friends and it's getting late. He's being a little clingy, but he makes some excuses like he hates "the day to have to end" and there's "never enough time to spend."

In the chorus, he wants "more… more…/more songs more warmth/more love more life." The chorus builds to a pounding conclusion as he also wants "not more fear not more fame/not more money not more games." And it's finished off with a nice 70's synthesizer riff.

In the second verse he sees "you – coming through the crowd/blue light silhouettes your head." He "wants to shout your name out loud," but he can't. He can only shout inside. The "you" here is possibly his wife, possibly a girlfriend. Shouting her name out in the bar would have been a demonstration of love, but he's conflicted, as becomes clearer in the second chorus. He wants "more current more spark." He wants intimacy "deep in the heart." But he doesn't want "more thoughtless cruelty" or "being this lonely." And there's that great synthesize riff again.

In the third verse, he asks himself whether he can "hear them talking?" They are his wife, or girlfriend, and her friends. Doesn't he "know what they say?" He thinks the worst. He decides that he's "a fool for thinking/things could be better than they were today," although it's hard to imagine that they could be much worse.

In the final chorus, he wants "more growth more truth" and he wants the chains around him to loosen. He doesn't want "more pain" or "more walls" and certainly "not more living human voodoo dolls." This song takes me back to the late 70's and my single days, hanging out in bars and "looking for love in all the wrong places."[17]

You Get Bigger as You Go[18] is about Bruce's breakup from his wife. The title image is like a cartoon shadow projected on the wall, which gets larger the closer the object gets to the source of light. The more distant his wife gets from him, the larger she looms in his thoughts. She is walking towards the light, and Bruce is left languishing in the darkness.

In the opening line of the song, Bruce is contemplating the irony that as he hates his wife, but "the luxury of hate is as exciting maybe as doing the dishes." He looks out the window and sees his wife walking away to "see a film/see some people see a man," and feels the jealousy like a "stab in throat twist in gut all too clear." But this is nothing new in the cosmic scheme of things. The "planet breathes exhaustion" and "staggers on." Bruce feels his "impotent" rage, but he's got "too many thoughts" and he's "too dogshit tired" for fighting.

In the second part, he says of her that "you get bigger as you go/no one told me, I just know." She is dragging "bales of memory" behind her "like boats in tow." Bale is an interesting word choice. Of course, it means a large package, like a bale of hay or cotton. But in archaic usage it also means a funeral pyre or large fire. And a third meaning is suffering and woe, as in baleful. Bruce may not have had all that in mind when he wrote these lines, but it supports the meaning of the song on a number of levels and was an inspired choice.

Each verse in the second part of the song starts with the line "you get bigger as you go." Bruce "spent all day afraid to talk," children "laugh out loud" at him, and he just takes it. After this there's a short instrumental break with a violin solo and then two more verses. The telephone "snarls 'don't touch me,'" and she moves "in waves like the midnight blues." He says spitefully, that she's the cause or the "vector of this weird dis-ease."

In the final verse, it appears that maybe he's been up all night watching TV "news reruns" and "dawn comes rainbow," which seems like a positive image. But he follows that by saying his "pain takes shape of grimy window." He can't fully appreciate the rainbow in his current condition, but perhaps it's a little better than the clarity of watching her walk away at the beginning of the song.

In *What about the Bond*[19], Bruce definitely has the blues, and delivers it in a funky, reggae package. He appears to be trying out his best arguments to save his marriage. There's slinky sax and smooth keyboards. In the first two verses, he talks about how "disharmony gives way to mute helplessness," and how "it's all too easy to let go of hope" and "think there's nothing worth saving."

Then the chorus kicks in and he sings about their wedding vows:

> What about the bond?
> What about the mystical unity?

He reminds her that they sealed their vows "in the loving presence of the Father," perhaps trying to make her feel guilty. This includes some fine backing vocals, like a good Motown tune.

In the next two verses, he mentions the "dysfunction of the institutions" and how the institutions ought to provide some assistance, but they've "got to find our own solutions." He mentions all the "confusion" and "pressure from all sides," which has to be the in-laws or friends butting in. He suggests that they need to focus and "head right down the centre/in the love that will abide." The chorus comes in again reminding her of the religious argument he's making.

He sings about how "man and woman" are "made to be one flesh" and he points out that "nobody said it would be easy." Can they really "let go now and fail the test?" In the final verse, he sings that "you could say" that "life is full of moving on." And you'd be right to say that, but "do you want the pain that's /already been spent/ to all be wasted?" He then sings the chorus twice to emphasize his point.

A reggae song may not be the best vehicle for getting down on your knees and pleading your case in this kind of situation, but it's a great musical package. The rhythms and the groove transport you to some mysterious place. In a romantic movie, Bruce and the band would be playing this song with his wife sitting alone at the front table in a small dark club and her heart would have been melted.

Unfortunately, life's not that simple or easy. I assume that most of these arguments were also used in private discussions and that they eventually failed. Whether they failed because it was too little too late or because the differences were much greater than he understood at the time, we'll probably never really know. As he simply notes in his memoirs, "how droll now to look back at my assumption that I knew what God did or did not want."[20]

I'm sure that Bruce spent many long hours contemplating the complexity of his life during this period. *Fascist Architecture*[21] examines some of the central causes of the breakup of his marriage in an oblique and less confessional way than the previous songs.   As Bruce has noted in a number of interviews,

> The image 'fascist architecture' came from Italy. It was stuff that was built during Mussolini's period that was a particular style where the buildings are really larger than life and what is supposed to celebrate the greatness of humanity actually dwarfs humanity. And it makes you fell tiny and helpless next to it. And everybody hates this stuff.[22]

This is certainly an unusual metaphor to apply to yourself, which he does in this song. A number of emotionally loaded words are suggested by the image: cold, impersonal, distant, and egotistical, to name a few. I would guess that these words and probably a few dozen more choice synonyms were thrown at Bruce by his wife, rightly or wrongly, in the period preceding this. But only Bruce and his wife really know the inside story and his memoirs, appropriately, don't fill us in on any lurid details. So, as all music listeners do, we fill in the blanks with our own experiences and find a connection.

Still, there are things that we do know about his life in this period. His daughter was born around the time that **In the Falling Dark** was released. His career had started to take off. He started touring farther from home in this period, including travel to Europe, the Northeastern U.S. and Japan. He toured in Italy and Japan in the fall of 1979. Bruce charted his first single in the U.S. in 1979 with *Wondering Where the Lions Are*. He was the musical guest on Saturday Night Live. He was probably feeling pretty good about himself and happy about all the opportunities that seemed to be opening up.

All of these things could have easily contributed to getting a bit of a big head. His wife probably did not travel with him as much, if at all, when he was on the road after nearly a decade of being constantly together. She was "stuck" raising their daughter while Bruce was off performing and probably partying in New York and Italy. This probably wasn't the life that she had imagined for herself. But Bruce suggests in his memoirs that the trouble went back even farther, even before his daughter was born.[23]

The song documents an emotional breakthrough that Bruce experiences. He realizes that he's built up these nearly impenetrable walls around himself and that he'd "too long been keeping my love confined." The last line of the first verse possibly addresses God or Christ, saying "you tore me out of myself alive."

In the second verse, he realizes that he's just been saved in the nick of time, "while the magnificent facades crumble and burn." Outside the walls, he experiences "the billion facets of brilliant love" and "freedom turning in the light."

In the bridge, he's exultant, like someone who has narrowly escaped certain death, with "bloody nose and burning eyes/raised in laughter to the skies." He's been anguished and depressed, "in trouble," and "through the wringer," but he's okay.

And, of course, in this moment of clarity, he wants to run and tell his wife and his "little girl" about this breakthrough. He was on the road when he wrote the song, far away from home. He wants to tell them that everything is going to be alright. "There isn't anything in the world/that can lock up my love again." I suspect that the song was written at a point where he still thought there might be hope for the marriage, but things didn't work out that way.

The Rose Above the Sky[24], which follows on the album, was actually written the summer before *Fascist Architecture*. Separation and Divorce never seem to follow a simple linear path. There's a weary resignation to the lyrics and the music. The placement of the song at the end of the album is perhaps an acknowledgement that the marriage has ended.

In the first verse, he notes that "something jeweled has slipped away" into the water. She laughs at his extended hands and he is left with "only air within their grasp." Looking at his wrists and empty hands, he contemplates suicide for a moment and the "fineness" of a razor's "slash."

The chorus offers some consolation. He will have to wait to die until "the rose above the sky opens/and the light behind the sun takes all." This reminds me of the "love that fires the sun" in *Lord of the Starfields*. The rose above the sky could be a symbol of God's eternal love, waiting for the right moment to take him home. Perhaps he is also hoping in his weariness for that "love" to "keep me burning" as it did when he wrote the earlier song.

In the second verse, he blames himself and his "gutless arrogance and rage" for the things that haven't worked out. He now prepares himself for a life carrying "the weight of inherited sorrow," towards his ultimate destiny. This is almost a mirror image of the "bales of memory" that his wife drags away in *You Get Bigger as You Go*.

The words of the chorus console him again. He sniffs "ozone on the midnight wind" and it reminds him "of the sea/and the mercies of the currents that brought/me to you and you to me." The sea is one of the bedrock images in Bruce's personal iconography. It is a symbol of joy and freedom that you can trace back to his earliest songs. He longs for that meeting and "the silence at the heart of things/where all true meetings come to be." Their love was not a mistake and he cherishes it deep inside himself.

Inner City Front, released in 1981, is one of Bruce's most electric, and in some cases electronic, albums. On this record, Bruce is starting to pick up the broken pieces that he shared in **Humans.** He seems to be on the rebound. As on that record, his guitar playing mostly takes a back seat to some of the other musicians, particularly Hugh Marsh on violin and Kathryn Moses on Saxophones and Flute. Bruce produced this album, the first time that he took the producer's chair on his own albums and the results are surprising. This is perhaps Bruce's most carnally exuberant album. It is certainly one of his most emotionally and biographically revealing albums.

You Pay Your Money and You Take Your Chances[25] is a little 4 minute movie, filled with jump cuts and cinematic details. The song opens with a jazz pop horn riff that is repeated throughout the song. In the first verse, Bruce watches as two women chase a man through the streets and alleys of Toronto. Perhaps he's been two-timing them. Bruce loses them in the night, and there's "just a deaf kid talking like Popeye to a large fleshy laughing man in a blue shirt." The chorus kicks in with the moral to the story:

> You pay your money and you take your chance
> When you're dealing with love and romance

The second verse is mostly just more atmosphere and scene setting. He hears a woman on the phone, her "laughter riding on its beam" of light spilling out of the kitchen. There's a sense of vertigo that he feels in "the maze of moebius streets" where "we're trying to amuse ourselves to death."

In the third verse, Bruce has returned to the bar to hang out with his friends. He watches them with both amusement and deep empathy and affection.

> Confused and solo in the spawning ground

> I watch the confusion of friends all numb with love
> Moving like stray dogs to the anthem of night-long
> conversations,
> of pulsing rhythms and random voltage voices

There is a level of observation of and empathy with the human world that is really new here in Bruce's work. There are some elements of it emerging in **Humans**, but it is in full flower here. Bruce has turned his gaze from the spiritual and inner realms to the dance of Maya with a vengeance. He's really drinking in this new experience, as if he has stepped onto an entirely new and undiscovered continent. He's there with his friends every step of the way, so he truly understands what they are going through, as he never really has before. He watches them as they try to make decisions:

> Stay or leave, give or withhold, hesitate or leap
> Each step splashing sparks of red pain in every direction
> And through it all, somehow, this willingness that asks no
> questions

He absolutely nails the awkwardness and anguish of trying to meet someone in a smoky bar, but the music is mostly lighthearted and somewhat breezy, like a jazz pop soundtrack.

Hearing *The Strong One*[26] for the first time is a little shocking for anyone who has steeped themselves in Bruce's other music. One of the last things that you would expect would be a sultry, midnight ballad with an electronic drumbeat and the staccato electric rhythm guitar. If this were a video, it would be two dancers on a darkened dance floor, with a hint of a spotlight, doing an erotic tango.

The song contains some of Bruce's most emotionally naked lyrics, such as the following from the first verse:

> When I was a torn jacket hanging on the barbed wire
> You cut me free
> And sewed me up and here I am

Bruce is laying out all of his vulnerability here. In the second verse, he lays out his own doubts and fears:

> Eyes fill with memories poisoned by intimate knowledge
> of failure to love
> Sometimes, sometimes, doesn't the light seem to move
> so far away?

This song, and these particular words, also had to be shocking for his ex-wife to hear. He never wrote a love song quite like this, or the others on this album, for her.

All's Quiet on the Inner City Front[27] takes the storyline from the first two songs a little further. Bruce finds himself in the kitchen at night with a billboard shining through the window. He's smoking a cigarette. He hears his lover; a "soft breath rises from the bed." And he's wondering what the heck he's doing there, with "a thousand question marks over" his head.

In the second verse, he turns on the TV, "but there's nothing new," just "the usual panic in red, white and blue." Soldiers are "marching in the square/knife-sharp trouser creases slicing air." Compare the precision of this image to the line in *Wondering Where the Lions Are* about the "young man marching helmet shining in the sun." On TV, he sees "private armies on suburban lawns" with their "shoulders braced against the tidal dawn." But here in this room "on the inner city front," all is quiet. Despite his questions, he "feels content" or at least thinks he is for a moment.

In the final verse, he hears a bell from the fire station and he "slip[s] through the door to the roof." He gazes at the billboard, at the sailor who "looks so self-possessed." He envies the fact that, unlike himself, the man in the picture "doesn't have a thing to forgive or forget."

On the surface, *Wanna Go Walking*[28] is a straight ahead three minute pop/rock song. It sounds a little like the Cars, a little bit retro and a little bit punk, but with more energy. He's out walking with his new girl. Setting the scene on some city street, there's neon reflected on an upstairs window and a "helicopter beats across the face of the moon." Bruce has "a hunger that sprawls like this galaxy." The chorus explains how he wants "to go walking" with her "through the movie/of the world." Like any good love song, it is evening and the moon is shining. But he's also got the flashing neon, a helicopter and his enormous hunger.

The second verse is all about her. He sees her and feels her everywhere.

> No matter what I do I feel your presence everywhere
> I'll be just standing around and your scent comes at me
> Out of nowhere
> I see your face on the wall -- in the magazine too
> Next thing you know the billboard out my window will be you

No question about it; he's in love. He's talked like this in his earliest love song, *Together Alone* from his debut album, where "all I can see is you/in a crowded subway train/or walking in the country rain." There the imagery was all soft pastels and here he's painting with bright, bold colors. But like the earlier song, this is a celebration of new love. It's also one of the few songs where Bruce actually names one of the characters in his songs. Aside from an occasional historical figure or Jesus, I can only think of four other songs where a person is named.[29]

Of course, Bruce is probably not capable of writing a simple three minute pop/rock love song. It's not all moons and balloons and the month of June. The third verse takes an immediate turn into uncharted pop song territory. Bruce still can't help but notice that the world is not perfect. So he has to point out that "today was a dog licking crap in the gutter of the street." This might have something to do with the song not making the charts. But all is not lost. He comes back with "tonight is a dancer oscillating on weightless feet." The world and our lives bounce between crap and effortless beauty.

In the final two lines, he tells us that the "fortune teller said you wouldn't end up with me." Bruce is not so certain. He reflects that "only God gets to say what has to be." Just as we careen between beauty and crap, there's the truth and stuff that you hear from less reputable sources. Bruce bypasses about 600-700 years of theological debate over determinism versus free will in the last line, but his point is clear.

Later on the same album, the song *And We Dance*[30] is jazz-inflected pop. Bruce is flying somewhere on a "midnight flight" to meet his lover. There's a nice melodic guitar solo in the brief intro. There's a full moon and "laughter in the air/ it's a party alright." Looking out the window he sees the "slate-blue clouds/iridescent sea." According to Bruce, "the band was flying from Victoria to Vancouver for a gig. We were the only passengers on the jet liner. We were drinking cognac. Drummer Bob DiSalle got to fly the plane. Is this what real rock stars do?"[31]

The chorus is buoyed by a nice descending guitar riff. In the second verse, he is thinking about fate. His mind wanders from the party on the plane, to somewhere "down in the realm of power" where:

> Somebody's manicured hands
> Play the Ace of Influence
> Against the Jack of Demands

Bruce reaches for the deck and "draws the seven of hearts." The forces of the universe work against love. There's the interplay of influence and demands. Bruce draws a middling card, but at least it's a card of love, and sevens can be lucky.

In the third verse, Bruce has doubts that this love will last, but for now it's good. He and his lover have "got this time/we've got this rhythm/till the whole thing comes apart/like light through a prism."

Along with *The Strong One*, *Loner*[32] is one of Bruce's most personal and emotionally naked songs. But it is also very different. This is a slow ballad, with a weary acoustic guitar strum. In the first two verses, he is observing people and things in the bus station. He sees "shark grins and sandpaper conversation" and "men's faces women's bodies on the magazine stand." He also sees headlines about distant unrest in places like "Sarajevo and Tehran."

The people he sees are "radiant angels," "earthly slaves," and "predators moving in their endless days." They work hard or just struggle to survive, trying to numb themselves with drugs, alcohol, or sex. But somehow, they'll never have "freedom from their pain."

In the chorus, Bruce tells us that he's "a loner/with a loner's point of view," but now he's "in love with you." There's none of his spiritual detachment left. He's thoroughly enmeshed in the dance of illusion and chained to the karmic wheel, just like the loners he's been watching at the bus station. The drums, piano, and violin kick in at the end of the chorus.

In the third verse, he turns inward but addresses his lover. He talks about "wild shadows, acid verbs." Perhaps some things were said in anger and that's why he's alone in the bus station. But he feels a stirring in his heart. There are "eyelids opening dans mon coeur." The verse switches to French in midstream. She has touched him "like the pressure of the stars on the darkness."

He finds himself alone "in the elevator and the empty hall." He doesn't know how he's "going to hear you when you call." He's in agony, living and dying "on the event horizon of your eyes." After the second chorus, Hugh Marsh's violin takes flight improvising over a verse. There's a repeated chorus and then the violin takes off again, playing over the piano, guitar and drums for a devastating solo of more than a minute and a half.

The Coldest Night of the Year[33] is R&B and jazz-inflected 60's pop/rock, featuring an electric violin and saxophone solo. The story is simple and straightforward; Bruce is alone on the coldest night of the year.

There are a couple of things that are especially interesting about the song. The opening lines of the song, "I was up all night, socializing/trying to keep the latent depression from crystallizing," shows the dramatic change in Bruce's life since his divorce. The loner who could sit for hours in the wilderness contemplating God and nature seems to be almost gone. In his place you have the guy who's staying up all night with friends to keep from being depressed.

In the bridge, he asks us to look at him and recognize his newfound wisdom. He says, "it's taken me so long to catch on to what's going on/inside this skin." And now he knows that in real love "there's nothing/but this suddenly compact universe/skin and breath and hair." There's none of the "love the Lord/and in Him love me too" from the not so distant days of *No Footprints*. The spiritual Bruce has gone AWOL. But we can twist this to make a spiritual point. In Zen, the idea is to engage fully in the moment. When you make love, you need to make love, and nothing else. However, I'm not sure that there's much spiritual about watching the "all night TV show/in the all night bar" and then driving everyone home.

5 *Lovers in Dangerous Times*

The intellectual runs away,
afraid of drowning;
the whole business of love
is to drown in the sea.

Rumi

On the road out of the depths of the personal hell of divorce, the world seemed to have changed. Starting over again in his late-30's, things outside himself appear to have come into sharper focus. Whether we are talking about spiritual or material issues, there seems to be a deeper understanding of the importance of people, both as friends and a community. The opportunity to travel presented itself and he embraced it, whether to play his music, commune with nature, or explore and discover the greater world. The hard-earned wisdom seems to color the songs, but there's also a newfound energy in the albums of the mid-to-late 80's.

Going Up Against Chaos[1] begins with a funky, syncopated guitar riff repeated about eight times before the piano joins in. It's a little like a rubber band being plucked. The basic guitar riff is repeated throughout the verses. At the end of the second verse the rest of the band joins in.

Simplistically, the song is about two lovers "lying in bliss," about to doze off under a giant moon. They're "lying on the mountain/by the satellite dish." The dish is "humming with the tremors of/every envy, rage, and wish." Also, despite their blissful condition, there's "a punch-up in the street." Outside their love nest, everything seems to be going to hell.

The bridge part changes to a more insistent rhythm and drumbeat. After the bridge there is an instrumental break with a dissonant, atonal jazz piano solo which emphasizes the idea of chaos. This eventually resolves back into the verses.

The first verse after the bridge sounds like a vision of paradise. He says that "we were bodies of light/like we'll be someday" and "the sirens and the curses/were light years away." They were innocent, like Adam and Eve in the garden. They didn't see any of this coming.

Then in an instant, they "were Lot on the mountain" and "Noah on the Ark/flying hand in hand/from the dog howl dark." They are fleeing the destruction of their world, chased by dogs and armed men. Lot of course was fleeing the destruction of Sodom and Gomorrah, which God was punishing for their iniquity. The flood was God pretty much throwing his hands up at the whole human experiment.

Sahara Gold[2] opens with a vaguely flamenco style riff on acoustic guitar which gives way to electric rhythm guitar and an insistent drumbeat. The title most likely refers to the gold carried by Berbers from Sub-Saharan Africa by camel across the desert, which eventually made its way to Europe through Arab merchants in Morocco and Algeria. This trade was at its height between the 7th and 14th centuries.[3] In any event, it's an exotic image for his lover's long blonde hair, which "tumbles down like Sahara gold".

At the beginning of the song, they are walking past a bar and hear the dance music and dogs barking. It is summer and a "hot night." The "streets are full of light." There are "carnival faces in Rembrandt light." This is such a great image conjuring up shadows and faces catching glints of lights from storefronts, neon signs and passing cars.

By the third verse, they are back at Bruce's place (or his lovers') and the rest of the song is a frankly erotic, but tasteful, telling of their wild lovemaking under the "half moon shining through the blinds." We know that it was wild, because at the end they have "animal grins and wild shining eyes" and they are "laughing and shouting" like they're "a hundred stories high."

Making Contact[4] was written on a trip to the island of Tobago in January, 1984. It has a nice Caribbean feel. The guitar is pretty much lost in the mix, which is dominated by keyboards, bass, drums and percussion.

This is a carefree song about splashing in the waves and making love. The "drumming of the surf" makes him want to dance. We really get the feeling of how "we move together like the waves/swimming in an ocean of love." But in addition to "one kiss from a smiling face" he sees "one world – one human race." On a spiritual plane, the song suggests that there are "so many ways to understand/one for every woman and man." He makes a good case that "making contact" is fundamental to being.

Lily of the Midnight Sky[5] is a song of the loneliness of being on the road. He's looking out the window as the "shimmering crescent moon recedes into working dawn." The view is a mix of urban detritus and trees and mountains. He sees "wave patterns among wave patterns/ particles disperse and rejoin." The feeling is the opposite of when he described "walls windows trees/waves coming through" in *Wondering Where the Lions Are*. Now, "the cold of your absence blows from/the silent TV, the parking lot/the balcony."

His thoughts crystallize in the chorus. He knows that he "can reach you if I try." But this "lily of the midnight sky" keeps "fading away" as dawn approaches.

He describes the sun as soldiers "shooting into a forest of flowers," emphasizing again that the light is the enemy, intent on destroying his midnight vision of the lily. The imagery seems like a description of how snow "petals float into pink crimson white" and they "flutter into mountainous distance...like a stadium full of applauding hands." Bruce is angry at the "marauding sun" and "raise[s] a fist." He's "the rag in a bottle of gasoline/longing to ignite." But he has no real object to focus his rage on.

He wants all of her "shining on the panther skin of night." Bruce is filled with an animal lust for her. In the last chorus he asks her to "spare a smile" as he "put[s] on my dog mask and howl for you" recalling the animal grins of *Sahara Gold*. Whatever reticence there was in his early love songs is gone here. He tosses out his inner feelings and thoughts with an almost primal intensity.

See How I Miss You[6] is a great little love song, with reggae guitar riffs and syncopated bass. The instrumental break is primarily handled by the keyboard player. Once again, Bruce is alone and missing his woman. Like many good love songs, this one starts with "rays of the moon" which "make magic in the streets of the city." But then he veers off and sees "the walking graffiti, survivalist bums" and "even the secret police" who "shout that you're the one." Who else but Bruce would link thoughts of his lover with such a motley crew?

In the second verse, the weirdness continues. He remarks that, "every psychopath gets his own magazine these days" and how he "just read about how I can kill in a hundred ways." This intermixing of seemingly random social commentary in a love song becomes more characteristic in Bruce's songwriting through the 80's and beyond. He seems to care less and less over time about what is "appropriate" to any specific genre of songs. From a commercial point of view, his music may suffer from this, but what comes through this is a fiercely independent spirit and voice trying to communicate the whole of experience, warts and all. It is almost an attempt to write without filters. In this, he is very much getting in tune with the Beat writers that he started reading in high school and continued to read throughout the 70's.

Kerouac and Ginsberg advocated writing fast and making few corrections. I'm not suggesting that Bruce followed that specifically, but we know that some of his songs are almost verbatim transcriptions of his notebooks.

In the final verse, he's watching a woman "in a tight sequined lizard dress." She "Tosses her scarlet hair like a sly caress." She may be a singer, or perhaps he's just overhearing her "midnight voice" that sounds to him " like some beckoning saint." She's "got something special, but you she ain't." Of course, this is more the description of a devilish temptress rather than a saint, but his resistance shows how much he really misses his lover.

The final verse reminds me of the mysterious woman in the early song *Golden Serpent Blues*. Bruce plays piano and croons about a woman who may or may not be his lover. The first few notes sound serious, stately and almost classical, but he quickly moves to a shuffling blues. Perhaps she's a waitress weaving through a crowd of people, as "she moves like a golden serpent all day long," and "she likes to give me honey when I'm down." And if he "ever was a king y'know she was the crown." She's clearly something special: "She can drive away the devil with a song." This isn't much of a love song, perhaps just an infatuation. But she has a way about her and he's noticed it and appreciates it.

By the time of his album **Big Circumstance**, a few years later, things have changed again. The two love songs on the album are again about separation. Bruce is far from home, in Nepal, and he's not sure if the relationship is over. There's an intensity and edge to these songs that is perhaps unmatched in his song catalog.

The song *Don't Feel your Touch*[7] is a beautiful acoustic guitar piece. Bruce is far from home and kisses his "departing companions" goodnight under the rising moon. He's alone and so very lonely, while "the night grows sharp and hollow/as a junkie's craving vein." He's missing his lover's touch. The image conveys his desperation and the pain of withdrawal.

In the second verse, he tells us that "being held in the heart of a friend is to be a king," but it's "the magic of a lover's touch" that he really needs. The "night grows clear and empty/as a lake of acid rain" and "the beauties of the world don't mean a thing." The friendship of his departed companions is not enough to sustain him.

In the final verse, he reflects on the sunset and the quick descent into night. He hears "a hint of chanted prayer" on the night wind. He says that he's "shattered heart and soul," which suggests that this is more than just being away from his lover. The relationship is over or he fears it might be over. Perhaps he's even travelled abroad to get away from the relationship. But he feels the loss deep in his gut and his brain and there's nothing he can really do about it.

Pangs of Love[8] was written in Nepal. In it, Bruce chronicles a sleepless night with rain falling "on this mountain town." The song is about the pain that you feel "when you give your love/but don't give all away." It's a beautiful and aching little love song; just two short verses, a long chorus and an understated acoustic guitar arrangement. The guitar is supported by bass, piano and light drums and percussion. The guitar solo is reminiscent of the 1970's work influenced by Django Reinhardt.

When we get to **Nothing But a Burning Light** the mood has changed again. Time has passed and Bruce is more settled, and based on the content of the songs, in a relationship again. There are still ups and downs, as in every relationship and every life, but overall it seems that life is good.

Great Big Love[9] is an exuberant love song, buoyed by Booker T. Jones' organ chops. Bruce is on his way home and can't wait to see his woman as the "evening sun slants across the road/painting everything with gold." The song was written in Western Manitoba, about 2100 km from Ontario, so Bruce was a long way from home. Perhaps he was stopping for the night.

In the second verse, Bruce is thinking about the state of the world and how he's "seen a lot of things…some bad but some good stuff too." He's "felt the touch of love in the works of God" and sometimes "in what people do." He admits that he "never had a lot of faith in human beings/but sometimes we manage to shine." The song is loose and conversational. He sounds relaxed.

In the third verse, he seems to be checking the scorecard for his life, which he likes "just fine." On a biographical note, I had no idea that Bruce was an avid horseman or into shooting or that taking those things away from him would make him unhappy. Indeed, he talks at length about getting into shooting in the 1990's in his memoir.[10] It's definitely in keeping with the Western themes and atmospherics of the album. Most importantly, he has "a woman I love and she loves me and we live on a piece of land." He decides that he's "a happy man."

One of the Best Ones[11] is another of Bruce's offbeat love songs. Who else would start a serious love song with the line "guess I'd get along without you?" There's a touch of sadness and doubt in the lyric that contrasts sharply with the preceding and following songs.

The "nine billion names of God" may refer, consciously or not, to a science fiction short story by Arthur C. Clarke, where Tibetan monks are tasked with writing down all of the names of God. They determine that there are nine billion names and that it will take 15,000 years to write them all down. They also believe that when they write the last one down, the universe will end. At the end of the story, the computer experts who help the monks speed up the writing process do see the stars going out one by one.[12] This is all very tangential to the song and it could just be a phrase that stuck in his mind, but his album notes suggest that he was a pretty serious reader of science fiction.

Somebody Touched Me[13] is another upbeat love song. It conveys deep feeling, but is neither as personal nor as interesting as either *Great Big Love* or *One of the Best Ones*. Some people have interpreted this as a religious love song, with the "somebody" being God or Christ. It works either way. That makes some people uncomfortable. For example, one critic suggested that "lyrically he's a male Amy Grant-a lot of his songs might appear on the surface to be about romantic love, but they're really about the other Great Big Love, or else about how the Big Guy orchestrates the romantic and spiritual order of things."[14] Yes, Bruce believes that Love is one of the central elements of the universe. It "fires the sun" as he wrote in *Lord of the Starfields*, but it's also a human emotion with romantic and even sexual overtones in Cockburn's work. In any event, Amy Grant is about the last songwriter I would think of when thinking about Cockburn.

Bruce's production of love songs was perhaps greater in the early 90's than at any time in his career and the 1994 release **Dart to the Heart** is dominated by love songs. These songs tackle many different aspects of love and longing.

Listen for the Laugh[15] is an ironic love song and a horn driven rocker. Discussing his inspiration for the song, Bruce said the following:

Man, being in love with somebody I wasn't supposed to be in love with and reflecting on what that meant, ya know? The love, the feeling of love was totally real and seemed kind of God given, but the object of that particular feeling was married to somebody else and there was nothing I could do about it. [laughs] So there's a kind of ironic sense of God laughing and love being a significant part of that laughter.[16]

Obviously, the song is about much more than that. Mostly, the verses are a catalog of what the laugh is not. It's not the laughter "of rain in the drain" or "a frightened mind." It's not the laughter "of the gloating rich" or the "sacred bitch." Nor is it the laughter of "the media king" and it most definitely "doesn't sell you anything."

To the extent that he can describe it, it's "more of a chain saw in a velvet glove," or "the wind in the wings of a diving dove." Last but not least, it's "balanced on the brink only waiting for a shove." You'd better listen for it. The sound is unmistakable.

All the Ways I Want You[17] is a song about missing your lover's presence. Bruce was on the road when he wrote this song. He's out in the hills, where "owls watch by night." In the first verse, he presents some incongruous details, like "down in town the bars are full/and the drunks are picking fights." He can't sleep or he's just up late and he hears the "2:19 freight train/moaning somewhere near." His whole world has "shrunken to/all the ways I want you." A decade earlier, he mused that:

> When two lovers really love there's nothing there
> But this suddenly compact universe
> Skin and breath and hair[18]

In the intervening time, he's experienced both the fullness and the emptiness of that truth. In the face of this compact universe or shrunken world, he still thinks about and sees the larger world around him. He notices that "stars look down and laugh at me." He hears the train whistle in the night and imagines the bars full of drunks. But those thoughts and sounds and sights seem only to accentuate his loneliness and fuel his desire for his absent lover.

The music is based around a beautiful acoustic guitar part with a number of lovely riffs. It's mostly finger picked, although it is a mix of plucked chords and single note runs rather than a traditional finger picking pattern. The guitar is accentuated by keyboards, electric guitar and pedal steel.

Southland of the Heart[19] is a song about offering a lover solace from the trials and tribulations of life. It's filled with beautifully crafted images of everyday annoyances, starting with the opening line: "when the wild-eyed dogs of day to day/come snapping at your heels." The images pile up through three verses to the final couplets:

> When the nightmare's creeping closer
> And your wheels are in the mud
> When everything's ambiguous
> Except the taste of blood

In the chorus, Bruce presents a picture of an oasis in the wilderness, "the southland of the heart/where night blooms perfume the breeze." He asks his lover to "lie down/take your rest with me." In subsequent choruses, he adds some details about this place of sanctuary. It's "where the saints go lazily" and "everyone was always free." There's a little bit of New Orleans in this mysterious place.

Musically, this is a country-folk piece, centered on the acoustic guitar. There's some nice organ work and pedal steel. Trumpet and saxophones punctuate the choruses and turnarounds.

Live on My Mind[20] is a wonderful, unhurried love song. He wrote it on a trip to Maui, before **Dart to the Heart** was recorded. While it would have fit in with that collection very well thematically, the arrangement would probably have been completely different. This arrangement fits easily with the fluid, jazz feel of many of the pieces on **The Charity of Night**.

The song has three short verses and a chorus. In the opening line, he sees his lover "standing in the door against the dark/fireflies around you like a crown of sparks." She blows him a kiss "that blurs my vision/blurs the human condition." In this dim, shadowy light, he sees the best of the human condition, the rest falls away.

In the second verse, he associates his lover with more imagery from his surroundings; she's "the ocean ringing in my brain" and his "island ripe with cane." She has the "scent of strange flowers," and he feels her "fluid motion like the wind in grass." In many of his earlier nature songs, Bruce anthropomorphizes nature, giving the wind, rain, sun and lightning human attributes. He also uses nature as a connection to the divine. Here, he is giving those natural and perhaps divine attributes to his lover.

In the final verse, he asks his lover to light him, "like incense" or "a candle", or "a searchlight." He wants her love to stoke his flames of passion and love. Compare this to *Lord of the Starfields* where he asks God to "keep me burning." He tells her that "time means nothing when I look into your eyes." In the chorus, he says that he wants to see her eyes "looking into mine." She is always "live on my mind." Her love obliterates time and joins them to the very heart of the universe.

The drums on this track utilize a more traditional jazz sound with lots of high hat and cymbals mixed in. There's also a fluid and melodic electric guitar solo and the vibes blend in with the percussion and the bass to give it a tropical lushness.

Mango[21] is a beautiful and erotic minor key ballad, mixing Bruce's delicately finger-picked acoustic guitar with Daniel Janke on the kora, a 21 string West African harp that looks a little like a banjo, but sounds somewhat like a harp.[22] Lyrically, the song is structured chorus, verse, chorus, verse, chorus, but the music for the repeated chorus sounds a little more like a verse and vice versa.

The song is an ode to female sexuality. The mango is a somewhat exotic, tropical fruit. His lover has "a mango in the garden" which is "sweet as can be." It is also "full of mystery" and "from the original tree." Most importantly, she "shares it with me."

He's got to have this mango and the verses suggest he is stealing into the garden late at night to have a bite. The moonlight betrays him as "tears of light poured over me/ and ricocheted all around." He's busted, but it doesn't matter, because this is not an unrequited love song. Margo Timmons of the Cowboy Junkies contributes steamy harmony vocals to drive home the song's message.

Isn't That What Friends Are For[23] is a long, mostly spoken word poem. Only the brief chorus is sung and Lucinda Williams adds a stunning harmony. It's a mellow, unhurried folk song with beautiful acoustic guitar work. In a radio interview, Bruce talked about the song at length and it conveys a lot about the life of the traveling musician. He reveals that:

> The 'you' in that song is my friend Jonatha Brooke who's [formerly] of a group called The Story... Jonatha and I had been going through similar things at a distance from each other (a couple years ago now), sort of upheavals in our respective lives and comparing notes over the phone for a while and we finally actually got a chance, after many months [to meet]. One of the weird things about being a touring musician is that you make friends with other people who do what you do but you only see them, you know, when you sort of flash past each other waving on the bus, or you know, at the occasional festival once in a while you get lucky enough that you actually end up in the same place at the same time with time to spend. Eventually you know, this happened, with me and Jonatha. While I was waiting for her to show up at the designated rendezvous point, I ended up writing that song based on our phone conversations and a few other bits and pieces from my notebook."[24]

The song is very much an intimate conversation with a friend. The rhythm is slow, almost hesitant, perhaps a little too slow and lingering a little too long.

Friendship and love is also the subject of the song *Look How Far*. Bruce says that he wrote the song:

when I was on my way to a seminar about religion and art. The idea for the song developed after a short meeting with Ani DiFranco (Canadian [sic actually American] folk-storyteller with her own record label, editor). You meet a lot of people in this business and once in a while you become friends or you want a friendship, but most of the time there is no time for that. I realised that this frustrated feeling, that there is never enough time, I experience a hundred times per year. Accordingly, I asked myself how it would be if I had enough time. It's not literally about Ani DiFranco in Look How Far. It could also be Jonatha Brooke, T-Bone Burnett or Jackson Browne, or all those others with whom I have worked. The image of "look how far the light has come" originally stems from the magazine, The Other Side, a Christian-left oriented magazine. The author wrote about the tough reality and asked how long the light takes before it reaches earth. It is a beautiful image and I use it in a different way, but it stems from the magazine.[25]

The song presents an idealized vision of being able to spend time with a friend or lover. They can sit on the rooftop and share a glass of wine and enjoy the "rays of the setting sun." There's "no desperation anywhere." There's nowhere to go, nowhere else to be.

They're caught up in the rat race; "so many miles, so many doors." Just to get through their lives they "need patience" as well as "force." And if they keep working at it, "all fall open in their own due course." Together at last, with a little time to spend, he sees her "limned/in light, golden and thin." It "looks to me/like you're lit up from within." In the chorus, which follows immediately after this he asks us to "look how far the light came/to paint you/this way."

Bruce pictures them 'in this light" with "friendship a fine silver web/stretched across golden smoky haze." This is the real thing; "this is simple/and this is grace." We need to recognize that "this light/is a guest from far away/passing through /the last whisper of day."

At the dawn of a new century, Bruce was still writing love songs and wrestling with the human condition. In the song *Open*[26], he starts each of the first three verses with the phrase "I never live with balance." In the first verse, he "always wake[s] up nervous" and he doesn't really breathe properly. In the second verse, he reports that he's "always liked the notion" of living with balance, but he has an "endless hunger for energy and motion."

The chorus is simply the word "open" repeated three times. In the third verse, he wants to "feel you near me," but then he tells us "there's an aching in my hipbone." He also says he wants to "let my heart drop open. It's early morning and he's just got up. He's not breathing properly and he's nervous. He's trying to open up his body and his mind and his heart. Perhaps his hip is aching because he is practicing yoga.

In the fourth verse, he notes that it's "daylight in the city." He hears a "thumping in the stairwell," which could be people coming and going in the early morning, or perhaps something more provocative. The next line mentions the "Kundalini sunrise". This is a great image. Kundalini is a life force or "psycho-spiritual energy"[27] that lies coiled at the base of the spine. When it is awakened through yoga, tantric sex or spontaneously, it rises through the spine, releasing the energy through the body and sometimes leading to illumination. The sun here is the kundalini energy rising in the morning sky to energize and illuminate us. I've always connected the "kundalini sunrise" with the "thumping in the stairwell," suggesting some early morning sexual activity. Regardless, all of it leads to "a clamoring of church bells," recognizing the intricate dance between the carnal and the spiritual.

In the final verses, he wants his lover to "come over here and kiss me" and he's "savoring your picture." Perhaps she's just been lying in bed in some tantalizing pose. The street is getting noisy outside. She gets up to come and kiss him and the "light comes at you sideways" and "enfolds you like a gown," the gown that she's most likely not wearing. Bruce said in an interview that it was just a picture and his lover was elsewhere, but in that case, his vivid imagination was working overtime on the morning that the song describes.[28]

Wait No More[29] is one of the most stunning and carnal love songs in Bruce's catalogue. The sound and rhythms are vaguely Middle Eastern, particularly Bruce's dobro and Hugh Marsh's violin accompanied by a propulsive beat from the bass, drums and percussion.

Bruce is "sipping wine with angels in this torch-lit tavern by the sea." Outside, "wild things are prowling – storm winds are howling." There's lightning and thunder and "everything's turning into pure crystals of light." The night is electric and the energy is surging all around them; "the heart is a mirror; it throws back the blaze of love."

In the second verse, Bruce asks the question, "What does it take for what's locked up inside to be free?" He wants the angels to "fold me into you, you know where I'm dying to be/ when my ship sets sail on that ocean of deep mystery." Again, he is seeking both freedom and enlightenment, in addition to sexual ecstasy.

In the third verse, his passion and lust have become more insistent and he asks, "What does it take for the heart to explode into stars?" Lightning is exploding all around them and it's "a kiss that lands hot on the loins of the sky." He feels "something uncoil at the base of my spine" and he cries "I want to wait no more/wait no more." This is another reference to kundalini, so he clearly had sex and Eastern Mysticism on his mind during the writing and recording of this album.

Without question the song is both spiritual and physical, both lust and love. The intensity of the storm reflects the intensity of the emotions at play. There's a deep congruence in the universe at this particular moment. The spiritual and physical dimensions are in sync. There's the possibility of a fusion of orgasm and enlightenment.

See You Tomorrow[30] is another song on resonator guitar. Ani DiFranco adds some quirky harmony. Julie Wolf adds some interesting keyboards and accordion. The song begins with an anecdote from his college years about a mercenary that he met, who was "pushing lethal steel." This friend of a friend took a liking to Bruce and wanted to hire him to help in "running guns to Cuba." It all sounded intriguing, until he "realized that his job would be trying to get between this guy and people who were trying to kill him"[31] Despite turning the job down, he "liked the thought of living that guilt free," as he tells us in the second verse.

After that long ago memory, he snaps back to the present, where he is on the street "watching the way the women walk. " It reminds him of his lover, but also of "all my sins." It also reminds him of "all my stalkers" and suggests that they make him a little nervous, as if he was indeed watching this guy's "back/while he did his deal." But whatever pain and guilt lies "on the horizon/can't sink me in sorrow," because he knows he'll be seeing his lover tomorrow.

Still, he's alone and looking "at that fat full moon" and he feels that "these chains of flesh are sour and sweet." Being mortal, these chains are man's fate; so "these we must explore." And in the end, he's "going to feel complete" when he does see her.

I'm not sure that the times became more dangerous in the 80's. After all, our generation, in the words of songwriter David Rodriguez, "grew up with the H-bomb and the Indochinese wars."[32] However, most of the love songs that Bruce wrote starting in the 1980's were more aware of the conditions and forces in the outside world than his previous works. Those forces intrude upon relationships, making love more difficult to sustain. There is great recognition in most of the later songs of this fragility, which give them more of an edge. Additionally, recognition that love can be fleeting sometimes gives it greater meaning and intensity in the moment. As he said so well, "one day you're waiting for the sky to fall/ the next you're dazzled by the beauty of it all."

6 Imperialism and Human Rights

Let us be those creative dissenters who will call our beloved nation to a higher destiny. To a new plateau of compassion, to a more noble expression of humanness.

Martin Luther King Jr.

Bruce released a trilogy of albums in the mid-80's which pick up and explore in depth themes of anti-Imperialism, Human Rights and Justice that he had hinted at in a handful of songs going back as far as 1971. At the risk of dredging up what some people might consider ancient history, some historical context is essential for appreciating major themes in Bruce's work, particularly the songs of the mid-1980's. Narrowly, these concern a critique of U.S. political and military activities in Latin America and the Caribbean and the impact of those activities on the poor and powerless. More broadly, these are connected across time and space to the issues of Native American and other Aboriginal rights, Colonialism across the Third World, Globalization, and the environment impacts of corporate greed. As he puts it in his memoirs, "These songs [on *The Trouble With Normal*, *Stealing Fire*, and *World of Wonders*] decry an abandonment by the powerful of a sense of *humanness* as they inflict widespread suffering, apparently without a second thought."[1]

Some of Bruce's earlier fans did not follow him in the new direction his music and lyrics took him in the 1980's. Whether this is because of the harder edge to the music (though in retrospect not really that hard edged), turning away from Christian or more clearly spiritual themes, or

103

political disagreement is unclear. It is likely some combination of these factors. This is the period when I became familiar with his music and I found it liberating. Here was someone telling truth to power. But, just as I might not have given Bruce a second chance if *Lord of the Starfields* had been my introduction to his music, some fans of that vein of Bruce's music were turned off by songs like *If I Had a Rocket Launcher* or *Call it Democracy*. The music of the 1980's is definitely different from the music of the 70's, both thematically and sonically. There are new issues and concerns and a change in focus, but the differences are perhaps not as great as they appear at first glance.

As early as 1971, Cockburn had criticized the U.S. war in Southeast Asia in his song *Go Down Slow* on moral grounds as well as poor execution, comparing the U.S. to keystone cops and schoolyard bullies. In 1975, his song *Burn* took on U.S. gunboat diplomacy and the CIA in Latin America in a gently satirical tone with an easygoing calypso beat. In the early 1980's, Cockburn had the opportunity to actually travel to Nicaragua, Honduras and the Mexico/Guatemala border at the invitation of Oxfam Canada.[2] He also had the opportunity to travel to Chile in 1983, barely a decade after the U.S. supported coup that put General Pinochet's government in power. Bruce had always resisted putting too much political content into his songs and had seriously contemplated not recording *If I Had a Rocket Launcher*. But, "in the sophisticated Latin American setting of Chile I understood that the distinction [between art and politics] was specious, that politics actually demanded art."[3] He describes these experiences in great, vivid detail in his memoirs.

The songs that resulted from those experiences are markedly different from his earlier protest songs. As a Canadian, Cockburn is free from preconceived notions of American exceptionalism and can more readily see the divergence between our rhetoric about freedom and the mixed record of our actions.

One of the songs that resulted from this trip was *Nicaragua* from the **Stealing Fire** album. The music for *Nicaragua* is centered on the acoustic guitar, with light percussion. The bass and keyboards are very much in the background here.

In the first verse of the song, Bruce paints a picture postcard of Managua, the capital of Nicaragua. On a cliff overlooking the city, "the U.S. Embassy frowns out over Managua like Dracula's tower." On the street, he sees a kid with a submachine gun, guarding "Fonseca's Tomb," who "at age 15 is a veteran of four years of war."

In the second verse, Bruce describes a vibrant street scene, with a "blue lagoon and flowering trees," but also "full of the ghosts of the heroes of Monimbo." He returns to the present for a moment, to talk about the "women of the town laundry" who "work and gossip and laugh at me." As he walks on, he sees the bullet holes on the building facades, and muses,

> For every scar on a wall
> There's a hole in someone's heart
> Where a loved one's memory lives

The events in Monimbo occurred only five years before, but even so, the mood is not of despair, but of hope. In the chorus Bruce channels the hope and anxiety that he feels in the streets:

> In the flash of this moment
> You're the best of what we are --
> Don't let them stop you now
> Nicaragua

In the final verse, Bruce is observing the streets again and mentions "Sandino in his Tom Mix hat" who "gazes from billboards and coins." Bruce reports the caption to these posters in Spanish that translates as "Sandino lives in the struggle for peace." A couple of lines later, Bruce tells us that Sandino "stood up to the U.S. Marines." Bruce returns from this reflection on the past, to a present, where "Washington panics at U2 shots of Cuban-style latrines," as they spy on revolutionary Nicaragua from planes and ships.

Bruce repeats the hopeful chorus after this reminder of the fragility of peace, under the threatening presence of the U.S. military.

The average American listener in 1984 (let alone 2012), would probably have been dumbfounded by this song. Many people who read the newspapers or watched some TV news reporting might have been dimly aware that the U.S. was supporting the Contras, who were fighting the "Communist" government in Nicaragua. Another small percentage might have also been dimly aware that the "Communists" had overthrown a U.S. supported government run by someone named Somoza. An even smaller number might have known that the Somoza government was a fairly brutal dictatorship.

Before looking at the deeper history that Bruce manages to encapsulate in this 5 minute song, let's dispose of some of the specific references. Fonseca, referenced in the first verse, was Carlos Fonseca Amador, who was a teacher and librarian who founded the Sandinista National Liberation Front. He was killed in the mountains several years before the Sandinista's were able to overthrow the Somoza regime.[4]

In the second verse, Barrio Monimbo was the site of a battle and massacre during the revolution in 1978 where the National Guard used tanks, helicopters and airplanes against the people of the village who fought back with rifles, handguns and Molotov cocktails. Hundreds, including women and children, were massacred.[5]

In the third verse, Sandino was a Nicaraguan national hero from the 1920's, who was captured in photographs wearing a broad brimmed cowboy hat. Tom Mix was a Hollywood actor who made hundreds of Westerns between 1920 and 1935 and who has been referenced or memorialized in both fiction and later movies.[6]

While the U.S. did not directly fight the Sandinistas in the 1980's, it is appropriate that the embassy is one of the focal points of the opening verse of the song. It is also appropriate in several ways that it is compared to "Dracula's tower." The historical Dracula was a very bloody ruler in Eastern Europe in the 15th Century, responsible for the deaths of large numbers of civilians, but also revered in Romania for driving out the Turks.[7] In the song the image connects to the lines at the end about spying, since vampires are shadowy creatures that go about their business in the dark. However, the centrality of the image of the embassy also relates to the long history of U.S. involvement in Nicaragua and Central America generally, a legacy that is little known by the vast majority of Americans.

One of many reasons the U.S. became involved in Nicaragua in the early part of the 20th Century, was because Nicaragua was considered as a potential site for a canal between the Caribbean and the Pacific Ocean, which was eventually built across the Isthmus of Panama. In 1909, a conservative Governor in one of Nicaragua's eastern provinces rebelled against the liberal president of the country. Though the rebellion was unsuccessful, a couple of Americans were killed and the U.S. Marines intervened and eventually drove the President from power. Over the next two decades, Marines were involved periodically in keeping the peace and making sure that Nicaragua was led by people sympathetic to U.S. political and business interests.[8]

Augusto Sandino was born out of wedlock in 1895 to a wealthy landowner and a servant girl. In 1921 he tried to kill a man who had insulted his mother, and fled to Honduras, Guatemala and later to Mexico. He worked for a while for Standard Oil, but also fell sway to the revolutionary fervor in Mexico. He returned to Nicaragua in 1926, just in time for another rebellion, this time by liberal rebels against the conservative government backed by the United States.

Sandino formed a small guerilla force and engaged in some failed attacks on government outposts. He then tried to join up with the main rebel forces and was initially rebuffed, but eventually was given a commission. He returned to the mountains and recruited more peasants to join his army and had considerable success attacking government forces. The rebels were well on their way to capturing Managua and ending the conflict, but the U.S. threatened to intervene and forced to two sides to the negotiating table.

The results of the negotiations essentially re-established the status quo. The conservative President was allowed to finish out his term and the rebels disbanded. However, Sandino and his army refused to lay down their arms and went back to the mountains. He continued fighting and the U.S. Marines continued to chase him for a number of years. By 1931, the U.S., partially in reaction to the Great Depression, decided it was time to pull back and all troops left after the 1932 election which installed a liberal government. Responsibility for dealing with Sandino fell to the National Guard, which was still advised by the U.S. military, and he was eventually assassinated at the order of General Anastacio Somoza Garcia in 1934. Somoza forced the liberal President Sacasa to step down in 1936 and declared himself President. He and his family ruled the country for the next 45 years, and many observers would consider it a brutal rule that disregarded the rights and aspirations of the Nicaraguan people, while the United States turned a blind eye to what was going on.

If you pick almost any country in Central America - Guatemala, El Salvador, or Honduras, for example - you will find similar stories. From the late 1890's through the early 1940's, Guatemala was ruled by a series of Military dictatorships. These governments were generally very sympathetic to U.S. political and business interests and there was very little need for a heavy handed policy from Washington.[9]

In 1930, General Jorge Ubico came to power with U.S. support and established one of the most brutal dictatorships in the region. He gave away land to the United Fruit Company and allowed U.S. military bases to be established. His policies sided with Urban and Landowning elites against the peasantry, particularly the indigenous Indian populations, who he considered no better than animals.

By 1944, his brutal and repressive policies were beginning to cause a serious backlash in the country and Ubico decided to step down. Because his handpicked successor was widely despised and had strong Nazi sympathies, Ubico eventually appointed a Military Triumvirate to rule the country. They decided to hold elections for President, but one of the Officers, Federico Ponce Vaides decided that he would take control of the government in July of the same year.

Jacobo Arbenz Guzman, who was born in 1913 to a wealthy family, had been a promising Military Cadet and served briefly in the Military before becoming a teacher at the prestigious Military Academy in 1937.

By 1943, he had risen to one of the top positions in the Academy. However, in the late 30's, he began to be acquainted with the writings of Karl Marx and other socialist theorists.

When Arbenz opposed the Ponce government, he was abruptly fired from his position. He left the country and began organizing other revolutionary exiles in neighboring El Salvador. Along with other rebels, they overthrew the Ponce government in October, 1944 and established a ruling Junta. They decided to hold democratic elections before the end of the year and a civilian leader was elected. Arbenz was appointed to head the Military. The new government initiated reforms to modernize the country. While these reforms were relatively modest, they infuriated large landowners and disgruntled military leaders. The U.S. government and U.S. business interests were also less than enthusiastic. The new government fended off some 25 coup attempts over the rest of the decade.

Arbenz was overwhelmingly elected President in the elections of 1950. He continued the reforms that had been begun in the previous administration and expanded the agrarian land reform efforts. He was viewed by the U.S. Government with increasing concern, both because of these reforms, and his tolerance of left-wing organizations and the Labor party. As part of the land reform, the United Fruit Company would have been forced to give up more than two-thirds of the land that it controlled.

In 1954, under the pretext of ties to the Soviets, the U.S. administration authorized the CIA to overthrow the government. Arbenz was forced to flee the country and another military government was formed. The reforms instituted by Arbenz and his predecessor were either weakened or discarded altogether.

Eventually, the country devolved into a period of almost endless civil war, starting in 1960 and not ending until the late 1990's. The civil war involved the government, right-wing paramilitary groups and left-wing insurgents and became one of many, bloody proxy Cold War conflicts with the U.S. supporting the government and tolerating the right-wing paramilitary groups and Cuba supporting the left-wing insurgents.

Hundreds of thousands of Guatemalans were tortured and killed, mainly from the poor and indigenous population. Many thousands more escaped to Mexico and other surrounding countries as refugees.

This history forms the backdrop for one of Cockburn's most well known songs, the unlikely "hit" *If I had a Rocket Launcher*, which also appears on **Stealing Fire**. The song chronicles Bruce's experience visiting refugee camps along the Mexico/Guatemala border. *Rocket Launcher* has a very distinctive finger-picked electric guitar part and a keyboard riff that sounds like tiny bells ringing. This is some of the most intricate guitar work that Bruce had done since the end of the 1970's. Here he plays multiple electric guitars, though the main guitar part could easily be done on acoustic guitar, which he has done many times in concert, although in concert he pretty much plays all the parts melded together. Here, he uses the overdubbing capabilities of the studio for maximum impact, to create a more complex, multi-layered sound.

Before explaining anything, Bruce drops us right into the action:

> Here comes the helicopter -- second time today
> Everybody scatters and hopes it goes away
> How many kids they've murdered only God can say

Bruce reacts to the scene in horror and says, almost as a matter of fact, that "if I had a rocket launcher, I'd make somebody pay." Over the next verses, he talks about torture, starvation in the camps, or "some less humane fate" that might befall the refugees. As he related in a 1992 interview:

> These people were dealing with this fear every day -- Guatemalan helicopters would fly over the camps, maybe drop a bomb on them, or some soldiers would kidnap some of the refugees, take them into the woods and chop them up...You know the scene at the end of the movie 'Apocalypse Now?' That's nothing compared to what I saw. [10]

In another interview, he talks of writing the song. "I was in a hotel drinking a bottle of Scotch the day after I came out of the refugee camps, and I was in tears thinking about it and writing this song. It doesn't get much more direct than that."[11] He also wrote in his journal about how he now understood how someone could kill another human being.

In 2010, he had this to say about the song:

> When I wrote that song, in 1983, it wasn't intended to be any kind of weapon. It was an expression of my own surprise at feeling so specifically a certain way, when I was confronted with the [Guatemalan] refugee-camp scene [in Mexico]. It's about a sense of outrage. I don't know whether I'm violent or not. I don't know if I have the talent for it. I think probably I'm chicken, if anything.[12]

Understanding the general outlines and knowing where Bruce's sympathies lie helps us to understand both this song and much of his work from the 1980's and beyond. I could dredge up similar examples from across the globe, where U.S. interests have clashed dramatically with the aspirations of poor people and others yearning for a better life, many of whom looked back at the American Revolution as an inspiration for taking up arms against brutal dictatorships.

Under the smokescreen of the Cold War, it was possible to frame the issue in terms of American values against sinister Communist plots to take over the world, and perhaps excuse the collateral damage, especially when most people hadn't even heard about it. One might even excuse aggressive support for providing a good environment for businesses like the United Fruit Company to thrive and prosper. I used to wonder how the U.S. government could have so consistently fought on the wrong side of these issues, particularly the harsh exploitation of poor people and overthrowing popularly elected governments. Didn't our government know that a backlash was inevitable? Hadn't they witnessed that backlash time after time, in country after country?

Then I wake up in 2012 and open the newspaper and read about the Republican war on working people and labor rights in Wisconsin and Ohio. Every day Republican candidates for President were calling a fairly moderate President Obama a socialist who is trying to destroy the country for trying to blunt some of the worst excesses of income inequality and preserve at least some of the legacy of the New Deal and Great Society. They also called him a failed economic leader for, apparently and with both hands tied behind his back, failing to rescue the country from the impacts of failed Republican economic policies. And I see that this history may not be such an anomaly after all.

Bruce's experiences in Central America, led inevitably to a broader critique of U.S. and First World economic interactions with the rest of the world.

> Through a growing familiarity with the Nicaraguan revolution, a recognition of North-South relations began to take shape. Nicaragua, the Philippines, Chile, virtually all of Latin America really, Indonesia, emerging African countries... Wherever you look you find the same financial interests at work. Working to get rich without controls, at the expense of the poor. When the poor complain, out come the troops, and then the arms companies get rich too.[13]

This critique shows up most forcefully in the song *Call it Democracy* from the album **World of Wonders**, without question the most strident and possibly controversial song in Cockburn's catalogue. The song is a polemic against the International Monetary Fund (IMF), which was created in 1944, under the auspices of the United Nations, to provide financial assistance to countries suffering from serious financial difficulties, usually an inability to pay debts to International banks and other countries. Countries that accept such assistance have been subject to economic and political conditions, which have usually been quite harsh. The impact of these conditions is usually felt disproportionately by the poor and working classes, who are subject to lower wages, longer hours, reduced working conditions, and other cost cutting measures.

In the first two verses, Cockburn comes out with rhetorical guns blazing. The IMF is a bunch of "international loan sharks" who are "backed by the guns of profit hungry military profiteers." They "rob life of its quality" and "render rage a necessity,/by turning countries into labor camps." They are nothing more than "modern slavers in drag as champions of freedom."

The chorus chimes in with "IMF, dirty MF," which "takes away everything it can get." In the end, he accuses the IMF of keeping poor countries "on the hook with insupportable debt."

After the chorus, he talks about the local leaders, that rotating cast of dictators that we met in Nicaragua and Guatemala, now spruced up for the Television age. They're really just "paid-off local bottom feeders" and their countries are "open for business like a cheap bordello." The IMF and the International Business elites pat themselves on the back and "call it Democracy."

In the final verse he looks in the eyes of children, "trying to make the best of it the way kids do," but he warns the elites that "one day you're going to rise from your habitual feast/to find yourself staring down the throat of the beast/they call the revolution."

At a live performance in 2000, Bruce had this to say about the song:

> That song came from the time of neo-conservatism, when governments supported business at the cost of lives and nobody gave a shit. We have since moved on to neo-liberalism, when governments support business at the cost of lives and nobody gives a shit; and I see we're moving on to neo-feudalism, that's the service economy coming at you. We will all serve. I'm not quite sure who we're serving.[14]

Bruce extends his economic critique to Free Trade in the song *Mighty Trucks of Midnight*[15]. It is not about the West, but musically it has many of the same sonic elements as the songs that precede it on the album **Nothing But a Burning Light**, including a fat TV Western-style signature riff. The beginning of the song is about the disappearance of industries in Canada as a result of Free Trade and agreements like NAFTA. The factories are moving away "down to Mexico where they work for hardly any pay." The whole country is being "sold down the river." And in the background, you can hear the "mighty trucks of midnight/moving on."

The second verse is somewhat puzzling and seems somewhat tangential to the subject at hand. "Wave a flag, wave the bible," seems to suggest some kind of protest, like the Tea Party, lamenting the fact that the jobs are disappearing and perhaps blaming it on our sins or lack of patriotism. Bruce doesn't want any part of it, saying "don't wave that thing at me." He then changes the subject to Love, which comes out of left field:

> The tide of love can leave your prizes scattered
> But when you get to the bottom it's the only thing that matters

Love is a powerful force and sometimes it leaves us battered and bruised. Still it is "the only thing that matters." Whatever we seem to do, the "mighty trucks of midnight" are "moving on" without us.

The last verse seems to rationalize non-action. We can't "make things last forever" and "it's a sin to try." In the end, we've "got to let go of the things that keep you tethered." You need to act with some "grace and then be on your way." This is a very Buddhist or Taoist view of existence and how we need to be detached and it's perfectly valid as a spiritual response. Of course, two "of the things that keep you tethered" are jobs and community, which are being destroyed by the forces symbolized by the Mighty Trucks.

This seems like two songs to me, about two completely different things. Why is it alright, even essential, in the song *Dream Like Mine* [discussed in the next chapter] for the Native Americans to stand up for their rights, protect their land and fight to restore the balance, but people losing their jobs and way of life to trade should just accept the fact and move on?

Is this cosmic payback for all of our complicity in taking the land from the Native Americans in the first place? I just don't see how this squares with Bruce's vision of justice. I can see, that like the Tea Party in 2010 or Trump in 2016, many protest movements wind up identifying the wrong problems and consequently come up with inadequate or bogus solutions to problems. But that doesn't mean that they shouldn't complain or even fight.

I can see a couple of distinctions between the two cases, but I don't agree with the argument that Bruce appears to be making. First is that many Native Americans have a sense of "the power of a thousand generations" and a connection to the land, which most Whites don't have. In *Dream Like Mine* the Native Americans are invoking their spiritual power to protect the land. In comparison to the land, businesses are a transitory thing, creations of man with much less permanence, and in many cases with an imbalance of power and rewards between ownership and labor. If the song's message was to suggest that we need to rebuild our communities and our economy or that we need to work together to find solutions, then I would be wholeheartedly in favor of it. But Bruce seems to simply be saying that we have to let it go.

The song *Trickle Down*[16] is about the way we structure our economy around keeping the top 1% fat and happy. We then pretend that benefits will trickle down to everyone else. To point out that this is just self-serving bullshit is generally shouted down with charges of "class warfare".

The song is one of two songs Bruce co-wrote with jazz pianist Andy Milne, who was introduced to Bruce by long-time collaborator and violinist Hugh Marsh. Hugh,

> called up one day and said, "There's this guy Andy Milne, and he's doing pretty neat stuff and wants to meet you." Soon after that we went to New York and Andy came to the gig and introduced himself, gave me a couple of CDs, and said he was interested in collaborating on some songs. The stuff he gave me was amazing. I'd been having this big, long dry spell, and I thought, "This is a gift, a chance to try something I've never done to a significant degree—collaborate with somebody else as a songwriter—and this is going to break the dry spell." We got together, and I had some lyrics that ended up becoming "Trickle

Down."[17]

The song is a jazz rap song. The arrangement is very dense and is propelled by Andy Milne's piano, lots of percussion and bass. Bruce and Andy trade solos during the instrumental break, the only place where the guitar really leaps out of the mix.

The song starts out with the "picture on magazine boardroom pop star/pinstripe prophet of peckerhead greed." Our minds leap immediately to billionaire icons like Donald Trump or Lloyd Blankfein of Goldman Sachs or even Bill Gates and Steve Jobs (sans pinstripes).

Pause to think of our bridges and roads falling apart in disrepair and "what used to pass for education now looks more like ignoration." We just "take the people's money and slip it to the corporation." If you are lucky enough to have a job, there's still "workfare foul air homeless beggars everywhere," while "picturephone aristocrats lounge around the pool." It's all a "big bucks shakedown," where you've "first got to privatize then you get to piratize." Those Somali pirates capturing oil tankers have nothing on Bernie Madoff, hedge fund managers, and other Wall Street tycoons. Similar themes are also explored in the songs *Slow Down Fast* and *Grim Travelers*. *Grim Travelers*, from way back in 1981, also interestingly associates International Bankers with Terrorists.

Bruce is not known primarily as an "environmental" songwriter, but he has always shown in his songs a strong appreciation for nature, and the destructive meddling of man. To the extent that he can claim the mantle, it is on full display in one of his most famous songs, *If a Tree Falls*, which manages to deftly connect global forest clear-cutting with the perversion of the global food supply, climate change, the devastating impact on indigenous people and rampant species extinction.

The words to the verses are spoken. There's a muted rage in the voice, spitting out lines like "ancient cord of coexistence/hacked by parasitic greedhead scam." The tragedy of clear-cutting, destroying the world's forests goes on across the globe, from Borneo to Brazil and even in British Columbia, we hear the "cortege rhythm of falling timber." Cortege is a word most often used for a funeral procession.

It's all about money and greed. He asks "what kind of currency grows in these new deserts." But it's just business as usual; "cut and move on, cut and move on." Business interests:

> Take out wildlife at a rate of species every single day
> Take out people who've lived with this for 100,000 years -
> Inject a billion burgers worth of beef

In the final verse, Bruce makes a spiritual connection to the environmental disaster that we are creating, his voice filled with despair. This force that we have unleashed is a "busy monster [that] eats dark holes in the spirit world/where wild things have to go/to disappear/forever."

Bruce's spiritual values form a strong foundation for his views on human rights, economics and the environment. His innate sense that all things and all people are interconnected on a spiritual level allows him to fully appreciate the beauty and value of the world and its inhabitants. It strengthens his critique of the global economic system, which is a perversion of that same view of interconnectedness. The economic system severs the spiritual connection and monetizes all the things and people, thereby reducing them to the lowest common denominator. It uses up their commodity value and then tosses them away. As a result, what is unique and meaningful is lost.

7 *Indian Wars*

My people are few. They resemble the scattering trees of a storm-swept plain.
The great, and I presume -- good, White Chief sends us word that he wishes to
buy our land but is willing to allow us enough to live comfortably.

Chief Seattle, 1854

While on the subject of human rights and economic justice, it would
be a grave oversight to forget the issue of Native American or aboriginal
rights and the dismal record of all governments on the American
continents in dealing with indigenous populations.   This is a tale that
goes all the way back to Columbus' "discovery" of America. By and
large, this tale is far better known than the others, but the brutality and
broken promises have tended to fade from our collective memory. There
are so few Native Americans left, after all, and in the U.S. most of them
are on reservations far from our population centers. When we think of
them at all, it is mostly as a cultural curiosity. Some politically savvy
tribes have created corporations that now receive large government
contracts based on their protected minority status. And of course some
tribes have made a lot of money by running casinos. Perhaps they will
ultimately buy back the continent by selling the white man fire water
and exploiting his addictions to slot machines and cards.

Bruce grew up in a community of primarily white people of European ancestry. He did not have any significant contact with Native Canadians throughout his childhood and even into early adulthood. This changed as he started driving across the continent on his early tours and walkabouts. He later described his initial contacts and how they led to his song *Red Brother, Red Sister*.

> In the early 70's, I met Native Canadians for the first time. I began to understand their situation and the history that led to it. There was this cab driver in Regina, an older guy, with a white duck tail gone yellow at the edges. We must have been getting the truck fixed or something, but he was taking us somewhere and recommending racially 'correct' establishments.[1]

The song is about racial insensitivity and discrimination against Natives. The first verse is about seeing Indian crafts in a Museum. There's a sign that "said wasn't it clever what they used to do." The second verse is about the encounter with the cab driver in Regina. In the third verse, he talks about going to a powwow where he "felt the people's love/joy flow around." Despite being moved by the ceremony, he feels nothing but shame at "how they used my saviour's name to keep you down." The song first appeared on Bruce's live album, **Circles in the Stream**, in 1977.

Hoop Dancer[2] was written on a trip to Japan in 1979, a few weeks before his song *Tokyo* and shares some of the same feelings of disorientation. The first part of the song is spoken over a repeated percussion and keyboard riff, almost like a computer generated electronic staccato droning, uniquely modern like the chuckle he talks about. There's a jazz bass and Hugh Marsh's violin floating over the top. Bruce is talking about jetlag and going for a walk. The streets and sidewalks are crowded and there's a "seeming infinity of white light and neon."

Out of nowhere, he has a "memory flash of prairie Indian/dancers...on a stage...surrounded by white faces." This is a vision of a tourist recreation of a real Indian ceremony, so it is not quite real. But into this "sea of mind" the "Hoop dancer struts in front." A transformation takes place on "a time line/something like vertical, like perpendicular." It cuts through the dancers, and "through the guilty, sentimental warmth of the crowd." And it reaches back and down to "some essence common to us, to original man."

> Where it intersects the space at hand
> This shaman with the hoops stands
> Aligned like living magnetic needle between deep past
> and looming future
> Butterfly pierced on each drum beat, wing beat, static spark,
> storm front, energy circle delineated by leaping limbs

The second part of the song is actually sung and takes us back to a vision of the Indians dancing on the prairie. The beat picks up and there is an actual melody that keeps up for about three verses. Then the melody disintegrates and the percussion and keyboard riff starts to reassert itself and the violin jerks and Bruce is brought back to the streets of Tokyo. But he can still see the Hoop Dancer vaguely "just beyond the clatter and cars" and he hears "the last long notes of wild voices ring/like Roland's horn."

You may wonder what Roland's horn is. Perhaps you might think of Rahsaan Roland Kirk, who was a jazz sax player who died in 1977. He was somewhat famous for playing two or more reed instruments at the same time, but was also just a very good musician. Bruce was familiar with him at least from his days at the Berklee School. But that's not what the reference is to. Bruce is mixing his metaphors here. Roland is the Medieval/Renaissance hero of such epic poems as the *Song of Roland* and *Orlando Furioso*. Among other attributes he carried a horn that was used to sound the charge or call for help. I'm not sure whether knowing that really enhances your understanding of the song, but it's an interesting aside.

Perhaps more interesting is whether or how the two parts of the song fit together. How does walking down the streets of Tokyo relate to the vision of the Hoop Dancer? I would argue that in both cases, there is the element of aliens coming together. Bruce is surrounded by a sea of Japanese; the Indian Dancers have their tourist crowd. In the ecstasy of the dance, there is a moment where the distance between them is erased. Bruce is similarly able to transcend the distance between himself and the Japanese crowds, becoming one for a brief moment.

Cockburn addresses the issues of Native Rights most directly and forcefully in his song *Stolen Land*, on the compilation album **Waiting for a Miracle,** released in 1987. The song opens by laying out the geographic and temporal dimensions of his story: "From Tierra del Fuego to Ungava Bay/the history of betrayal continues to today." Tierra Del Fuego is at the southern tip of South America and Ungava Bay is on the northern coastline of Quebec. Then Bruce calls on ghosts to lay out his thesis:

> The spirit of Almighty Voice, the ghost of Anna Mae
> Call like thunder from the mountains -- you can hear them say
> It's a stolen land

Almighty Voice was a Cree Indian born in Saskatchewan in 1875, who was killed by Mounted Police in 1897. He spent a couple of years as a fugitive after being accused of killing a government cow in 1895.[3] Anna Mae was an Indian activist in the 1970's in both Canada and the U.S. She was found executed in South Dakota in early 1976.[4]

We have "apartheid in Arizona", and there is "slaughter in Brazil," but "if bullets don't get good PR there's other ways to kill." In the chorus, he recognizes the problem and the intractability of finding a real solution. It's a:

> Stolen land -- but it's all we've got
> Stolen land -- and there's no going back

In the third verse, Bruce has a vision that encapsulates this history of betrayal with striking images:

> In my mind I catch a picture -- big black raven in the sky
> Looking at the ocean -- sail reflected in black eye --
> Sail as white as heroin, white like weathered bones --
> Rum and guns and smallpox gonna change the face of home
> In this stolen land...

In most of Cockburn's work, the sea and sailing are images of freedom and being at peace and centered in one's spiritual being. But this is a vision of death. The sailing ships that crossed the oceans carrying explorers and settlers, as well as rum and guns, changed the face of the continent and brought about a precipitous decline in the Native population over the last 500 years, with smallpox and other diseases being far more deadly than guns. The raven could be an Indian shaman transformed into a bird, flying through the spirit world and seeing in the flash of a moment the entire unfolding of this terrible tragedy.

In the final verse, Bruce talks directly to the audience to establish additional rapport. He's told us all these terrible things that we really don't want to hear about. We probably want to go back to our sit-coms and sports and forget about life for awhile. He says to us sympathetically, "If you're like me you'd like to think we've learned from our mistakes." Then he ends the verse by asking us to help:

> So now we've all discovered the world wasn't only made
> for whites
> What step are you gonna take to try and set things right
> In this stolen land

The song ends on another chorus and we're reminded of our dilemma and our opportunity to "set things right."

The album **Nothing But a Burning Light** leads off with the song, *A Dream Like Mine*, based loosely on:

a Canadian novel by M.T. Kelly. The setting is a Native

American community in confrontation with industrial interests and the law over land use in their area. They're losing, so an old man of the tribe, kind of a shamanistic character, conjures up out of dreams a sort of eternal warrior figure to come to life to try and right the wrongs that are being done... It was that sense of community, that sense of an unbroken link to the past that caught my attention.[5]

The song is fairly simple, starting out with a chorus that describes the power of his dream, which gives him the strength and courage to stand up for what is right. Then in the first verse, he talks about another dream, where he sees things as they used to be and "things were different before." In the dream, "the picture shifts to how it's going to be/balance restored." The second part of the verse, which is almost another chorus since it is repeated, he further delineates what makes the dream special. He tells us that,

> When you know even for a moment
> That it's your time
> Then you can walk with the power
> Of a thousand generations

This is really about our perception of the universe that surrounds us and breaking through the barrier between the material and spiritual dimensions to understand that all things are connected by powerful webs of energy and spirit. This insight transcends the nominal source for the song; it is not just a song about a story that he read in a book.

In the second verse, he contemplates the beauties of nature: the rocks, grass, soil, river and sky. He tells us that he "never thought of possession, that all this was mine." The irony, of course, is that when you don't try to possess things then they sometimes become truly and completely available to you.

As with all the songs on **Nothing but a Burning Light**, this one has a very distinctive sound. The interplay between the bass, the organ, and the electric guitar creates a very strong and lush atmosphere. The main guitar riff is very simple, but has a very classic Western feel to it.

Kit Carson[6] continues with one of the album's main themes, the ongoing conflict between Native Americans and the White men. If you grew up in the 50's, you probably watched a lot of movies and TV that romanticized the men like Carson who tamed the West. Generally, you had positive views of these characters, and Bruce was no different.

> I grew up with the Western hero, who was thought to be basically a good guy, saving maidens in distress on the railroad tracks. When you hear the real story, he was sort of an unsavory character. He befriended the Navajo long enough to learn their ways and learn where they all were. He then offered himself to the U.S. Cavalry to drive the Navajos off their land and betrayed the people who were good to and accepted him. He was responsible for a large number of the deaths, including burning their villages, poisoning their waterholes and the general dislocation of their culture.[7]

There was some discussion on the Humans list-serv several years ago about how Carson's descendants were thinking of suing Bruce for defamation. In the same interview quoted about, he says that he got the story of Carson from a Navajo Indian.[8] I've read good and bad things about Carson and it appears that he may have been somewhat more sympathetic to the Indians than the average Westerner of that period, but certainly by today's standards, his actions are pretty much indefensible.

This is not one of my favorite songs by Bruce, even though I sympathize deeply with the characterization of the conflict between the Native Americans and the U.S. Army, regardless of Carson's actual role. I feel that as a song, it editorializes too much and tells too little of the story. I simply can't believe that the President would say anything like "make my great lands barren for me," or that Carson would accept the task from the President and remark that "my fall's not yet complete."

The actions and motivations are highly stylized and the story is boiled down to a very elemental form, almost like a Kabuki drama, which is more dance movement and music than story.

Despite this, Bruce almost redeems the song, with the final verse, where he shies away from judgment and simply says that "somewhere there's a restless ghost/that used to bear his name." In other words, Carson is paying for his sins. The musical arrangement is quite good. The blues electric guitar plays off the organ. There's a shaker that sounds almost like a rattlesnake and an acoustic bass that sounds a little like a very deep moaning violin.

Indian Wars[9] at its heart is a folk acoustic ensemble piece with Bruce on Guitar and lead vocals, Jackson Browne strumming a resonator guitar and singing harmony, and Mark O'Connor playing a wonderful country-folk fiddle and mandolin. As the title suggests, it continues the Western theme, invoking the long conflict between the Native Americans and the White men.

The verses tell a tale of a life of hardship and struggle. The Indians live "out in the desert where the wind never stops." They are just "a few dozen survivors." It's "never been easy…but the pulse of the land is the pulse of their lives."

The tone of the song is one of weariness, which is encapsulated in the chorus: "you thought it was over but it's just like before/will there never be an end to the Indian wars." They've been beaten down, yet they are "ragged but proud."

In contrast to the history, what we've grown up with in the cinema, and the "poison and flame" that we heard about in *Kit Carson,* the nature of the war has changed.

> It's not breech-loading rifles and wholesale slaughter
> It's kickbacks and thugs and diverted water

The verses conclude with the thought that the treaties that the Indians signed were mostly worthless pieces of paper. They could have been drafted "in sand," since the agreements were rarely kept and were often rewritten a few years after they were signed to grant more concessions to the White Man or to move the Indians to even more remote reservations.

For me this is a much more effective song than Kit Carson. It's not flashy or dramatic, but it paints a vivid picture of the hard life that many Native Americans have. I remember visiting Old Oraibi in Arizona years ago. My wife and I were driving around the countryside, in a vain attempt to find some "real" Indians.

We had driven about 160 miles that day and wound up at a Hopi Cultural Center in Northern Arizona. This was a small museum, gift shop and restaurant in a modern building. After eating lunch, we asked the hostess where we should go to see something more authentic. She suggested that all the tourists went to Old Oraibi, which was about eight miles further up the road, or to Walpi, which would have been about 35 more miles.

Old Oraibi is a pueblo on the top of Third Mesa, which has been continuously occupied since at least 1020 AD. We drove off the main road onto a bumpy dirt road when we reached the village. Before you reach the village, there is a stone house with a big sign out front, saying that all non-Hopi should go no further. You must leave your car and get permission from the chief to walk to the village. You must also promise to take no photographs, do no sketching, nor make any other kind of recordings. This is a sacred place to the Hopi.

We signed the guest book, pledged to be good and walked down the dirt road to the village. The village would have been a photographer's dream, although not in the sense we were expecting. As you walked down the road, the sheer poverty and desolation of the place made you feel that you had somehow violated the present, rather than the spirits of the past.

Many of the old adobe huts were abandoned, crumbling, and roofless. Some were patched up. Sitting outside one hut, on the second level, a young looking man was carving a Kachina doll. We kept walking and tried not to stare, even thought it was interest that we felt, rather than the invading eye of the tourist.

The site overlooks a wide valley. You could see to the horizon for almost 270 degrees. The second mesa looms to the northeast. This was a landscape of dry grasses and stunted shrubs, difficult and lonely. A young boy was listening to rock music and shining his motorcycle outside another adobe. A couple of cinder block houses were mixed in, looking somehow cheap and flimsy next to the poor adobe which had served so well for a thousand years.

Aside from about five Indians and a couple of tourists, we saw no one. The village seemed almost like a ghost town. We felt uncomfortable and disappointed, like voyeurs.

We got in our car and drove off. It rained some as we drove and you could see the rain coming across the plains, with the sunlight chasing it from behind. We saw a double rainbow across the whole late afternoon sky. Bruce would've written a song.

Anyone interested in the water rights issues in the Southwest should check out the great novel *The Milagro Beanfield Wars* by John Nichols. It's a beautiful evocation of place and the struggle for the soul of the country between poor Latinos, developers, young hippies, and politicians. His whole trilogy is a great read, though in the end it can be pretty depressing.[10] If you are interested in the collision between the past and present in Native American life and culture, Leslie Marmon Silko's book *Ceremony* is also a very good read.

How do we get beyond these divisions? How do we heal the wounds and move forward? Bruce may suggest a path in *Put our Hearts Together*,[11] a reggae tune from the early 1980's. Bruce wrote the song while on vacation in the Caribbean, so he was probably hearing a lot of reggae and related Caribbean musical styles. The first verse is a laundry list of things we don't really need, such as: "trade expansion," drug addicts and dealers, conquistadors and "the Inquisition", macho western gunslingers, hate, "reactionary politicians", jihad and the "IRA."

In the chorus, he tells us that the answer is "to put our hearts together." And we need to dance and "get a rhythm that will shake creation."

In the second verse, he lays out his vision that multi-culturalism is destiny. We don't need, or want, "supremacy of pink people." As he puts it "the whole of history is a growing together." Racial purity is a myth and the basis of backward and destructive ideologies like Nazism and the KKK.

After the second chorus, the third verse attacks unequal gender roles and patriarchal social norms, like the 1950's idea of "woman in kitchen, man in palace," with everyone "worshipping the performance of the phallus." He also takes a shot at warmongering politicians as "limp lance phallocrat[s]," with their "finger on the trigger."

His song *To Raise the Morning Star*[12] continues the thought. It starts out with intertwined bass and two electric guitar riffs and drums and keyboards join in. As he described it,

> the phrase, 'to raise the morning star' comes from the Australian aborigines. They sing to raise the morning star, literally. And of course, it's a beautiful image. That image went with the rest of the song, which was a kind of imaginary vision I had. The place I used to live in downtown Toronto had a roof where I could stand. One night when I was looking at the lights of the city, I began thinking about all the people who were sleeping. All of them were dreaming; wishing things were better. And in their dreams, they were trying to make things better. Their dreams and wishes were trying to light the skies.[13]

He goes on to say that it's "a God song of mine." This is a very mystical song of almost boundless spiritual depth. The last verse returns to the idea of a multiracial, multi-cultural paradise that he also sang about in *Put Our Hearts Together*:

> Singing for the yellow and the brown and the black
> For the red and the white people, too
> Dovetailing strong points with the things we lack
> Singing for the people like me and you

8 Meditations on the Journey

If someone is dying in the south,
goes and says there is nothing to fear.
If there is a dispute or lawsuit in the north,
goes and says to stop being petty.
And when there is a drought, he sheds tears.

Kenji Miyazawa[1]

Throughout his career as a songwriter and performer, Bruce has tantalized his audiences with glimpses of spirit in the ordinary moments of life. He has also tried to articulate for us what he feels his place is in the world, and by extension we can perhaps glimpse what our place is in the world. He's taken us on a magical journey, from the Mountains of Nepal, to the beaches of the Caribbean, to African lowlands, Iraq, Cambodia, and Nicaragua. He's taken us inside refugee camps in Mexico and Honduras. And we've walked the back alleys of Toronto and the pine forests of British Columbia with him. He's reported on and examined those journeys, those many footsteps.

Lovers in a Dangerous Time[2] is the first Bruce Cockburn song that I ever heard, or at least that I was aware of hearing. I was hooked from the opening electric guitar and bass riff. I stood in the room transfixed by this music. In 2010, Bruce said of this song that:

129

When I wrote that, I was thinking of kids my daughter's age. She was quite young at the time. But, for any given individual, the world has always been a place where you could die. That's the baseline. At times we can ignore that, more than other times. There are times when fear is in the air, and, of course, there's always people around willing to exploit that, and enhance it, if need be.[3]

In the sense that he describes it here, you could consider that notion of dying as sort of the background radiation in the Universe, a constant hum that more often than not we are only dimly aware of. We get inured to it. In the 60's and 70's it was the fear of nuclear annihilation. Starting in the 1980's it was more likely things like AIDS or exotic viruses like Ebola. The last decade or so, it has been more the fear of terrorism or less tangible fears about Global Warming, Peak Oil and economic collapse.

The line that encapsulates the song for me, is "one day you're waiting for the sky to fall/the next you're dazzled by the beauty of it all." That sense of heartbreaking beauty, the razor's edge of experience, where joy and sorrow are so close they almost touch is one of the things that make Bruce's music and poetry so vital and intense. Bruce tells us later in the song, that in order to see that beauty, sometimes we have to act boldly and "kick at the darkness/til it bleeds daylight."

Gavin's Woodpile is a song filled with anger, but it is also meditative, with just Bruce and his acoustic guitar. It starts out with a bluesy riff. The blues phrases continue throughout the song, but the music is more a mix of jazz, blues and folk. The story of the song is simple. Bruce is chopping wood outside his father-in-law's house near dusk. [4] As he works, "visions begin to crowd my eyes/like a meteor shower." The soil beneath his feet "seems to moan… like the wind through a hollow bone."[5] In his mind he sees "figures like Lappish runes of power." Then he's brought back to the moment by the sound of the wood and a distant voice "scolds a barking dog."

His mind wanders off again and he "remember[s] a bleak-eyed

prisoner" that he had met and how "you drink and fight and damage someone/and they throw you away for some years of boredom." He has "no job waiting so no parole" and "over and over they tell you that you're nothing."[6] Bruce "toss[es] another log" on the woodpile and sees the inviting "lamp-warm" glow of the window of the cabin. There's a chill in the late afternoon air.

In the next verse, he remembers a room with a crackling fire and "coloured windows shining through the rain/like the coloured slicks on the English River." The pollution in the river is causing people, mostly Native Americans, to get sick and die. And he angrily remembers "some government gambler with his mouth full of steak/saying 'If you can't eat the fish, fish in some other lake." It's a vivid memory, painted with just a few quick brush strokes. He comments in his memoirs that, "in 'Gavin's Woodpile' I was able to harness my anger and effectively represent it; you can hear it in my voice, certainly in the words, and perhaps even in the guitar's intentionally slicing sound, but I'm not trying to persuade people to act as much as to paint as vivid a picture as I can."[7]

Bruce throws more logs on the pile "and the stack of wood grows higher and higher/and a helpless rage seems to set my brain on fire." He feels paralyzed and "cursed with the curse of these modern times."

He stops and looks around him, noticing the "distant mountains, blue and liquid." They seem to him in a flash "like a stairway to life." But a train whistle distracts him and he sees "three hawks wheel in a dazzling sky." He's just about to make a connection, but "a slow motion jet makes them look like a lie." But he manages to keep these human intrusions from overwhelming him.

In the next moment he sees "a narrow path to a life to come ... explod[ing] into sight." In his celestial vision the "mist rises as the sun goes down/and the light that's left forms a kind of crown." It's "a sign of hope," and "the earth is bread, the sun is wine."

Faith and the beauty of nature allow Bruce to overcome his depressed thoughts about the poisoning of the English River and the wasted life of the youthful prisoner. What's not so clear is how faith might actually solve these issues. At best, we might say that by "lifting the curse of these modern times," faith may give someone the hope and clarity to make a positive impact on the world.

Rumours of Glory is one of Bruce's more hopeful sounding, but entirely enigmatic songs. He has said that one of his intentions was to demonstrate "that however negative we can be, we can also depend on each other and are capable of great love."[8] Bruce "got the idea for the 1st verse on a bitter winter night somewhere on Highway 7 between Toronto and Ottawa. Got the 2nd verse from NYC. Got real reggae players to record it,"[9] none of which actually tells us what the song means or even what it is about.

In the first verse, Bruce is alone and sees "two vapour trails cross the sky/catching the day's last slow goodbye," above "the dark town."[10] Based on the comment quoted above, he is driving into the city. He's feeling peaceful and calm and the "skyline looks rich as velvet" and "something is shining/like gold but better." That shining something is "rumours of glory." But they are just rumors, not facts. Obviously, he senses something, perhaps a little bit of hope emanating from the dark sky and city. But why does he use the word "rumour"? Rumors are talk on the street, often of questionable validity. How can he be so certain that what he is feeling and seeing is not only "shining like gold," but that it's also "better"?

The second verse describes a crowd of people dispersing, perhaps from a demonstration. Some are happy and some are cursing. Other than this brief sketch, we know nothing about them, although Bruce says that "each one [is] alone yet not alone." He sees and senses something more, but there's a sense that he is simply observing them, like a naturalist observing animals in the wild. In his memoirs, he had this to say about his experiences in the early 1980's: "As always, I rummaged for answers through alleys of the spirit, but now humans – lots of them – and their habitat became central to the explorations."[11] At that time, Bruce was really only beginning to seriously pay attention to other people, but he always had great observational skills. "Behind the pain/fear etched on the faces," he glimpses those same shining "rumours of glory."

In the final verse, he asks us directly if we "see the extremes/of what humans can be?" In "that distance" between the extremes "energy [is] surging like a storm." If you try to touch it, you might get burned, but underneath "it's shining like gold but better."

The song is obviously very important to Bruce, either as a song, a metaphor for his life, or both. After all, he named his memoir after it. The reggae beat is infectious. He clearly wants us to feel something positive, which he felt in the moments that inspired the song. And maybe that is all that there is to the song and all it is about. He has a strong "feeling," more than just a hope, that people can be more than they appear to be in random moments. But we unfortunately know how well that "Hope and Change" thing can work out.

Glory is another interesting word. It has both secular and spiritual connotations as well as positive and negative meanings. It can be pride, ambition, and boastfulness or it can be about worship, praise and honor. Bruce is clearly employing the word in the positive senses and it is hardly a stretch to see "like gold only better" as God shining through his creation, but the religious sense is far more muted than in his songs from the 1970's.

Child of the Wind[12] is a wonderfully complex, yet simple folk song. Musically, it is very simple. Bruce plays a resonator guitar and he's backed by Booker T. Jones on organ, Mark O'Connor on violin and Edgar Meyer on acoustic bass.

In the first verse, Bruce catalogs some of the things that he loves the most. They include "the pounding of hooves", "engines that roar" and "the wild music of waves on the shore." In addition to these delights, there is also "the spiral perfection of a hawk when it soars," and last, but not least his "sweet woman." The roaring engines surprise me a little, but given all the driving and touring that Bruce has done over the years, and his affection for the Beats, I guess an appreciation of roaring engines is not so hard to fathom.

In the second verse, he sticks to a single subject, the subject of roads, which follows from the roaring engines and horse's hooves. He defines two types of roads and notes that they call out to him:

> There's roads and there's roads
> And they call, can't you hear it?
> Roads of the earth
> And roads of the spirit

This suggests to me the famous Robert Frost poem about two road diverging in the woods and how taking the road less traveled made all the difference. But Bruce draws a further distinction, that "the best roads of all/are the ones that aren't certain." And he says that's where you are most likely to find him until he dies. That sense of comfort with uncertainty and even a need to seek it out pops up again and again in his songs.

In the chorus, he tells us to "hear the wind moan/in the bright diamond sky" and he sees the desert mountains spread out in front of him. He realizes that he'll "be a child of the wind/till the end of my days." Again and again, Bruce uses diamonds as a favored symbol for beauty and a dazzling white light; illumination of life's mysteries.

In the final verse, he imagines the earth from a vantage point in space, as a "little round planet/in a big universe." Is it "blessed" or is it "cursed"? It depends what evidence you look at, "but even more it depends on the way that you see." Looking at it as "a child of the wind" it probably looks more blessed than cursed. Ever the wanderer, the song was written on a Christmas Eve in Tucson, Arizona.[13]

The "wild music of the waves on the shore" can be lonely and haunting, as well as beautiful and comforting. *Planet of the Clowns*[14] is one of the most plaintive and haunting ballads that I have ever heard. The song opens with a lonely, minor key riff on electric guitar. Bruce is alone on an empty beach on a tiny island at the very edge of civilization (Canary Islands), thinking about the fate of the earth and man's destructive power. He stares into the moonlight, pressing his hands against his eyes, "probing in his heart with longing." He watches his footprints disappear in the surf, "grain by grain."

Then the minor key switches to major and intensifies as the chorus begins. The "waves roar on the beach." The image that Bruce conjures here is uncharacteristic for him. Instead of the waves being some expression of the grandeur and beauty of nature, they roar "like a squadron of F-16's." The image intensifies the despair of the song as the earth is under attack. We can only wonder at the things we humans have unleashed on each other and the planet.

The verses continue. Bruce turns from his introspective meditation to world affairs. "Government by outrage/hunger camps and shanty towns" hints at the tragedy of war and refugees. But Bruce maintains a little hope that "dignity and love [are] still holding."

His thoughts turn to the planet and he imagines it from space:

> This blue-green ball in black space
> Filled with beauty even now
> battered and abused and lovely

The chorus intrudes again and the F-16's of his imagination strafe the beach once more. Finally, he suggest that we each "in our own heart" are desperate to know "where we stand" against the violence and destruction. But then he calls us, including himself, a "planet of the clowns" as he stands there at the sea's edge in his "wet shoes."

This is a harsh and despairing judgment, especially from Bruce. I think what he is trying to convey is that there should be no question at all about which side we stand on, but the world is filled with war, hunger, refugees, toxic waste, and other unimaginable horrors. As a species, can we really be this heartless, cruel, and careless? While the song is not directly about environmental issues, the environment is certainly under assault and the earth is suffering collateral damage in man's seemingly endless wars.

As a songwriter, one of the interesting things about this song is that the lines of the verses don't rhyme. I'm not entirely sure how he pulls this off without our really noticing it. I think it has something to do with using only three lines in the verses instead of four, and obviously the pacing of the delivery is important, but this gives it a very intimate and conversational tone that suits the song very well.

Another similarly haunting song, expressing similar views about the fate of the "battered and abused and lovely" planet is *Beautiful World* by Eliza Gilkyson.[15] When I heard it for the first time, it reminded me of Bruce and this song. It is packed with the same world-weary sense of despair and loneliness, and the same sense of the earth under attack by the forces of man.

Bruce has said that he was reading Doris Lessing's science fiction novel Shikasta at the time he wrote this song. He remarked that "it's very poignant and disturbing, but beautiful at the same time. Somehow that all went together with the imagery of the place, being on the beach under the moon" and the "sense of standing on the edge of space."[16] Many critics have found Lessing's book incredibly bleak, and some of that bleakness may have contributed to the sense of isolation and despair over the human future that bleeds through the song.

Among other things, *Pacing the Cage*[17] is at least in part about middle-age and its frustrations. You're not sure how to get out of the place you suddenly find yourself in. As the song opens, he's watching a sunset. The "sunset is an angel weeping, holding out a bloody sword." If the sword is pointing to anything in particular, he can't make it out. If we take Bruce at his word, this is as much a literal description as it is a metaphor. In the context of the song, it appears that the angel is weeping for the same reasons that Bruce is "pacing the cage." Among those reasons are the frustrations of the modern age, growing old, ennui, the problem of identity, and simply how to pass through this uncharted territory we call life to get from Point A to Point B.

In the second verse, he uses a great metaphor for the modern problem of identity. He says "I've proven who I am so many times/the magnetic strip's worn thin." We have passports, driver's licenses, credit cards and a host of other identification. And sometimes even that is not definitive enough. Bruce commented on this idea in an interview:

I think the metaphor has more to do with presenting ID or

constantly having yourself identified as someone who's worthy to buy this object or that object or cross this border or that border. And I was thinking, too, of my own chameleon nature when I said that, as much as anything, and that's what's been changing -- and periodically does change.[18]

In the last verse, the song echoes the 23rd Psalm: "though I walk through the valley of the shadow of death, I will fear no evil."[19] As Bruce puts it, "sometimes the road leads through dark places/sometimes the darkness is your friend." He follows that with an anachronistic metaphor: "today these eyes scan bleached-out land/for the coming of the outbound stage." His future is in front of him, looking like a desert, but he's not going to get there in a car or a plane, perhaps because in the old West, they won't ask for any credentials. He can simply disappear.

He says in his memoirs that an upset fan called it "a suicide note."[20] He also notes that his girlfriend at the time knew that their relationship was over when she heard the song, saying, "a happy person is not going to write something like that."[21] I don't really agree with those sentiments. There can be a lot of bullshit and frustration in modern life and this song expresses them eloquently and perhaps as perfectly as anyone could ask for. As Bruce sums it up, "I wasn't contemplating suicide, but the song is about waiting to get out of here. Is 'out of here' out of your skin, out of a situation, out of town? You choose."[22]

Bruce plays acoustic guitar on the song. Rob Wasserman contributes a low-key bass part, although there's a nice bass solo on the instrumental break. There's a whisper of keyboards playing very ethereally in the background that you may miss, unless you listen carefully.

In *Understanding Nothing*[23], the verses are spoken over acoustic guitar and electronics, giving the song an exotic sound. Piano punctuates the chorus. This is a meditative song, written from notes he took during his trip to Nepal in 1987. He finds himself in a harsh, but beautiful landscape far away from civilization, feeling something akin to PTSD as the "momentum of civilizations/threw me too far over this time... /and I hang here/In this mountain light/a balloon blown full of darkness." He needs to let go.

In the chorus, he laments that "All these years of thinking /ended up like this/in front of all this beauty/understanding nothing." The feeling of the song suggests that Bruce is slowly unwinding and healing, the meditation and the simple beauty is relaxing his heart and bringing him back to life. And it does the same for us.

Closer to the Light[24] is a song that Bruce wrote about the death of his friend, singer-songwriter Mark Heard. It's a beautiful acoustic ballad on the mysteries of life and death, friendship and loss. Bruce's acoustic guitar is the clear focal point of the arrangement, but if you listen closely, you can hear some of the things that T Bone Burnett does particularly well as a producer.

The first thing that you notice is the organ, which is very restrained and atmospheric. Then there's the light touch of the bass, a shaker, and minimalist drumming with occasional swelling cymbals. Then Colin Linden pitches in with electric guitar that delicately echoes the main acoustic riffs. If you listen to the song superficially, you might even think that it's just acoustic guitar and vocals or you might be only dimly aware of some other instrumentation. The layering of all these sounds in a way that supports the main thrust of the song as played on the acoustic guitar is very impressive.

He starts out the song with an interesting view of death: "there you go/swimming deeper into mystery." Then Bruce tells us that he:

> Stared at the ceiling
> 'Til my ears filled up with tears
> Never got to know you
> Suddenly you're out of here

Death is a mystery, but it's also an ocean, the same sea that Bruce has long equated with both spiritual and personal freedom and enlightenment. His ideal of love and life seems to be to go beyond the known into the mystery, to understand the very heart of the universe, "the love that fires the sun."[25]

Perhaps his most well-known song on death is *Joy Will Find a Way (A Song about Dying)* which is a beautiful song of comfort for the dying. The lyric is just a short verse and chorus. The verse compares death to lying down to go to sleep:

> Make me a bed of fond memories
> Make me to lie down with a smile
> Everything that rises afterward falls
> But all that dies has first to live.

While the first two lines are comforting and warm, the last two lines are a little more intellectualized, rationalizing more than comforting. We can apparently take some solace in death, because it means that we were alive, but it seems clear that Bruce has his doubts.

The chorus tries to paint a more positive picture of death and resurrection.

> As longing becomes love
> As night turns to day
> Everything changes
> Joy will find a way

After an instrumental break, the chorus is repeated with ethereal backing vocals. The guitar part is a fairly simple, slightly percussive riff repeated over and over with only slight variations throughout. There are bells, possibly vibraphone, and other bits of percussion thrown on top to fill out the sound and accentuate the movement of the piece. While Bruce may be trying to convince himself of his faith and overcome his own doubts about death, the music is fully positive and joyful.

Bruce has said the song:

> owes its guitar part to a record that I had way back when featuring the music of Ethiopia. And there was a guy that played something called the Harp of David which I think was really a

kind of kalimba-like thing. It certainly sounded like that. I don't know what he was singing about, but he played a really great groove that was almost exactly, by some strange chance, what you hear in the background ..., played on the guitar.[26]

Bruce had to be joking when he said that this sounds like something he had heard by "some strange chance."

The song *Use Me While You Can* is mostly about his experiences on a trip to Mali. In a press release for the album release, Bruce says that:

> All the images are about the transitory nature of things. In that part of the Sahara you really have the sense that when you pick up a handful of sand, that it really is the 'dust of fallen empires,' and of cultures that came and went. There were people living there when it was grassland. An ancient presence is there, and yet it can only be felt because there's no sign of it now, no living vestige of it, other than what's left of Timbuktu.[27]

The first half of the song is spoken followed by four verses. In the spoken word part, Bruce describes the exotic scene of looming cliffs and blowing sand. He sees a "milk-white camel" with a "turbaned rider, blue robe billowing." He "wears a sword and a rifle on his back" and has a transistor radio "hanging from his neck." He "blink[s] and like ghosts, they're gone." He watches a woman who "hoists her water bucket onto her head/and strides off up the trail."

The verses begin and he sings that the sun is "a steel ball glowing/behind endless blowing sand" and he feels the "dust of fallen empires slowly flowing through my hands." He sings to us and perhaps to God to "use me while you can." He longs to pass the gift on to us.

The "moon behind dry trees" is like a "pearl held in black fingers" as night falls. His heart is like a "bird inside the rib cage" and it is "beating to be free." Again he tells us to "use me while you can."

In the bridge section, he tells us that he's traveled to many lands; he's "had breakfast in New Orleans" and "dinner in Timbuktu." He's even 'lived as a stranger in my own house." A "dark hand waves in the lamplight," divining the future as the "cowrie shell patterns change." All he can be certain of is that "nothing will be the same again."

In the final verse, he hears a "bullet in a sandstorm/looking for a place to land." He muses that a "full heart beats an empty one." And one final time, he asks us or God to use him. Bruce describes his trip to Mali and Timbuktu in great detail and notes,

> The sands that surround us, metaphoric and literal, will not wait around. It's a law. The hourglass trickles, deserts grow. Everything is temporal. When the Harmattan blows, we really do choke on the dust of fallen empires... the herders I saw were roaming the Sahel as their ancestors did seven thousand years ago, when it was grassland.[28]

Bruce plays blues-tinged resonator guitar for the basic guitar part and 12-string guitar as well. The kora also plays a prominent role in the arrangement, weaving in and around the guitar. Bass, drums and organ fill out the sound. Lucinda Williams contributes a haunting backing vocal.

Bruce wrote the song during a relative period of peace in Mali and Timbuktu, and was thus able to concentrate on the environmental devastation that the area foreshadows. He also had a chance to jam with West African bluesman Ali Farka Toure, some of which was filmed by the 'River of Sand' crew.

The 1990's, partly because of the relative peace, was also a time of cultural revival and preservation in the area. Timbuktu had been a great center of Muslim learning for centuries, but also instrumental in preserving non-religious texts and culture. They spent a great deal of time over the centuries translating ancient texts from Greek and Middle Eastern languages and the clerics and scholars often debated secular subjects. This is talked about in great detail in the book, "The Bad-ass Librarians of Timbuktu" by journalist Joshua Hammer. The book also describes how Timbuktu became something of a tourist haven in the late nineties, even spawning an annual Rock festival. The peace started to unravel in small ways starting after 9/11 when some of the desert tribes became radicalized, leading to occasional kidnappings of Westerners, usually with ransom in mind.

The situation worsened in 2012 after the fall of Gaddafi's government in Libya. Many desert tribesmen had been in his employ as mercenaries and when he fell, his arsenals were left unguarded and the Bedouins made off with whatever they could grab and disappeared back into the desert. The former rebels made common cause with some of the splinter Al Qaeda groups and decided to reopen the Civil War in Mali. The rebels and fanatics managed to take over much of Northern Mali, including Timbuktu, but it was the Al Qaeda groups that seized control, with their strict fundamentalist ideology and practices wreaking havoc on the relatively liberal Malian populace. They imposed severe punishments for things like listening to music or smoking. The only acceptable 'music' was chanting passages from the Koran. They gruesomely cut off hands or feet as punishment for stealing. The horrors of their reign of terror are described in detail and highly recommended to anyone concerned about ISIS and similar terrorist groups.

Ali Farka Toure died of cancer in 2006, but his family and friends continued his musical tradition. Harmer notes that in 2012, "jihadis threatened to chop off the fingers of Toure's proteges if they were caught so much as lifting a guitar." They also, "destroyed instruments and sound equipment, and burned down rudimentary recording studios."[29] The jihadis were driven out by French commandos not long afterwards.

The book is a fascinating read for the historical and cultural background on Timbuktu, the race to save extraordinary manuscripts from the ravages of time and harsh desert conditions, and for the discussion and details of the Al Qaeda takeover. These were truly souls who had turned their backs on love.[30]

The Charity of Night[31] is another one of those songs that Bruce has taken great pains to point out that it's all true. It's a series of vignettes; memories from his past. The first takes place in 1964 when Bruce was traveling around Europe after high school. The second takes place in 1985 and the last at an undetermined time near the present. The verses are spoken.

The first vignette is the story of Bruce walking alone in the cold streets of a Stockholm late at night. A man in a car stops and offers him a ride, but also wants something more and the car follows him across a bridge. Eventually the car stops and the man gets out to approach him. In the song at least, Bruce has a gun and draws it, "sight blade bisecting yellow forehead." In his memoirs, Bruce tells us that "no shots were fired."[32] He also writes at length about his first European adventure.

The story ends abruptly and the chorus comments on the action. The song is about the "haunting hands of memory", "the damage and the dying done" and "the clarity of light." The chorus ends by evoking a party scene with "gentle bows and glasses raised/to the Charity of Night." With the help of the night and sleep and dreams we manage to survive and put troubling memories in their place.

The second vignette recalls events in in Honduras as part of a fact-finding mission with Oxfam Canada.[33] He's in a hotel room "crosswise in a hammock in the hot volcanic hills. /It's 3AM the night after the air raid." He is recalling something that a woman told him about the "A-37s, like ugly gulls, make a dozen swooping passes over some luckless town." He hears "lascivious laughter" floating "on the darkness from the police station next door." The memory ends when "a pig suddenly screams."

In the third, erotic vignette, he is making love to a woman; "Tongue slides over soft skin/Love pounds in veins, brains buzzing balls of lust/Fingers twine in wet hair." What should we make of this song and these three stories? They all involve lust. The first also involves a clear-cut sexual predator and a threat of manslaughter. It's an intriguing story that Bruce had perhaps been struggling for years trying to find a way to get it into a song. The second is ambiguous, perhaps simple flirting in the hot night against the backdrop of war, perhaps something unsavory. The third is consensual sex. The first two are disturbing memories and the third ends with an "ecstatic halo of flame and pheromone." It's a good memory, but there's a hint of regret. It may or may not be about a very significant affair that Bruce had with an unidentified married woman in the 1990's, which he describes at length in his memoir.[34] The affair may have ended about the time the song was written.

I've never been able to make up my mind about this song. It lends the title to the album; a suggestion to us that it is either the most important song on the album or that it somehow provides some perspective on the songs. Having pondered it seriously, probably to the point of overthinking it, I'm not sure it adds up. The pieces are intriguing, but leave you wanting more clarity. The music is also not so compelling as to hold it together on its own.

Tie Me at the Crossroads is something of a throwaway song. It's not intended to be taken that seriously, though we should check his last will and testament to see if he really does want to be tied "at the crossroads" when he expires. It's a ragged garage band rocker. Everybody in the band and in the studio contributed backing vocals. Bruce had this to say about the song in an interview at the time:

> Although I want to be taken seriously, some people take it too far and start investing my insights with greater power than they ought to. At that point, you have to chuckle. It's great for other people to take you seriously, but you'd better not be guilty of doing it to yourself.[35]

Often songs are just products of the moment that bring them to life. They can document a passing thought or a feeling. They can be profound or beside the point. Of course, this is also an admonition to me and anyone else not to take ourselves so seriously.

But taking the song seriously for a moment, it does have some points to make. First, the crossroads are significant in the blues. Allegedly, Robert Johnson sold his soul to the devil at the crossroads in exchange for magical guitar powers. Bruce certainly has extraordinary guitar talent, but he usually makes light of it and here, he makes light of it musically. But even that talent and the music that will be his legacy, may not last. We can never be certain. So, among other things, he wants us to know that he "loved you all in my particular way."

There's a hint of "what is this all for" in the song. We live our lives, even lives of great accomplishment, and what are we left with when it's over? Who will remember us? Certainly not just so that "the kids that pass can scratch their heads/and say 'who was that guy?'"

In having his body taken to the crossroads, he emphasizes the fact that life is a journey and specifically the fact that he has been a wanderer. At the crossroads, we are faced with choices. It implies a beginning, or a continuation, rather than an ending. Perhaps I should not end this section on one of Bruce's "lesser" songs, but it seems an appropriate place to pause in this discussion on his meditations on life and the place that death has in life.

9 *World of Wonders: Spirit in the Later Works*

... you feel like you're swimming in an ocean of love
And the current is strong
But all that remains when you try to explain
Is a fragment of song

Paul Simon, *The Afterlife*

In the early to mid 1980's, Bruce turned his gaze more and more to the outer world and conflicts in his own life. Religious and spiritual imagery doesn't disappear from his work but it takes a less prominent role. More and more, starting in the 1980's the spiritual imagery is mixed with social commentary and the images are drawn from a variety of traditions. While Bruce continues, at his core, to be a Christian, he embraces and respects the variety of religious and human experience. As he puts it in his memoirs, his perspective, at least in the new millennium is that, "The 'spiritual' songs are about celebrating the Divine and our place in the cosmos, and doing so from a place of seeking, from a desire to know, as best we can, the heart connection with God, however one might define such an entity."[1]

At the beginning of *World of Wonders*, Bruce is standing on a bridge. Bridges connect things, like the past and future, or different places. They are suspended in space and time. Here, he is standing "before the cavern of night/darkness alive with possibility." The dark is not always to be feared anymore. The unknown can be exciting as well as dangerous.

In the chorus, he tells us that we live in a "world of wonders," as

146

smoky horn riffs blow over the top of the bass, drums, guitar and keyboards. This is tightly arranged jazz, direct and to the point. In the verses, repeating staccato keyboard riffs are the primary musical backdrop.

He catches the sound of a saxophone, possibly a street musician, as it "slides though changes." It's "like a wet pipe dripping down" his neck and it "sounds like danger." He says that he "can't stop moving till I cross this sector of this world of wonders." There's a mixture of fear and excitement. Is he hurrying to keep ahead of something dangerous or is he plunging across a dangerous unknown territory? Interestingly, he doesn't use a saxophone in the mix of instruments on the recording, constructing the horn parts with trumpet and flugelhorn.

In the next verse he sees "a rainbow in a bead of spittle" and "falling diamonds in rattling rain." The rainbow is a glimpse of beauty in a totally unexpected place. The second image is one of Bruce's favorite images, diamonds created by the interplay of light and water. After seeing this beauty, he's "dazzled with my heart in flames." He realizes now that beauty and wonder are everywhere. This is one of those good days when you're not "waiting for the sky to fall."[2] The diamond image also connects the song back to three earlier spiritual songs: *All the Diamonds*, *Dialogue with the Devil*, and *Man of a Thousand Faces*.

In the last verse, he has a "moment of peace like brief arctic bloom" as he watches the "sun going down." The brief rain has passed, night is coming on, and his heart is filled with love and calm. He uses a similar image in the song *Nanzen-ji*, where he has his "mind swept clean like arctic sand." In *Understanding Nothing*, rhododendrons blooming in a spring snow remind him of seeing a "single orange blossom/at the wrong time of year." When he blinked, it was gone.

This song is, to me, a crystallization of many of the elements of Bruce's songwriting and thinking. It is not overtly religious, but it is certainly spiritual. It is a simple experience, walking across a city bridge as night is falling. It's a brief moment and his heart is pierced by ephemeral images of startling beauty. Despite his urge to move forward, he always has a choice. He could retreat back across the bridge to safety

James A. Heald

and a well worn path. As with *All the Diamonds*, the narrative elements of the song are stripped to the bare essentials. There is not a wasted word in the song. Bruce is on a journey and presented with choices.

Looking back at the other songs where he uses the diamond imagery, we can see other parallels. In *Man of a Thousand Faces*, he has a vision of where he needs and wants to be, but he has no bridge or clear path to get there. The city is a distraction, filled with temptations and false knowledge. I'm also reminded of his marvelous image of "the maze of moebius streets" to describe the city and aimless wandering in *You Pay Your Money and You Take Your Chance*. In *Dialogue with the Devil* he is standing on a rock in the middle of a stream, contemplating suicide and trying to make sense of his life and regrets. He again has a vision of the city, which is pure distraction and temptation. After the conversation with the Devil, he has a clearer vision of the way forward and is buoyed by the spirit of nature that surrounds him. *All the Diamonds* starts out with him expressing what it is that he values most in the world. He then tells the story of how he lost his way when he "ran aground in a harbour town." Again, the city or town is a distraction along the way. In that song God sends a ship, giving him the means to pursue his journey to the end.

In *World of Wonders*, the city is no longer the same distraction. It's not clear that he has any pre-conceived notion of what is about to happen or "should" happen. He is simply open to possibilities and his awareness is heightened. He still feels a "chill" and senses danger. Unlike in his earlier songs, the city can even be beautiful in its own way as he has his "nose to this wind full of twinkling lights." He realizes that he can find the spirit anywhere, even in the most unlikely places. And he seems more content in realizing that it only or mostly comes in brief flashes. As in *All the Diamonds*, rather than retreat to safety, he is willing to move forward into the unknown. He embraces the uncertainty.

These themes find many echoes in the later works. The spiritual songs are less about religion with a capital "R" and more about being open to the spirit that surrounds us. Recognizing the spirit is a gift. His song, *The Gift*[3], was inspired, at least in part, by Lewis Hyde's book of the same name, a book "which tries to reconcile the value of doing creative work with the exigencies of a market economy."[4] "The gift" can be described as spirit or inspiration or the touch of the divine. It comes and goes. The only thing you can be certain of is that it keeps moving and it must keep moving. If you try to hoard it or keep it for yourself, it slips through your fingers like sand.

Echoing some of the themes he laid out in *If a Tree Falls*, on the same album, he points out that:

> In this cold commodity culture
> Where you lay your money down
> It's hard to even notice
> That all this earth is hallowed ground

We can't seem to recognize all the gifts, beauty and wonder that surrounds us every day of our lives. Whatever happens in this life, "the gift moves on regardless/tying this world to the next." The connection to spirit is always there, whether we see it or acknowledge it. As Bruce puts it in one of his darkest songs, we "ride the ribbon of shadow/never feel the light falling all around."[5] The music in this little gem of a song is joyful noise. There's a repeated electric guitar riff, grinding, syncopated bass, noisy percussion like banging on tin cans, and keyboards.

Broken Wheel[6] is a reggae song from 1981 where Bruce is surveying the state of the world and is distraught about the condition of things. He sees us,

> Way out on the rim of the galaxy
> The gifts of the Lord lie torn
> Into whose charge the gifts were given
> Have made it a curse for so many to be born

He asks how he's "supposed to feel/way out on the rim of the broken wheel," comparing the spiral Milky Way to a broken wheel. Here the galaxy is sort of like a flat tire coming off its rim. The second and third line refer to Genesis 1:26 where God creates man in his likeness and says to "let them have dominion over the fish of the sea, and over the birds of the air, and over the cattle, and over all the earth, and over every creeping thing that creeps upon the earth."[7]

Despite this dark imagery, he feels that things are going to change or at least feels that they can change, but it's not going to be easy. A lot of blood may be spilled and we may have to go through many trials to get it right and "no adult of sound mind/can be an innocent bystander."

In the bridge, he says that "you and me – we are the break in the broken wheel" and a "bleeding wound that will not heal." This bleeding wound is a reference to the stigmata, which are supposed to be marks on a person, similar to the wounds that Jesus suffered on the cross. Bruce then asks Jesus for help. "Lord, spit on our eyes so we can see/how to wake up from this tragedy." The image comes from Mark 8:23 where Jesus spits on the eyes of a blind man, then touches him and heals his blindness.

In the final verse, Bruce repeats lines from the second verse and the bridge. He asks for direction. Because "trial comes before truth's revealed," it is difficult to know what actions to take and how you are "supposed to feel." Despite the dilemma, you "can't be an innocent bystander/in a world of pain and fire and steel." You have to try and do something to make things right.

The Light Goes on Forever[8], from the same period, is a song about man's hunger to reach the truth and how difficult it is. In the first verse he talks about the Shaman who "clambers up the world dream tree/looking for clues about what is to be." His "chants and trances give his spirit wings for flight," but the "wings [are] still shackled to history" and "the chain of events is broken so easily."

In the second verse a native "skull-drum skin…sends out ripples in the gathering night." There is "music rising from the bones of saints" and also "from the pungent smell of sad sweet poems and paintings." In our world of darkness, we have a whiff of the divine and we can almost hear it and smell it and taste it. Bruce asks permission to "rest in the place of the light."

In the chorus, Bruce reveals that "God waves a thought like you'd wave your hand/and the light goes on forever." The light is always with us, "through the burning and the seeding/through the joining and the parting." These thoughts are similar to the Pete Seeger song *Turn, Turn, Turn* which has its origins in Ecclesiastes.

In the third and fourth verses, Bruce paints a very dark and despairing picture of human striving. First, he talks about the Gypsy searching "through the cards for clues" and the alchemist searching "for eternal youth." Unlike the shaman or the saint, we can see that these are really pointless exercises, but Bruce isn't holding them up for ridicule. In the next line he says that "human reaching almost makes it but not quite." And then he says, "you live and it hurts you, you give up you die." It's hard to put a positive spin on that thought, though perhaps you can argue that he's really saying that you have to fight through the pain and keep going. And perhaps that is what he means when he then asks to "rest in the place of light." He needs to rest up for the difficult journey ahead.

The next verse is also about the human condition; how we are "fugitives in the time before the dawn/backed up to the wall with weapons drawn." We're in the dark, we can't see, and we're in a struggle to the death with unknown forces.

The chorus repeats with some changes, reminding us that the light is always there. In the final verse, he holds out some kind of hope. He talks about the "uptight lawyer on Damascus road/becomes a nexus where the light explodes." This is the Apostle Paul who was struck blind on the road to Damascus and became one of the leading missionaries of the new Christian religion. Bruce describes this as "Infinity stoops to touch the human mind." There is hope that anyone can be a focal point for the light.

The chorus repeats a final time. What the song seems to be saying is that despite all of our striving, no matter how grounded it is in spirit (shamans and saints), we really won't make it through unless we are touched directly by God.

Another way of looking at this is that the light is always there; it "goes on forever." We're already there and we don't have to do anything but open our hearts and our eyes. We are blinded to the fact, by all of our struggles and by looking in the wrong places, whether in the cards, or the formulas of alchemy. The more we fight, the more we back ourselves into a corner in the darkness.

Bruce is "ranting about religion"[9] in *Shipwrecked at the Stable Door*. The song starts out with a man twirling a rose in his teeth and gets "his tongue tied up in thorns." This man is later seen begging and telling all who will listen that "it's horrible to be born." He is referring to the physical pain of birth and leaving the womb, but he is also referring to life, where one has to make choices and where one sometimes makes poor choices, such as twirling a rose in your teeth.

The physical sensation of birth is again alluded to in the second verse, where "Big Circumstance comes looming like a darkly roaring train" that "rushes like a sucking wound across a winter plain." You are tossed out into the world without any bearings; "wherever you are on the compass rose/you'll never be again."

In the chorus, Bruce tells us that we are "left like a shadow on the step/where the body was before." This is an allusion to Hiroshima, where "the white hot bomb blast left people's shadow's imprinted on concrete."[10] We are also "shipwrecked at the stable door."[11] The world seems to get us both coming and going. Birth is a shipwreck or a "sucking wound" that sounds like a "darkly roaring train." Our lives are also these same things, each moment bringing unexpected twists and turns.

In the third verse, we start again with "Big Circumstance." This time it has "brought me here." Bruce wishes it would "send me home." Unfortunately, he "never was clear where home is," although he seems certain that "it's nothing you can own." Home, as he's describing it is not so much a place, as a state of mind or condition, a realization of your place in the world. Home "can't be bought with cigarettes or nylons or perfume." This is an interesting allusion to Post World War II Europe where GIs bought "love" with cheap luxuries that were non-existent in the broken post-war economy. In any event, the best that you can buy "is a voucher for a tomb." Death is the only certainty.

In the last verse, the poor and the meek are "blessed" and they will inherit "the kingdom/that the power mongers seek." Also blessed "are the dead for love/and those who cry for peace." Finally, he blesses "those who love the gift of earth;" those who would be good stewards of the environment and care for it properly. Bruce wishes that all of these blessed folks have "their gene pool increase." We are back to the painful fact of birth. Somehow through the miracle of the cycle of birth and death, and the miracle of the birth of Christ, we can hope that good will triumph over evil and that love will conquer greed. Bruce says in his memoirs that the Christian Right was "spiritually shipwrecked, foundering on shoals of their own ambition and indifference, slick and ridiculous in their genuflections to greed," which links this song specifically to his more direct critique of fundamentalism put forward in *The Gospel of Bondage* from the same album.[12]

Skipping forward to the mid 1990's, Bruce makes a number of references to the 23rd Psalm in *Strange Waters*. The most obvious reference is in the chorus, where he says that "You've been leading me/beside strange waters." Bruce uses "strange" instead of the biblical "still." The next reference is "where is my pastureland in these dark valleys?" This refers back to two lines in the psalm: "He maketh me to lie down in green pastures" and "though I walk through the valley of the shadow of death, I will fear no evil."[13] In the modern world, the world experienced in this song, it seems like the "valley of the shadow of death" is nearly everywhere.

Like the psalm, Bruce mixes beautiful and positive images with negative images. He starts out the song with two images of the beauty of nature: "a high cairn kissed by holy winds" and "a mirror pool cut by golden fins." Most of the rest of the images in the song are of either of ugliness, danger or ambiguity; "alleys where they hide the truth of cities", "rifled roads and land-mined loam," a "forest in flames", and "the concrete fields of man." The "concrete fields" are his modern substitute for the "green pastures" of the psalm, neither comforting nor comfortable. Even one of the "positive" images has an undercurrent of pain, as he remembers that he has "burned in love till I've seen my heart explode." But as he said of God's love way back in *Lord of the Starfields*; "oh love that powers the sun/keep me burning." And in *Wait No More* he asks, "What does it take for the heart to explode into stars?"

The message of the song and the psalm are basically the same. Through good and bad, through times of danger and moments of beauty, Man has survived because God is with him and has kept him safe. However, unlike the psalm, this is not a quiet meditation.

Musically, this is a slow-burning rocker. It starts out with Bruce finger-picking on a resophonic guitar. There's a slight hum of electric guitar in the background. The drums kick in after the first verse and pick up in intensity throughout the second verse. Ethereal, delayed background vocals come in on the second chorus. There's another intense, heavily distorted electric guitar solo. The backing vocalists also provide a haunting wordless chorale during the solo.

The song *Last Night of the World* collects images and thoughts from a seemingly ordinary, sleepless night. Bruce is drinking rum at three in the morning and the radio is playing. The music is 90's alternative rock, the kind of things you'd most likely hear on satellite or college radio.

At midnight, he'd been out watching the people in a bar "fusing the spaces between them with bar-throb bass and laughter." Bruce wonders what he would do differently if he knew this was the "last night of the world." He decides that he'd probably do more or less the same kinds of things, unless he had the chance to have champagne with his lover. Bruce has said of this song on a number of occasions, that:

> The champagne notion, actually, I owe to Sam Phillips, who's a great songwriter and a good friend. She toured with us some years back and at one point, she saw me carrying this backpack that I'm always lugging around loaded with books and useful things.... And she said, 'What are you carrying in that thing anyway?' I said, 'It's everything I need for the apocalypse.' And she just stopped and looked at me and in my mind, I picture her putting her hands on her hips and kind of giving me this

quizzical expression, and she just said, 'What do you need for the apocalypse besides champagne and a couple of glasses?' And I thought that was the most succinct statement you could possibly make about the correct attitude toward the end of the world, so that's where that came from.[14]

In the third verse, he reveals a little bit about himself and how "as a child" he learned "not to trust in my body." And like most of us, the things that we learn as children stick with us and in some ways come to define us. But he is almost looking forward to the "day when we all have to be pried loose," because maybe it will take us "from mystery into mystery … another step deeper into darkness/closer to the light."[15]

In the fourth and final verse, he thinks back to his times in Central America and the stories that he heard and how heartbreaking it was to see "the flame of hope among the hopeless." Looking back on that, it was a moment of great significance in his life, "the straw that broke me open."

Everywhere Dance[16] is one of Bruce's more successful attempts at a kind of cabaret-style jazz. His style and overall intensity just doesn't really fit well into a crooner vibe. He's not Sinatra or Michael Buble. I just can't picture him in a tux or even a suit (I've seen pictures and he just doesn't look very comfortable), but here it works.

In this song, "the dance is the truth and it's everywhere." It's the dance of Maya; the illusion that is the truth. The "translucent moon floats in waves of blue air." The dance is a "pas de deux in stark silhouette /pulsing against a clear orange sunset." The duet is the dance of the duality of the phenomenal Universe. The dancers' "bodies shape the spaces they're in" and "the limbs slide smooth through unresisting air."

In the last verse, we see the dance "in grains of sand and Galaxies/in plasma flows and rain in trees," and "in the ebb and flow of dying and birth." The accompaniment is just Bruce on acoustic guitar, Andy Milne on piano, and Gregoire Maret on harmonica. The harmonica is wistful and the melody teeters on the edge of joy and despair.

Boundless[17] was the result of collaboration with Annabelle Chvostek, formerly of the Wailing Jennies. According to the liner notes, this was mostly lyrics by Bruce. This song is marked by strong religious and spiritual imagery and is probably the song, aside from *Iris of the World*, that many long-time fans will gravitate to on the album **Small Source of Comfort**. It is certainly the "deepest" song on the record; open to many interpretations depending on your spiritual bent.   It begins with Gary Craig on chimes. Then the guitar and mandolin come in. Drums and bass follow after the first verse.

Bruce is driving through the country.   There are "horses in the meadow by the highway side/and a Church of Christ in a double-wide." It's cloudy and there's chill in the air. He sees a "red-winged blackbird" outside a "ghost town gutted like a dried-up mine." A train speeds by and he sees "stark faces in the windows." As he sees all this, it reminds him that "we love our blindness and we love our pain." The benign rural landscape of horses gives way to a poor church and the desolation and despair of a ghost town.

He gets out of the car and stands "by the lake sucking poison mist." He has his "lungs clenched tight like an angry fist." He's "picking at sores in the hope they heal." He's "hungry and harrowed and caught in the wheel." This could be samsara, the Karmic Wheel of life, or perhaps the *Broken Wheel,* where he wrote almost thirty years earlier:

> The gifts of the Lord lie torn
> Into whose charge the gifts were given
> Have made it a curse for so many to be born

We've poisoned our lakes and rivers and done our best to trash the earth, and we're left with ghost towns and "picking at sores" that won't heal; not unlike the "bleeding wound that will not heal" as he put it in that earlier song.

In the fourth verse, there's an echo of the line in *Wait No More;* "lightning's a kiss that lands hot on the loins of the sky." Here, Bruce says that he "feel[s] these serpents of desire ripple my skin like ropes of fire." Despite these carnal desires, "all I ever wanted, all along,/was to be the 'you' in somebody's song." He just wanted to be thought of and to be loved? Really?

In the chorus, he starts out speaking of "seven dances for the spirits/running a race, running a race." Are the spirits running a race or are we? These two lines are repeated, but the second time the dances are "for the saints." The chorus ends with the line, "looking for the stillness in the womb of space/ Boundless/ boundless." While the first lines of the chorus are somewhat cryptic, the race could be interpreted as the frantic pace of modern life. Seven is a very common number in the bible and according to some commentators is a symbol of completeness and perfection.[18] We are all seeking "the stillness." We are seeking to touch the Infinite, to be one with the "boundless" presence. Bruce has told us before that space is the realm of the *Lord of the Starfields*. After the chorus there's an instrumental break with a mandolin solo by Annabelle.

In a recent interview, Bruce explains the origins of his image of the seven dances. He was on a trip to Venezuela unofficially monitoring the election that put Hugo Chavez back in power and was being:

> guided around by a couple, an American woman who was married to a Venezuelan guy who was a musician and who had a youth group in a city west of Caracas ... and we went to that town and he got his youth group to perform for us and what they were performing was dances and music based on, well not based on, it was a recreation of music of the coastal Afro-Venezuelan culture and their spirituality, which is like a lot of other spirituality in that region, defined as a mixture of African and Catholic, pretty much. So the Saints acquired the attributes of African gods and the gods acquired the faces of Catholic Saints...

> There was a cycle of dances, of seven dances, that went with this and these kids got out there and they ranged in age from eight to their late teens, so some of them were really great dances and the dances were very interesting. Some of them involving kind of

sword displays and some very sensual stuff and all of it celebratory, so that's where the image of the seven dances of the spirit came from.[19]

Back on earth and back in the present, "the howling wind, it sings to" him. The "sky looks troubled," but Bruce feels free. He's had "visions and feelings and ink on my hands." In the final line of the verse he suggests that "you can travel forever and never land." I'm not sure how comforting that is. Bruce is a nomad, one of a tribe "following our own song lines." Perhaps we'll make it home, perhaps we won't.

In the final verse, Bruce returns to the star fields and to the *Broken Wheel*. He sees, "in the crashing chaos where stars are born/the strong get fed and the weak get torn." This is the world where "no adult of sound mind/can be an innocent bystander." We're all guilty and we'll be judged "by the children of our slaves." The final image of the song, before the last chorus, is of "the cosmos eating its tail/circled like the lip of the holy grail." The serpent eating its tail is a symbol of eternity or the cycle of life, death, and rebirth. We may travel forever and never land. The grail, of course, is the chalice from the Last Supper. Is the wheel still broken in this vision? The song fades out after the chimes enter again.

In a 2006 interview with Cathleen Falsani he talks quite a bit about his then current views of God. While he still considered himself a Christian at the time, he was sometimes uncomfortable claiming to be one because there are a lot of Christians who "would probably be offended at me using that word about myself."[20] In describing God, he "like[s] the Kabalistic view of God as 'the boundless,' which is basically a way of saying, I think, that there's no image that applies at all and there's no limits and every image that you could possibly think of is going to have limitations."

In a very recent interview, Bruce characterized his views on religion as follows:

> To me, everything in life is a process. There is no stopping point; you never land. If you think you've landed somewhere, watch out, because God or whoever is gonna pull the rug out from

under you, and you are going to have to start thinking again, trying to understand how you fit into things.

Cockburn says he doesn't care whether people believe he's a Christian or not.

> "What's important is recognition that there is a spiritual side of life, and that needs to be paid attention to," he says. "There's a real distinction between materialism and a sense of the cosmos being a deeper place than that. If it's a deeper place, then what does that ask from us? I don't know the answer. I'm still working on it, and that is perhaps why people are willing to listen to the stuff I put into songs."[21]

As I have tried to point out, Cockburn has always expressed a fairly idiosyncratic version of Christianity. He's been very open to alternative expressions of faith and spiritual connection. He has certainly not been afraid to challenge Christian views that he feels gets in the way of truth, justice, and love.

Bruce and Fundamentalism

In a 1992 interview, Bruce said that he had tried for a little bit to be a fundamentalist. However,

> in the end I was completely unsuccessful at being a fundamentalist because what a fundamentalist really is is somebody that takes the Bible literally, who takes the traditional teachings literally, and I couldn't do that. I don't think that's what it's supposed to be at all, and I just grew up as too much of a free thinker to be able to submerge myself in a belief system without any question, and I also don't think that's what we're asked to do as Christians at all, either. But some people do think that.[22]

Justice[23] is one of the first songs where this strong questioning, as opposed to doubt, really comes to the forefront. It's a reggae song that makes a pretty definitive statement about how religion, in particular, has been perverted and manipulated to justify injustice and terror and a whole host of ills. The first verse is a laundry list of ideas that have been distorted, beginning with "what's been done in the name of Jesus", and followed by Buddha, Islam, man, liberation, civilization, race, and peace.

In the chorus he notes wryly that "everybody loves to see/justice done/on somebody else." Mankind is good at creating slogans to whip up anger and justify terrible things against people who don't look quite like us or don't think quite like us or dress like us. And so we'll ignore most, and sometimes all, of what Jesus said or Buddha said, if there's an opportunity to beat somebody up.

In the final verses, he says that we have to live with what we've seen and "what we've been." I'm not sure that what has preceded this gives any hope that we really are that reflective and willing to take responsibility for our actions and how we use words. Then he takes a shot at those who think charity is about the bare minimum, like letting someone in need use "a toilet and a telephone." Ultimately, we need to look deep inside ourselves and "search the silence of the soul's wild places/for a voice that can cross the spaces" to bridge the gap between the word and meaning and also to bridge the differences between us.

Gospel of Bondage[24] is a chilling song, all the more chilling living in the U.S. during another period in our political lives where religious fundamentalism rears its ugly head. This is a different kind of rant about religion. At a concert where he was introducing the song when it was newly written:

> he called Pat Robertson a "grinning skull" and said of the candidate's reactionary evangelist brethren, "They scare the hell out of me and also irritate me, because I've gotten tired of saying, 'Yes I'm a Christian but I'm not one of them.' So here's my way of saying fuck you' to them."[25]

The song is basically about Fear and Terror and a pre-enlightenment view of religious virtue as a cure for all the real and imagined ills of modern society. In the key passage, he says:

> We're so afraid of disorder we make it into a god
> We can only placate with state security laws
> Whose church consists of secret courts and wiretaps and shocks
> Whose priests hold smoking guns, and whose sign is the double cross

Written more than a decade before September 11, the Patriot Act, waterboarding, and Abu Ghraib, this is shockingly prophetic. This kind of reactionary Old Testament fundamentalism and biblical literalism is definitely not the answer in Bruce's view:

> You read the Bible in your special ways
> You're fond of quoting certain things it says -
> Mouth full of righteousness and wrath from above
> But when do we hear about forgiveness and love?

As he said in another interview, "the message of Christ is so evidently love and freedom, I just don't understand how anyone can read into the message and get anything but that."[26]

Soul of a Man is a blues song by Blind Willie Johnson. Bruce has not recorded too many cover tunes in his career; for his own releases I can only think of three. According to some interpretations, the soul is "nothing but a burning light." I have always interpreted that line to mean the Bible is "nothing but a burning light," which would make it a caution against literalism. It reminds me of the Zen notion that doctrine is only a "finger pointing at the moon." Here is the relevant verse of the song and you can decide for yourself.

> I read the Bible often
> I try to read it right
> As far as I can understand

It's nothing but a burning light

This is great acoustic blues picking on the resonator guitar, with only some minimalist, hypnotic drumming and percussion backing Bruce up.

Put It in Your Heart[27] starts with a rush of percussion and drums, soon joined by Bruce's urgent 12-string guitar pounding out the simple 7-note riff that draws us right in. We can feel something big happening, whether it is wonderful or terrible. This is the psychological heart of the album **You've Never Seen Everything**, perhaps the best song to come out of 9/11. The song begins with Bruce staring "into the flames/filled up with feelings I can't name;" those terrifying images of dark smoke and flame billowing out of the gaping hole in the side of a massive skyscraper.

Emerging from that image, "behind the veil are seen/love's ferocious eyes" and the words that come to his ears tell him to "put it in your heart." But how do we fit such a thing into our hearts? How do we come to terms with that kind of horror? How do we make any sense of it at all? And to even think about forgiveness, how can we manage that?

These were, without question, "terrible deeds done in the name/of tunnel vision and fear of change." They "surely are expressions of/a soul that's turned its back on love." But these deeds were also done in the name of God. Think back to Bruce's song *Justice*. "What's been done in the name of Jesus" and Buddha and Islam? Once again, Bruce tells us to "search the silence of the soul's wild places/for a voice that can cross the spaces" that separates us as people, and religions, and "tribe and state."[28] And he hears that voice in this song.

Here, he finds solace in "all the sirens all the tongues/the song of air in every lung." We have each other, whether it is "Heaven's perfect alchemy" or chance. Something greater than ourselves has brought us together, "me with you and you with me." This event has drawn out of Bruce some of his greatest poetry and an almost perfect melding of sound and sense. At the very end of the song, it sounds like there is a beautiful horn part, but it is not credited. The only other thing I can think of is that it is somehow Hugh Marsh's violin. Whatever it is, it is a wonderful touch.

Bruce struggled to write this song, even thinking "that it would be pathetic to address such an event in a song."[29] Later, he was attempting to meditate and "let thoughts and images rise to the surface of consciousness, the phrase 'put it in your heart' floated past."[30] He notes that he had used dream therapy to unearth "buried sources of pain" and realized it could apply to external as well as internal sources of pain, buried or out in the open. Finally, "without thinking, I began to put images and feelings together, and the song took shape."[31]

In his recent song *Each One Lost*[32], Bruce is witnessing a ceremony honoring comrades fallen in battle. He takes another shot at fundamentalist religion, whether the Taliban or those like Jerry Falwell and Pat Robertson in America.

> Some would have us bow
> in bondage to their dreams
> of little gods who lay down laws to live by
> but all these inventions
> arise from fear of love
> and open-hearted tolerance and trust

There's a touch of righteous anger in his voice and he follows these thoughts with the lines: "Well screw the rule of law/we want the rule of love." He suggests here that we are, or should be, fighting for love. We're still fighting the battles of 9/11 as he so beautifully portrayed it in the song *Put It In Your Heart*.

10 *Instrumental Music and Jazz*

A poem should be wordless
As the flight of birds.

Archibald MacLeish, *Ars Poetica*

Whether for instrumental pieces or songs, the music has always been an important component of Bruce Cockburn's work. In a recently published interview, he had this to say about his instrumental music:

> I went to music school to study composition because I imagined myself making instrumental music, jazz mostly. It turned out not to be the direction. The love of music without words has always been there. The obvious difference is that words can pin your imagination down; ideally that's what they are supposed to do. Or fire it up in specific directions. With instrumental music it's more about the feel, the mood. You can analyze the music intellectually, but being non-verbal it has a different kind of effect on you.[1]

Bruce began playing the guitar by learning the music of Chet Atkins and other similar artists that were popular in the late 50's. Through Atkins music, he was introduced to jazz standards and, at least second hand, to guitarists who influenced Atkins, like Django Reinhardt.[2] He was introduced to acoustic blues and finger-picking hanging out with folk musicians who were playing at local coffeehouses in his home town.

The 50's are an interesting decade musically. Jazz, Country, and Folk music were all quite popular and had homes on radio and the new medium of television. The jazz crooners from the 30's and 40's were still popular. There was a lot of cross pollination going on between genres. Western Swing incorporated Jazz into Country. Rock and Roll brought elements of the Blues into the mainstream, at first tentatively and then more aggressively in the late 50's and 60's with the emergence of Chuck Berry. Shows like American Bandstand fueled the commercialization of Rock and Roll and also introduced white audiences to Black artists.

The evidence suggests that Bruce lived and breathed the guitar almost from the moment he first picked up the instrument. It's not clear when exactly he started to dabble in alternate guitar tunings. However, he was writing and performing his own songs in alternate tunings at least by the time he recorded *Sunwheel Dance* in 1971.

Alternate tunings give the guitarist different sounds to work with, and can make certain combinations or sequences of notes easier to play. It is often a way for the guitarist to play more open strings. Playing a note on an open string generally sounds brighter than playing the same note with your finger holding the string down.

Perhaps the simplest of alternate tunings (in some ways hard to consider an alternate tuning because it is so commonly used) is Drop D tuning. In this tuning, the low E string is tuned down a whole step to D. This gives the guitarist a nice, resonant D bass note when playing in the key of D or D minor. Bruce uses this tuning in songs such as *Tibetan Side of Town, Mistress of Storms,* and *Mango.*

Another type of alternate tuning is the Open Tuning. In an open tuning, all the strings are tuned so that when strummed you are playing a chord, which is not the case for standard guitar tuning. This also allows you to play any major chord with a single barred finger. Open D (DADF#AD) and Open C (CGCGCE) are two very common open tunings that Bruce uses. Open D and Open E are essentially the same, tuning strings down for D and in E the 3rd and 4th strings are tuned up. You can

165

also use a capo with Open D to achieve the same results as Open E. Tuning strings down in Open C, particularly the low E string, can cause several strings to be a little loose and slack, which presents some issues for guitarists. Bruce uses Open D or E for *Sunwheel Dance*. *Foxglove*, *Sunrise on the Mississippi*, and *Soul of a Man* are examples of songs played in Open C.

The last tuning that I'll discuss here is something that might be called Drop F# tuning. Bruce may have come up with this one on his own. In this tuning, the G string is tuned down a half step to F#. Bruce often uses this to play songs in the key of E, which adds an open 9th to the E chord and allows you to easily rock between an E minor 9 and E major chord. F# is part of the B major chord, and is the 6th for the A major chord. A and B are the two other major chords in the Key of E. Bruce uses this tuning in songs like *Cader Idris, Last Night of the World, Don't Feel Your Touch, Parnassus and Fog*, and *Fascist Architecture*. He recently said that,

> For me, you change one element of the guitar, then all of a sudden there are all these sonic possibilities that weren't there. If you're a flatpicker, it probably doesn't make much difference. But for fingerpicking—where one of the sources of color is the degree to which you can get the strings to ring against each other—changing one string can really make a difference.[3]

This appreciation for minute sonic shadings is an important element of Bruce's musical palette. It doesn't mean that he can't just let go and play loose and ragged (think *Tie Me at the Crossroads* or the solo on *Night Train*), but when he does you know that he intends to do it.

Bruce has also had an interest in world music, spicing up his music with echoes from various cultures. *Ting/the Cauldron*[4] is an early, meditative instrumental piece with an eclectic and exotic Eastern feel. It sounds by turns Middle Eastern, Oriental and even African. There are gongs, cymbals, marimbas and other assorted instruments supporting Bruce's guitar. This is also the first song to show the influence of Django Reinhardt on his playing, adding Gypsy jazz to the eclectic world music mix. Oriental and Middle Eastern influences pop up from time to time in Bruce's music.

Water into Wine[5] is a solo acoustic guitar instrumental piece in Drop D tuning from **In the Falling Dark**. It starts off with a free form and abstract introduction that lasts for about 1:45. There are some hints of Middle Eastern influence in a few places, as you might expect from the title. It varies melodically between light and dark moods. The main body of the piece is a very melodic and structured section or sections. You can almost pick out alternating verse and chorus sections with a more improvisational section in the middle. It provides a good transition to the more intense lyric-driven songs that follow on the album, such as *Silver Wheels* and *Gavin's Woodpile*.

Deep Lake[6] is a languid instrumental. Bruce plays the acoustic guitar and is supported by bass, dilruba and percussion. The dilruba is an Indian stringed instrument played with a bow. The bass is very whispery and the percussion is minimal. The dilruba gives a slight droning and echoing effect to the guitar playing and becomes more prominent as the song progresses, giving it an exotic sound. It is as if you are sitting in front of a still lake in the early morning watching the mist rise.

Jerusalem Poker[7] starts with a humming keyboard, soon joined by drums, percussion and hand claps. After a few bars, the acoustic guitar comes in. There's a horn that harmonizes with the main guitar riff. This is a very intricate and moody piece, with an improvised section in the middle. The title is suggestive of a high stakes game played out against an ancient and mysterious landscape. Perhaps you can pick out the Jews, Arabs, and Christians in the distinctive musical riffs.

The song *Ancestors*[8] is another experimental piece. This time it is just Bruce on guitar and Gary Craig on singing bowl and chimes with lots of delay and echo effects on the guitar. There's a vaguely oriental sound to the whole. There's a long improvisational section in the middle. Perhaps the echo and the singing bowls are like our ancestors calling us from far away, or the skulls whispering in *Postcards from Cambodia*. The connections we have with all other things in the Universe also carry across time. The effects here are similar to those used in *The End of All Rivers*, though Bruce doesn't play against the echo in this piece.

Sunwheel Dance[9] is a classic example of Bruce's Celtic and folk style. He has mastered the interplay of thumb and fingers to manage the bass and melody parts without the need for overdubs or sidemen. Bruce credits a guitar player in the Carolinas named Fox Watson[10] who was, "given to rendering traditional fiddle tunes on the guitar in a graceful finger style that seemed to float like the wings of a gull."[11] Bruce later "fooled around with what [he] could remember of the technique and came up with"[12] several pieces, including this one. In addition to searching out the mysteries of the universe, Bruce has also been on a quest to find fresh new guitar approaches, unique rhythms and striking soundscapes to expand his own musical horizons. On the same album, Bruce also shows a fluid mastery of Celtic guitar picking on the song *My Lady and My Lord*.

Night Vision starts off with the sprightly, solo guitar instrumental *Foxglove*[13], one of three instrumentals in the collection. Like *Sunwheel Dance*, this is very much influenced by Irish fiddle tunes and Fox Watson. Also, like *Sunwheel Dance*, it is not quite one and a half minutes long.

After these early experiments with Celtic music and fiddle tunes, there is nearly a twenty year break before Bruce recorded another instrumental that wasn't influenced by jazz in some manner.[14] For lack of a better term, *When it's Gone, It's Gone*[15] ventures into Americana or roots music. It is an ensemble piece with Bruce playing acoustic and electric guitars. It is an unhurried finger picked and melodic composition. There's a touch of atmospheric organ, bass and a plaintive violin. As the title suggests, the music is wistful and a little mournful.

Train in the Rain[16] is a solo acoustic guitar instrumental in Drop D tuning, unlike anything that he had recorded since the mid 1970's. But it is also different from most of the 1970's instrumentals. It is much more traditionally structured as a piece of music. There is no improvised lead section. There's a short introduction, then the main part of the song, which follows an AABAB structure (or verse-verse-chorus-verse-chorus, if you prefer). At the end there is a short coda, which repeats the introduction. This is much more akin to compositions by people like Leo Kottke than his previous Django influenced jazz works. It is somewhat comparable to the Appalachian/Celtic pieces like *Sunwheel Dance* and *Foxglove*.

Sunrise on the Mississippi[17] is very similar, though with a lighter tone. It is in Open C tuning. It was written in St. Louis, apparently inspired by looking out of his hotel window and watching the sunrise. Like *Train in the Rain*, it is traditionally structured and has no improvisational section. It also follows an AABAB blueprint. Both of these songs are very much in keeping sonically with the folk and roots spirit of the album **Dart to the Heart**.

Islands in a Black Sky[18] is another early piece, where improvisation is an important part of the composition. In a 1993 interview, James Jensen told Bruce that it "sounds a lot like Michael Hedges."[19] Bruce responded that, "If you ask Michael Hedges he would probably tell you it reminded him of him too because he has publicly said he owes something to my early stuff but I haven't discussed it with him really."[20] As he got older, Hedges incorporated a much more percussive guitar style that really punctuated his melodic runs, sounding at times like he was trying to rip the strings off the guitar. Bruce's style is more fluid and melodic throughout this piece, but with his trademark bass lines and lead playing. This is a minor key rumination, very haunting and mysterious. With an interesting combination of Celtic and somewhat dissonant modernist sections, it stands out from his purely folk and also his jazz work and runs for almost eight minutes.

This is a complex piece which has at least six distinct sections. The first section has a dark melodic part, which perhaps is meant to evoke the black sky, followed by a somewhat brighter phrase. This is repeated and the whole section lasts about a minute. This is followed by a more edgy, insistent set of phrases that are repeated over and over for about 45 seconds finally resolving into a slower and more melodic short section. This is followed by another intricate and intense section which is punctuated by strumming and is repeated.

After this comes the longest section, which is a mix of patterns and free-form lead guitar including some vaguely flamenco riffs with a strong plucked bass line throughout. This is similar to passages in other works like *Mistress of Storms* or *Tibetan Side of Town*. This is followed by another brighter melodic section that eventually transitions back to the opening part, which is played through once at the end.

Elegy[21] is a solo acoustic guitar piece that first appears on the album **Speechless.** This is a very mournful tune and has some similarities to the Black Sky sections of *Islands in a Black Sky*. It opens with two formal sections and at about 1:30 starts an improvisational section and then after about a minute repeats the opening sections. The improvisational section is much more melodic than *Islands in a Black Sky*. Imagine a cold and overcast November day. The leaves are falling.

The song *Salt, Sun, and Time* is a slow instrumental waltz played on a single guitar. Bruce has said that the song is about "Sea travel, hanging out on the coasts of northern Europe. The title came from a phrase in Loren Eiseley's book, *The Immense Journey*."[22] Eiseley was a well known anthropologist and nature writer who wrote and published from the 1950's until his death in 1977. The *Immense Journey* was his first book, published in 1956, and "was a collection of writings about the history of humanity."[23] The song and the album can be viewed as a meditation on the interaction of the momentary and the timeless and sits well with Eiseley's lyrical meditations on the evolution of the planet and its inhabitants and his vision of it all as a continuous journey through time and space.

Red Ships Take off in the Distance[24] is a rousing duet with acoustic guitar and bass. The bass playing is very much in the jazz tradition and there is a pretty lengthy bass solo, though the song itself is not really jazz. Perhaps you could lump it in with New Age Jazz and the kinds of things that are typical of a lot of his compositions that combine elements of jazz, rock, folk and blues using the acoustic guitar as the instrument of choice. This seems more rock and folk with a touch of jazz, especially in the improvised sections. Fellow Canadian Don Ross does a beautiful solo guitar version on his 2010 release **Breakfast for Dogs** though he foregoes trying to arrange and mimic the bass solo.[25]

There were three instrumental compositions on **Life Short Call Now.** *Peace March*[26] is a lively piece. Bruce is playing acoustic guitar over light, shuffling percussion. There are muted keyboards that come in during the middle of the piece, giving it a little extra depth and color. The music seems more organized than most peace marches that I've been involved with. In places, it reminds me a little of a piece by Andy McKee called *Art of Motion.*[27]

Jazz first comes to the forefront on Bruce's album **Night Vision.** As with much of Bruce's music, his jazz songs are an eclectic mix of jazz styles with songs that vary from a more traditional jazz, the gypsy jazz of Django Reinhardt, jazz of the 1950's and 60's, jazz fusion, 70's pop jazz, and even some avant-garde.

The original version of *Mama Just Wants to Barrelhouse All Night Long*[28] is languid blues played by a jazz quartet. The music evokes a bygone but indeterminate era. The musical palette is made up of brushed drums, piano, bass, and low-key electric guitar. Bruce is playing the crooner. The song starts out with him, "up the road on easy street/watching everybody stand around and cheat." A man tells him to "move along/down to the corner where you belong." A lot is happening, and Bruce sings plaintively that "Mama just wants to barrelhouse all night long." In other words, she wants to hang out in a juke joint; dancing, drinking and having a good time. You feel like you're in a 1930's movie.

In the second verse he hears a "siren choir", because "some fool tried to set this town on fire." The "TV preacher screams come on along" as if it's a party, but it makes Bruce "feel like Fay Wray face to face with King Kong." He's between a rock and a hard place, but "mama just wants" to party, so he probably just gets dragged along.

In the third verse, Bruce wonders what he is and feels like he's "living in a hologram" where "it doesn't seem to matter what's right or wrong." The contemporary image goes almost unnoticed. It's a dog eat dog world where "everybody's grabbing and coming on strong." But "mama just wants to barrelhouse," so what can a poor boy do? While the song is definitely the blues, Bruce spices it up with a lot of jazz substitutions in the chords, for example using an E-minor 9th instead of an E7.[29]

Déjà Vu[30] is a piano and guitar jazz composition. This is more formal jazz for the cabaret rather than the juke joint or smoky jazz basement club. The lyrics are impressionistic, little word pictures like the Imagist poets of the early 20th Century. The song starts out with swirling piano and intricate guitar on top of a little slack bass. It ends with a romantic burst of piano followed by chimes and electronics that suggest the "music box melody" of the final line of the song. Bruce says that some of the atmosphere of the lyrics and music comes from Lawrence Durrell's books *The Alexandria Quartet*.[31] I'm not sure that this style suits Bruce especially well as a singer. It seems a little mannered and stuffy. The song merges right into the instrumental *Lightstorm,* which is a short little jazz fusion piece, heavy on the drums, electric guitar and bass.

The song *Rise and Fall*[32] was recorded in 1999, and was distributed on the Japanese release of **Breakfast in New Orleans** before being included in the **Speechless** compilation. In this jazz composition, acoustic guitar is joined by stand-up bass, drums and percussion. Structurally, it is based on a verse-chorus-verse-chorus pattern, with drums, percussion and stand-up bass joining on the second verse. At about 2:00 it transitions to an improvised section, which is primarily an acoustic guitar solo. At about 4:30 it switches to acoustic guitar playing chords, roughly the same as the verse and chorus part with a bass solo. Between 6:30 and 6:50 the improvisation transitions back to the main part and the ensemble plays a verse and chorus with a very brief coda to end. Imagine yourself in a smoky little basement jazz joint near the end of the night when everyone is in a slightly mellow, but melancholy mood.

King Kong Goes to Tallahassee[33] is a playful little lazy blues composition. It's in no hurry to get where it's going. In an interview, Bruce said it:

> was inspired by Pulitzer-winning American author Robert Olen Butler and Ottawa poet Bill Hawkins. The music was written to accompany a spoken-word performance by Butler, who lives near Tallahassee, but the title was inspired by *Dancing Alone,*

[2005's] retrospective volume of Hawkins' poetry. In the 1960s, Hawkins was Cockburn's bandmate in the legendary 1960s Ottawa group the Children.

"Reading the poems in the new book, there are several references to Tallahassee," Cockburn explains, "and then he had a whole series of poems that involved King Kong as the perpetual frustrated outsider. So it seemed like if I was going to put in Tallahassee, it would be nice to have King Kong."[34]

The song has a similar feel to the song *Mama Just Wants to Barrelhouse All Night Long*. The song is in Drop D tuning.

Don't Have to Tell You Why[35] is a lazy and mellow acoustic jazz piece. You can definitely hear the influence of Django Reinhardt on the lead guitar part, but this is definitely more 1970's jazz than the time-gone-by 1930's. He wants to be out of the city, away from the hustle and bustle of the "man-made" sounds of a fountain, the "parties full of fair-weather friends," and "chasing after every trend." What he really wants is to "stand where the sea-spray gleams like fire", or on "some hillside in Wales," or "at the rainbow's real end with you." This was written after he returned from an extended trip to Europe. He wants to take his wife back to some of the special places and relive their magical moments together.

Rouler Sa Bosse[36] is a light and bouncy finger-picked jazz tune that evoke pre-war Paris, complete with a clarinet solo. The title comes from "an expression used in France in the 20's 30's and 40's meaning 'rambling' or 'moving around,'" although it literally means "rolling your hump."[37] It's in standard tuning in the key of A minor, giving it a wistful tone, as if he were thinking longingly of the places he has rambled.

The instrumental *Bohemian 3-Step*[38] is the first of the five very strong and engaging instrumentals on **Small Source of Comfort**. The arrangement is just guitar with a touch of light drums. The song starts out with Bruce's thumb playing the base line. The opening section is a little discordant and dark in tone, followed by a more melodic, upbeat section. These sections alternate like a verse and chorus. There is an improvisational section in the middle.

Lois on the Autobahn[39] is another instrumental, written for his mother who died in 2010. It's a jazz tune supported by Jenny Scheinman's violin. The collaboration really shines on this piece. While the guitar work could stand on its own, it would really lose much of its beauty without the violin part, particularly the nice harmony call and response on the main riff and her solo. Bruce plays the baritone guitar and Colin Linden plays bass. Gary Craig supplies some very light percussion, perhaps a conga. The song evokes a relaxed drive on the open road.

Comets of Kandahar[40] is another instrumental showcasing Jenny Scheinman's sometimes dissonant jazz violin over a strong, insistent drumbeat and, of course, Bruce's steady guitar. There are also some vaguely Middle Eastern accents to some of the violin riffs. It was inspired by the planes taking off at night from the airbase in Afghanistan and Bruce described it in a press release as "Django meets John Lee Hooker."[41] The Hooker reference is probably to the fairly minimalist guitar part throughout most of the song, while Django takes over in the solo. As she does so well throughout the album, Scheinman does her best Stephane Grapelli to Bruce's Django.

Nude Descending a Staircase[42] is a fairly recent jazz instrumental piece named after the famous 1912 cubist painting by Marcel Duchamp. It starts and ends in a burst of static, the sound of a person trying to tune in to a radio station. They ultimately land on an otherworldly jazz station and this combo, playing a piece with maybe a 1950's or 60's Wes Montgomery jazz groove. Bruce plays electric guitar, supported by bass, drums, percussion and Jon Goldsmith on Fender Rhodes. The sound is drenched in echo. There are some horns that chime in near the end. The piece is not nearly as abstract or angular as you might expect from the title. It's actually quite melodic and perhaps even danceable.

Clocks Don't Bring Tomorrow -- Knives Don't Bring Good News[43] is piano-based jazz rock with a fairly contemporary sound, with tastefully restrained electric guitar, bass, and drums. It was written in 1969, but not recorded until 1973; perhaps Bruce didn't feel that it could be pulled off without a full band and a bigger budget. The lyrics are a little like Sartre's play *No Exit*. There are a number of characters stuck in a room, each distrustful of the other and not really knowing what they think themselves. The characters are waiting in the darkness, longing for the light, but are fearful of the future and not sure what to do. He concludes by despairing that "all we know is that we're here until we are set free."

The song ends with an instrumental break that lasts more than three minutes. It starts out with electric guitar in the lead over the piano for about a minute. The music gets quieter for about a minute and the guitar and piano are pretty much sharing the attention. The piece ends with the piano moving to the foreground for a big finish.

Seeds on the Wind[44] is a haunting modern instrumental. It starts out with synthesizer, chimes and discordant guitars. Then the synthesizer fades and the guitar becomes more melodic. As the synthesizer fades out altogether, we have two guitar parts, a driving rhythm and an intricate, layered lead part. There's a mix of things that you might call folk music, giving way to modern jazz, and then a more mellow 70's jazz. The music speeds up and then slows down and finally stops.

I can hear some similarity, particularly in the modern jazz and discordant part, to the acoustic guitar work of John McLaughlin who played with Miles Davis in the late 60's and had his own fusion band, the Mahavishnu Orchestra in the early 70's (check out *My Goal's Beyond* from 1970 for an example of his acoustic work). Bruce's music here is a little more melodic and accessible than McLaughlin. There is a similar feel to his song *Nanzen-ji*.

The instrumental *Cala Luna*[45] was issued on the 2002 re-release of **The Trouble with Normal,** but had been available on a German release of the original album. The title is Spanish for "moon creek" or "moon cove". There is an acoustic guitar at the center of the mix, but also lots of cymbals and other percussion, with bass and keyboards. There's a lot of atmospheric electronic background as well. It a haunting tune that conjures up visions of the jungle and a deserted beach with the moonlight shimmering on the water. If you think of it alongside *Tropic*

Moon, from the same album, the hint of mystery in the song becomes a little more menacing.

The End of All Rivers[46] is an interesting experimental and improvisational piece that makes significant use of echo and delay. Bruce gets to play on top of the echo of riffs he's already played. It's a bit of a gimmick, like Roland Kirk playing two saxophones at the same time, but if the result is good music, then I'm not going to argue with it. Perhaps the title has something to do with the closing line of his song *Feast of Fools*: "It's time for us all to stand hushed in the cathedral of silence waiting at the river's end."

Parnassus and Fog[47] is a guitar and violin collaboration from the recent **Small Source of Comfort**, with a little bit of accordion and barely noticeable electric guitar from producer Colin Linden. Bruce also plays harmonica. From the liner notes, the song is about "San Francisco magic and mystery." The song alternates between a lazy morning on a porch swing and a bit of restlessness or anticipation. I catch a touch of Zen in Bruce's improvised solo in the middle, a stillness that bridges the two moods. As noted earlier, this is another of Bruce's compositions in the idiosyncratic drop-F# tuning.

Giftbearer[48] is a joyful, high energy jazz celebration, an instrumental tune that combines marimba or vibes, bells, flugelhorn, flute, bass, with light drumming, high hat and other percussion. It has a tropical jungle rhythm and the horn floats beautifully on top of the rhythms. Bruce's guitar is very submerged in the mix. Sonically, the song looks backward to songs like *Joy Will Find a Way* and forward to the songs **Dancing in the Dragon's Jaw**. It would fit very well with either of those albums and makes you want to dance and sing. It makes me think of a beautiful sunset on a tropical beach, with the stars popping out and music from a native band drifting in on the warm breeze.

In *Radio Shoes*[49] Bruce experiments with 70's-80's instrumental jazz-rock fusion. It opens with piano, drums and bass. After a few measures the rhythm guitar joins in, followed by flute. Bruce solos on electric guitar. Here, he's funkier than Pat Metheny, but in that vein of melodic interplay of guitar and piano that he used previously on pieces like

Badlands Flashback and some of the songs on **Night Vision**. About halfway through, Hugh Marsh joins in on electrified and distorted violin, giving it a little bit of a Jean-Luc Ponty vibe for about thirty seconds. Though Bruce dabbles in Jazz fusion on a number of earlier songs, this is a fairly unique piece in his catalog. It's also one of the few pieces from the early 80's where he really lets himself go on guitar, even if it's only for about a minute.

The only instrumental on the 1996 album **Charity of Night**, *Mistress of Storm* is an upbeat duet with Jazz virtuoso Gary Burton on vibes. The vibes and acoustic guitar play off each other to wonderful effect. The song is in Drop-D tuning and is a minor key jazz composition with a significant improvisational section where Bruce and Burton both take turns on lead. The improvisational section is darker in mood than the opening and closing sections. The only time that I've heard the piece live, was in 1998 at the Birchmere, in Alexandria Virginia and Bruce performed it solo. It would be interesting to know if it has ever been performed live with vibes. That would be great to see.

Down to the Delta[50] is a contemporary jazz instrumental jam with acoustic guitar backed by upright acoustic bass, drums and percussion. Bruce said that it:

> is kind of a free for all, especially on the drum and percussion end of it. It's basically an improvised jazz piece with a melody at the beginning and end. If we had more players, we could have stretched it out to a whole side of an album; that is if we still had sides.[51]

There's a bowed bass solo part in addition to the guitar improvisation.

If Bruce wanted to, he certainly has enough quality material to release a follow-up to his beautiful compilation **Speechless**. Indeed, he's released about half an album's worth of new and varied instrumentals in his recent studio albums.

11 Live Recordings

...let this be my epitaph: THE ONLY PROOF HE NEEDED
FOR THE EXISTENCE OF GOD WAS MUSIC"

Kurt Vonnegut Jr., *A Man Without a Country*

I first saw Bruce Cockburn live in Austin, Texas in about 1990. He was there solo and the show was sponsored by a local radio station KGSR. The song that I remember most from that concert was *Tibetan Side of Town*. What impressed me the most was that he had played it solo and it seemed to contain all the elements of the previously released studio version. And I remember going back home and listening to the album and realizing that he played essentially the same thing that he played on the record, but it was covered up to a large extent by the other instruments that had been layered on top of it. When I have heard him play the song in subsequent concerts he has generally played it solo or with minimal accompaniment. Perhaps he realized that the studio additions may have actually subtracted from the impact of the song rather than enhanced it.

Most of us who listen to music, love to hear the music of our favorite artists live. Whether it is the intimacy of a small concert venue or an arena full of screaming fans, or the sunshine or cool evening breezes at a Festival, live music offers us something elusive that often doesn't exist in even the best of studio recordings. There is sometimes an element of risk. Can the artist actually pull off some of the riffs that you heard on record? Does the energy of the crowd inspire them to sing or play even better than on the record? Are they great at improvisation and are the live shows filled with extended jams, like Phish or the Grateful Dead?

Live music has also become ubiquitous in our media saturated culture thanks to the cell phone and other cheap digital recording devices. Bootlegs and You Tube videos abound, though the quality is all over the map. Just about all of Bruce's concerts, at least in recent years, have been bootlegged and many are available on the internet. It would be impossible to assess more than a fraction of this material and so I will limit my remarks here to the officially released live collections in Bruce's catalog.

While listening to these songs again, particularly the studio versions, they really cried out to be played live in front of an audience. Of course, that is true of all Bruce's music, but it really hit me this time.

Circles in the Stream (1977)

Circles in the Stream was recorded in concert at Massey Hall in Toronto April 8-9, 1977. The musicians are Robert Boucher on bass, Pat Godfrey on electric piano, marimbas and vocals; Bill Usher on percussion and backing vocals; and Bruce playing acoustic and electric guitars, and dulcimer. Massey Hall was originally opened in 1894 and has a capacity of more than 2700.[1]

The concert opens with a short bagpipe introduction, something that you are not at all likely to expect from a Bruce Cockburn studio recording and probably not from one of his concerts. His music kicks off with *Starwheel*, which was originally recorded for **Joy Will Find a Way**. On the studio recording the bass is fairly conventional and the acoustic guitar is much more prominently showcased. There are some haunting, mostly wordless background vocals.

On the live version, the bass playing is more fluid with a bit of a jazz feel. The keyboards on the instrumental break combined with the bass make a very pleasing transition to the final verse. Compared with the live version, the studio version seems a little stilted.

This is followed by *Never So Free*. The studio version, from **High Winds White Sky**, uses two acoustic guitars playing in counterpoint. This is a strategy that Bruce employs more than a few times on his earlier albums to great effect. There is a beautiful, fluid interplay between the two guitars. The pace of this song, both in the studio and on stage is very deliberate.

The live version adds some minimalist percussion (mostly cymbals), while bass and marimbas fill in for the second guitar from the studio version. This recording has a very different texture and feel, but both are very good. I think the studio version is extraordinarily beautiful, but I would have loved being at that concert.

This is followed by three previously unreleased tracks, starting with the instrumental *Deer Dancing Round a Broken Mirror*. The title "comes from a Japanese children's story by a man named Kenji Miyazawa who was one of the most brilliant writers of any sort around, wrote a lot of children's stories with many dimensions to them beyond the obvious..."[2] Bruce also cited Miyazawa as an inspiration for his song *Incandescent Blue*.[3]

The piece is in Drop-D tuning. It is not unlike some of his other instrumentals like *Sunrise on the Mississippi* or *Train in the Rain*. The driving, propulsive rhythm provides a good contrast with the previous track and the laid back track that follows. This is the only released version of this song.

The song *Homme Brûlant* was also not previously or subsequently released. It was written only a month before this concert in March 1977.[4] Perhaps a studio recording exists somewhere in the either Bruce's or True North's archives, but, at least for now, this will have to do. This is a good example of 1970's era jazz fusion. The interplay of the bass, guitar, percussion and keyboards reminds me of late 70's Pat Metheny and other similar pop/rock/jazz artists.

Bruce introduces the song as a love song. The lyrics, in French, employ imagery that reminds me of several other early songs, such as *Man of a 1000 Faces, Dialogue with the Devil,* and *All the Diamonds.* They also have a dream-like or psychedelic quality, as when he says, "The City/open-mouthed/seems to be drinking/The Milky Way…" and "in the glow/You call me/Dressed in/Rainbows/And I'm burning."[5] By the end, he's a "sparkling/Sea Green" river and his lover, or perhaps God, is "the ocean I'm seeking." This is a good piece, very well performed and recorded, so perhaps there was never any need to do it again.

Free to Be is another piece that has not been released in a studio version. This is a full band piece with guitar, drums, bass, and marimba. The acoustic guitar part is finger-picked. The lyrics talk about the contradictions of this world, and specifically how we need to learn our limitations, chill out and "grow up." This is not the most memorable or meaningful tune Bruce has written, but it is a nice change of pace between the languid *Homme Brûlant* and the acoustic blues of *Mama Just Wants to Barrelhouse.*

The studio version of *Mama Just Wants to Barrelhouse All Night Long* from **Night Vision** is an almost perfect piece of jazz arranging with the piano front and center, supported by subtle guitar, fluid bass lines, and restrained brush drums. This is also some of Bruce's best singing, especially because we don't think of him as a jazz crooner. It's not Sinatra, but it is perfect for the mood and it feels absolutely genuine. The recording transports the listener to a smoky basement jazz club in the 40's or 50's.

The live version has just Bruce, by himself, on acoustic guitar and vocal. The vocal is very close to the studio vocal, with perhaps a little more of an edge. In the music, the blues elements come to the forefront and we can see that the song is really a 12 bar blues with jazz chord substitutions. The guitar work is excellent throughout with a strong solo and fills. It is completely different from the studio version, but also wonderful.

This is followed by the solo acoustic guitar instrumental *Cader Idris,* named for a mountain in Wales. Bruce's fingers are playing "eighth notes and the thumb instead of playing an alternating bass is playing a harmonized melody."[6]

This is a beautiful and complex piece, alternating between fast and slow and structured and more improvisational sections. Perhaps the changing moods and tempos of the piece suggest his memories of hiking up the mountain. Frankly, it almost seems impossible that it is just a single guitar. Given the quality of the performance and the recording it is not that surprising that he never released a studio version.

Arrows of Light presents an interesting case study for evaluating the differences between a live performance and a studio recording. In very many ways, the recordings are very similar. The instrumental arrangements are virtually identical, employing dulcimer, bass and percussion. The live version adds keyboards near the end, but in a distinctly subordinate role. The bass players, though different, are playing the same notes, including a three note figure that is played throughout.

The major difference between the two recordings is that the studio version uses a female harmony singer who sings the entire song, but rather than layering the voices together, she is singing behind the beat, sometimes substantially so. That gives it the effect of an echo and allows the vocalist more freedom in the choice of notes to sing and in the phrasing. This results in a very complex, but also very pleasing effect. The other structural difference between the two recordings is that the dulcimer part in the studio version is more complex, including more single note runs and other effects.

If you listen to the two pieces casually and not back-to-back you would probably think that they are indeed essentially the same. And yet there are some differences that might lead you to prefer one over the other, such as the backing vocalist noted above. The bass players play the same notes throughout, but their styles are very different. In the studio version, the notes are shorter, making the bass part a little choppy sounding. In the live version, the notes are longer and the bass sound is fatter, both of which add to a sense of flow. This probably also has an impact on how the percussionist plays (it was the same percussionist on both recordings), though I haven't compared the percussion parts in any detail. The bass also seems more in sync with the dulcimer, which is not totally surprising.

I would bet that in the studio version, the parts were recorded separately with Bruce recording the dulcimer and his voice and the bass and percussion parts being overdubbed later. To me, Bruce's vocal also sounds stronger on the live version, perhaps picking up on the energy of the crowd, but also the energy of the players on stage with him. I prefer the live version.

One Day I Walk is a country-folk tune from the **High Winds, White Sky** album. The studio version has a real country feel emphasized by the Mandoline Banjo and Mandolin. The tune has a nice lilting acoustic guitar part. Bass and percussion come in on the second verse. There is also a harmony vocal on the chorus. On the live version, keyboards substitute for the Banjo and Mandolin. There is no harmony vocal. It's well played, but the country feel of the studio version is mostly missing.

The studio version of *Love Song*, also from **High Winds, White Sky,** is a short acoustic gem with two acoustic guitars playing counterpoint to one another and with one guitar in each ear if you are wearing headphones. This stereo mixing practice has largely fallen out of favor, at least the extreme version of it employed here (and on the other songs I've talked about here). We are rarely, if ever, in a situation listening to two guitars with one guitarist on each side of us. As a result, the sound of the two instruments is rarely so clearly separated.

One of the highlights of the live version, at least for me, is the one-minute introductory piece, written by Gilles Binchois who was "born around 1400 and was one of the leading figures of the Burgundian School of Renaissance Music."[7] The live version transitions immediately into *Love Song*, which starts with just acoustic guitar and bass. Keyboards add additional depth starting at the second verse.

Red Brother Red Sister shifts again to just Bruce on acoustic guitar and vocals. It's another song which was not previously released. There is a studio version that was probably recorded around the time of *In the Falling Dark*, but not released until 1981 on the *Mummy Dust* compilation. The studio and live versions have largely the same intricate acoustic guitar part. The studio version adds bass, drums and harmony vocals on the chorus. It was later included on the 2002 reissue of *In the Falling Dark* as a bonus track. It's a strong piece and a little puzzling that it wasn't released earlier, but it doesn't necessarily add a lot to the performance on the live album.

We might expect that the versions of *Lord of the Starfields* might be very similar, given that it was recorded only about a year before. A few things are mostly the same, particularly the vocals. On the studio version, the bass guitar is very percussive and almost aggressive. This is emphasized even more by the congas and other percussion. Both, in my opinion, overly dominate the mix, where the voice and guitar should be more the core of the song. The guitar part is nice, but it is fairly repetitious and could use a little more variation and dynamic changes.

The live version is very different, beginning with an introduction, lasting more than a minute of free jazz with the bass, percussion, keyboards and acoustic guitar all playing prominent roles. The song also ends with a long, jazzy acoustic guitar solo. In the body of the song, the bass playing is more fluid and laid back. The acoustic guitar part is a little looser and while largely the same as on the studio recording, just seems more relaxed. I would say that the percussion parts and the keyboard parts are maybe a little too busy. Less might have been more. And, as with the studio version, the vocals could be more prominent in the mix. However, in my opinion, this is one of the songs where the live version is clearly superior to the studio version.

Over time, *All the Diamonds* has become one of Bruce's signature songs. The studio version has two acoustic guitars playing intricate, complementary parts in counterpoint. At several points later in the song, there is also a little bit on synthesizer. But this part is played so briefly that it doesn't really register unless you are listening very carefully. I have to scratch my head a little bit and say, what was the point?

The live version is just Bruce on guitar. It is very beautiful and I doubt very much if anyone missed the second guitar or the synthesizer, especially since Bruce's vocal is probably superior to the studio version.

The studio version of *Dialogue with the Devil* from **Sunwheel Dance** is just Bruce on acoustic guitar and voice. The song sounds as if it was played live in the studio. This live version is largely the same, though it clocks in at more than two minutes longer than the studio version. It is still just one guitar and one voice. The guitar sounds a little more electrified with the bass and middle accentuated. There is a very long, good guitar solo before the last verse and this definitely makes use of some kind of effects pedal which creates something of a popping percussive sound. It could be something that the percussionist is doing, but it seems like it would be very difficult to keep that in sync with the guitar.

This solo guitar piece is followed by the band performance of *Joy Will Find a Way*. The studio version is an acoustic recording featuring a very staccato, almost frenetic guitar part. There is light, varied percussion and bells throughout and there is a harmony vocal part sung throughout the entire song. Bruce's vocals seem relaxed and fluid.

The live version is significantly different. The guitar part is not as rough as on the studio version. The bass guitar adds a strong underpinning to the performance and marimba and shaker substitute for some of the staccato energy. The audience also contributes vigorous clapping on the beat, though their energy flags after a couple of verses and the clapping dissipates. Bruce sings the song without any additional harmony or backup. The song ends with raucous clapping and yelling from the audience, as they demand an encore.

The final song is *God Bless the Children*. The studio version of this song from **Night Vision** is largely strummed acoustic guitar and voice. Starting with the second verse, there is also barely audible, atmospheric electric guitar which fades in and out through the rest of the song.

The live version makes full use of the band to enhance the sound without turning it into something else entirely, such as a rock song. The core of the song is still the strummed acoustic guitar and Bruce's voice. However, from the first note, he uses cymbals for emphasis and the bass guitar adds depth and propulsion to the arrangement. Keyboards join in about halfway through the song, also in a very supportive role. The album ends on a very high note.

I've talked a lot about how the songs on this release compare to previous studio releases, if they exist. That's all well and good, but to evaluate this release as an album, does any of that matter?

The first thing that you need to look at when evaluating an album as a collection of songs, all things being equal, is the quality of the songs. Bruce was able to select his songs for this project from seven previous albums, in addition to recording several previously unreleased tracks. If not the best of the best, these songs are right up there at the top of his catalog. We may quibble at a few choices. Why not *Going to the Country* or *Silver Wheels*, to pick two possible alternatives? But these are good choices and the performances are uniformly excellent. There may have been other songs recorded at the two nights, but they were not chosen, whether for quality of performance or simple lack of space.

I have not been able to locate a set list from the Massey Hall concerts, but one exists from a performance a month later at the University of Alberta. In that concert, Bruce performed all but one of the songs that appear on **Circles in the Stream**. The missing song was *Dialogue with the Devil*. However, he also performed *Silver Wheels, In the Falling Dark, Gavin's Woodpile, Vagabondage,* and *Can I Go With You*, so it is certainly possible that they performed additional material at Massey Hall. According to Bill Usher, who was in the band and also produced a radio special on the tour, the recordings from the first night at Massey Hall were not usable, though even today he is not sure what the problem was,[8] but Bruce says in his memoirs that he " was nervous and didn't perform very well on the first night."[9] That's somewhat difficult to believe, but it's not out of the question, so it's as good an explanation as any.

Bruce Cockburn Live (1990)

This album was recorded live at Ontario Place in Toronto, August 14-15, 1989. Bruce performed at *The Forum*, an outdoor concert venue on the site, which has since been torn down.[10] On this album, Bruce plays electric and acoustic guitars, harmonica, bodhran, and wind chimes. Fergus Jemison Marsh plays Chapman stick, midi stick and contributes background vocals; with Michael Sloski on drums, percussion and background vocals.[11] The Chapman stick is an electric stringed instrument with either 10 or 12 strings that essentially combines bass and guitar. The player can use it to play either bass or guitar or both depending on their skill. There is also flexibility in tuning the instrument, which would make it even more versatile in skilled hands.[12]

The album opens with *Silver Wheels*, which starts out on electric guitar with no accompaniment, just like the original studio recording from **In the Falling Dark**. Bass and drums join in on the second verse. There's a long electric guitar solo at the end, essentially substituting for the trumpet solo on the studio recording.

This is followed by *World of Wonders* played with the full band, including a substantial electric guitar part. Bruce uses the harmonica for color and to partially substitute for the horns of the studio version. There's also a brief harmonica solo. Fergus Marsh covers the bass with his Chapman stick and there's a strong drum beat rocking us along. The original studio version of the song doesn't have much of a guitar part, but is driven by bass and/or stick, keyboards, and horns.

Harmonica is also a featured instrument on the version of *Rumours of Glory* which follows. Bruce plays acoustic guitar. There's bass and drums and even a harmonica solo. This is a very solid version of the song.

Next up could be the definitive version of *See How I Miss You*. The finger picking is impeccable and very fast, a really fine example of Bruce's impressive fingerstyle guitar work. Stick and drums join in to flesh out the arrangement, but the guitar is front and center. The studio version, from **World of Wonders**, is completely different. It has a pronounced Latin flavor, with lots of percussion and keyboards, doing their best marimba impression, with a fairly minimal guitar part.

This is followed by *After the Rain*, which Bruce performs solo, on acoustic guitar. Bruce cracks that "It's a union break for those guys," in his introduction to the song. This recording really showcases the beauty and complexity of the guitar part, complete with a guitar solo at the end.

Call it Democracy is also a solo guitar rendition. The guitar and particularly the vocals sound very intimate, with a nuance that you'd expect at a much smaller concert venue. It's also interesting that he chose to sing what is arguably his most ferocious song completely stripped down, especially when he had a band ready and able to perform it. But he may have wanted to put a really different version of the song out there.

The band returns for *Tibetan Side of Town*. This is a really good example of the versatility of the Chapman Stick (or the midi stick) where Fergus Marsh is playing both bass and filling in with something like high end keyboard fills and even a solo. The drums and stick provide a strong bottom end to anchor Bruce's extended guitar solo. Bruce also manages to add some wind chimes played with his feet. This is a really excellent version of the song.

Wondering Where the Lions Are comes next. The song starts out with just Bruce on acoustic guitar, but the drums and stick come in on the second verse. This version ends with Bruce sort of scatting while his bandmates play and sing the chorus over and over.

This is followed by an excellent band performance of *Nicaragua* from **Stealing Fire**, a good song that has perhaps not aged well because of its topical content. However, it contains some really startling images of that place and time. What is really impressive to me about the song is how it captures the fragile beauty of people's hopes and dreams and contrasts it with the sinister forces, primarily the U.S. government, arrayed against them. The version is very similar to the studio version of the song.

If I had a Rocket Launcher features Bruce on electric guitar and starts with no accompaniment. The band doesn't kick in until the first chorus. Stick provides both the bass and also something like high pitched keyboard fills, which provides a very nice sonic effect on the ending. The guitar solo is one of Bruce's best and the vocals are really good, filled with passion.

The stick and drums provide a very solid base for the reggae song *Broken Wheel*. Fergus Marsh contributes excellent, atmospheric instrumental work on the bridge.

Stolen Land follows, featuring Bruce on vocals and the bohdran. As he said in notes from his songbook *Rumours of Glory*, "Trying to make this song work for a subsequent solo tour, I discovered that if I played a Bo Diddley beat on the bohdran, the Irish drum, I could sing the song with it. It appears that way on the live album."[13] If "Bo Diddley beat" doesn't really mean something to you, go listen to the song *Who Do You Love*. The studio version appeared on **Waiting for a Miracle** and is a very electronic funk song, with Hugh Marsh playing electric violin and keyboards and synthesizers. There's a little bit of a very distorted guitar solo near the end of it, but Bruce mainly contributed the vocals.

To Raise the Morning Star, originally released on **Stealing Fire**, features Bruce on electric guitar using lots of effects, along with the bass part from Fergus Marsh on stick. There's an extended rock guitar solo. No other description fits, given the distortion and other effects.

Bruce opens *Maybe the Poet* playing the signature riff at the beginning on harmonica, which he plays off and on throughout. He also plays very distorted electric guitar. This is very different from the original version on **Stealing Fire**, but I'm not complaining at all.

The album ends, somewhat curiously, on the Monte Python song, *Always Look on the Bright Side*. Bruce plays acoustic guitar, starting out solo for the first verse which is played slowly and theatrically for emphasis. The band joins in at the chorus and the piece settles into a show-tune jazz groove. This is one of the few songs Bruce has ever recorded on one of his records that he did not write. He rarely even performs a song by someone else in his concerts, though I did hear him play Pete Seeger's *Turn, Turn, Turn* around the time that he recorded it for a tribute album. In any event, this is a good song to end what some may consider a pretty heavy concert or album, injecting a little humor at the end, even if it is a song about death and how "Life's a piece of shit, when you look at it."

This is possibly Bruce's most electric, rock oriented album, at least to this point, despite a handful of acoustic pieces in the middle. It definitely rocks harder than any of his previous studio albums. All of the songs on this album were released after **Circles in the Stream**, except *Silver Wheels*, so this is a pretty good record of his work in the 13 years between the two albums.

One very curious omission from the album is a version of *Lovers in a Dangerous Time*, clearly one of Bruce's signature songs from the 80's, though you could also make strong cases for *Fascist Architecture*, *The Trouble with Normal*, and several other songs from **Dancing in the Dragon's Jaw, Humans, and Inner City Front**. Admittedly, that's a nice problem for any artist to have: too many stellar songs.

Again, I have not been able to locate a set list from these performances. A performance at the Maine Festival three days before has nine of the same songs released from these concerts, with the addition of *Lovers in a Dangerous Time, All the Diamonds, Shipwrecked at the Stable Door, Don't Feel Your Touch, If a Tree Falls*, and *Peggy's Kitchen Wall*. A show two weeks later at the Greenbelt Festival in the UK has eight of the songs recorded on **Live**, with a few different alternative choices, such as *Radium Rain, Where the Death Squad Lives, Lord of the Starfields*, and *The Gift*. Recordings of some of these songs may, or may not, exist from the performances captured for **Live**.

You Pay Your Money and You Take your Chance (1997)

This "short" six song CD was recorded live at the Barrymore Theater in Madison, WI on May 3, 1997. It features Bruce Cockburn on guitars (acoustic, electric and resonator) and vocal, Steve Lucas on bass, and Ben Riley on drums. Steve and Ben also contribute background vocals.[14] The concert from which these songs were taken was from the album tour for **The Charity of Night**, and not surprisingly two of the six songs are from that album. Bruce reaches back to the 1980's for the other four songs.

The CD kicks off with a raucous, loud version of *Call It Democracy* featuring very distorted electric guitar. This is quite possibly the most ferocious recording that Bruce has ever made or released of any song. Bruce really lets it go on the guitar solo which ends the song. It is an angry call to arms and unfortunately, the subject matter is just as relevant today in the Age of Occupy Wall Street and the Age of Trump as it was when it was written.

Next comes a full band version of *Stolen Land*, more of a straightforward rock version than the funk-based studio version that he released on **Waiting for a Miracle**. Again, the guitar is heavily distorted. Like the other live version, this version has kind of a Bo Diddley beat and guitar. The overall volume of the piece is not as high as the first cut. The guitar solo is kind of abstract. This is a two chord song, so there's a lot of freedom for the guitarist, especially one as adept as Bruce.

Strange Waters begins with Bruce on resonator guitar with lightly played cymbals added for atmosphere. The bass and drums join in on the second verse. The song bears very strong resemblance to **The Charity of Night** studio version, which isn't that surprising, since this version was done about a year after that album was released.

This is followed by a rousing and succinct version of *Fascist Architecture*. This is true to the studio version, minus the keyboards, which are admittedly a very nice touch. Still, the live version sounds complete and the more complex arrangement of the studio version can seem a little cluttered when they are played back to back.

You Pay Your Money and You Take Your Chance has Bruce on acoustic guitar. The opening solo has a vaguely Middle Eastern flavor until he settles into the main riff of the song, at which point the band joins in. The fairly short guitar solo continues nodding towards the Middle East.

The studio version of this song, from **Inner City Front,** starts with horns and features them throughout, including a cool trumpet solo, that gives way to Hugh Marsh on electric violin. The song ends with a keyboard solo followed by keyboards and horns playing the main riff over and over. The original version of the song was much more smooth than this one.

Bruce straps on the resonator guitar for the CD finale, an extended jam on *Birmingham Shadows*. There's some intermittent percussion and the bass joins in on the second verse. As on the studio version from **The Charity of Night**, this is a relaxed, spoken jazz-inflected song. The guitar solo is free jazz and there seems to be a tempo change during the solo.

Bruce is in excellent vocal form on this CD and the band is really tight. The CD was culled from a concert where Bruce played 20 songs plus 3 encores. Included in the show were versions of all the songs from **The Charity of Night** except *The Coming Rains*.[15] If these recordings are any indication, this was a great concert. If the tapes still exist in Bruce's or True North's archives, hopefully some of the rest of this will see the light of day someday.

Bruce Cockburn Live on World Café (2002)

This CD was recorded and aired on World Café on September 25, 2001, just two weeks after September 11. It was released as a special companion disc to his compilation CD **Anything Anytime Anywhere**. The CD intersperses interview questions and responses with solo acoustic performances of five songs and an instrumental interlude. This is no doubt similar to many radio appearances that Bruce has made over the years. There are probably dozens of examples and I have listened to many of them, which I have found through the Cockburn Project, the Bruce Cockburn facebook group, and the Humans listserv on Yahoo.

The first interview snippet is called *Thoughts on September 11*. The host notes that the broadcast was originally scheduled for September 13 in Baltimore, but had been postponed. He then asks Bruce what he was doing on September 11. Bruce says that he was driving from Montreal to Vermont to see his girlfriend and then planning to drive on to Baltimore for the show. He says that he turned on the TV before leaving and saw the plane hit the second tower and thought that he really needed to get across the border before things tightened up. There wasn't much traffic and the crossing was uneventful, but then the radio appearance was cancelled along with some other gigs that he had in the DC area the following week.

He then talks some about terrorism in general and the only time that he had guns pointed at him directly, which was in the late 70's in Italy when the Red Brigades were active and Fascists blew up the Bologna railway stations while Communists were shooting off people's kneecaps, which led to the police really being on edge. He also talks about protecting civil liberties and how much power we allow police to have. The host points out that he had described the Italian incidents in one of his songs, which leads to him performing his song *How I Spent My Fall Vacation*.

Of course, the song is about much more than what happened as he traveled through Italy and Japan in the late 1970's. The series of vignettes that make up the song are framed by his watching Ingmar Bergman's classic film *The Seventh Seal* in a cold movie theater somewhere in Italy. The original studio version appeared on **Humans** and on that version Bruce is supported by light drums, bass, keyboards, backing vocals and towards the end, violin played by Hugh Marsh. The arrangement is very balanced with none of the instruments overpowering any of the others. It's a very satisfying version where all the elements pull the recording together into a coherent whole. This solo version is certainly satisfying as well. As always, the guitar work is impeccable and Bruce's voice is in good form, although there's a touch of a rasp in it. The two things I miss the most from the studio version are the backing vocals and Hugh Marsh's violin.

This is followed by a discussion with the host about *Bruce's Sabbatical*. Apparently at the time Bruce was largely taking a year off from touring and recording to recharge his batteries, meditate on the state of his life and the world and hopefully write a few songs. He notes that because of personal and other issues that wouldn't interest anyone else, it had actually been a somewhat more stressful year than anticipated, although he did manage to write a few new songs. They also discussed his new record deal with Rounder Records and the compilation disc that was going to be released in early 2002, for which this live disc was a companion.

Anything Anytime Anywhere is a very nice little love song that was originally slated to be included on **Dart to the Heart**, but they didn't get a recorded version that they were happy with. The acoustic version here has a vibe that would have fit right in with that collection. It has a timeless quality. The studio version of the song has a more distinctive late 50's and early 60's sound encompassing R&B and roots.[16]

Backup vocals are provided by the black a capella gospel group the Fairfield Four. The sound fits comfortably with the sound developed in his work with T Bone Burnett on **Nothing but a Burning Light** and **Dart to the Heart** and also Bruce's work on **Breakfast in New Orleans**, especially his cover of *Blueberry Hill*.

This is followed by a discussion of Bruce's experience on a major label and how other singer-songwriters were briefly on the majors until the labels figured out that they couldn't sell enough records to make it work. Bruce also talks about how he found his voice in the late 60's. These issues are described at length in his memoir, but he relates here that he started writing when he was in the band The Children, first putting music to words by the poet Bill Hawkins and then writing songs on his own. And there is also a discussion of his album **Dancing in the Dragon's Jaw** and how, for him, it summed up all of the things he was trying to do in the 1970's and how he got his first serious radio airplay with *Wondering Where the Lions Are*.

Creation Dream is a beautiful acoustic rendering of a song first recorded on **Dancing in the Dragon's Jaw**. The guitar part is virtually the same, but the original is a full band version including marimba, bass and drums and while the guitar is certainly audible on that version, in some way it gets a little bit overshadowed by the other instruments. The vocal is also lower in the mix than I would have liked. This version stands completely on its own. You don't miss the other instruments at all.

Creation Dream is followed by a short instrumental fragment titled only *Instrumental*. It is actually a one minute instrumental fragment of *The Trouble With Normal*. This is followed by a brief discussion of **the** inspiration for *Celestial Horses*.

This version of *Celestial Horses* is a beautiful and complete version that easily stands on its own. The pacing and phrasing of this and the studio version are almost the same; indeed, the pace of studio version may be even more languid. It beautifully captures the mood that you would think you'd experience sitting alone in a wild hot spring at sunset and dusk in the mountains watching the moon rise. The big difference for me is the great violin accompaniment by Hugh Marsh on the studio version. Another, nearly identical solo version was also released on **Slice 'O Life**.

This is followed by a brief discussion called *Thoughts on singer-songwriters today*. Bruce notes that as he travels and performs at Festivals and other venues that there seems to be a great deal of creative energy out there. Recognizing that they are running short of time, the host notes that he had been thinking a lot since September 11 about *The Trouble With Normal*. He notes that terrorism may be part of the "new" normal and it is getting worse.

On cue, Bruce performs the song to end this CD. It is quite interesting, particularly because Bruce pretty much plays the arrangement from the studio version with only his guitar. What's mostly missing from the studio version is guitar, which he either barely played (some electric guitar fills) or is so buried in the mix beneath the bass, drums, and keyboards that you just can't hear it. For no other reason, that makes this an essential recording for his fans.

At the very end, the host thanks Bruce for helping World Café celebrate its 10th Anniversary and asks what he's up to next. He replies that he'll be doing some concerts with artists like Emmy Lou Harris, Steve Earle, Nancy Griffith and others for the Campaign Against Land Mines.

As a radio broadcast, it is likely that it was not as well recorded as his own records, and he certainly had very little control over the recording process. All the same, he and True North had to be reasonably satisfied with the recording to bring it out, even as a bonus disc. While the interview materials are interesting, especially those that touch on Bruce's inspiration for several of the tunes, I'm not sure how many people will continue to listen to those bits and pieces. For most of us, it's still about the music and there is some excellent music here.

Slice 'O Life

Bruce's most recent live release is the two disc solo recording **Slice 'O Life** from 2009. While all of his live releases except **You Pay Your Money and You Take Your Chances** contain solo acoustic tracks, this is the only full release with just Bruce and his guitar. It also encompasses tracks from just about the whole of his career, going back to the **Night Vision** album from the mid-1970's.

I guess it is obligatory for a Live CD to begin with raucous applause as the artist or band takes the stage. I'm not sure how much it actually contributes to making you feel like you are in the audience, but that's how this CD starts.

The music actually starts with *World of Wonders*, which has been completely reimagined and rearranged as a solo guitar piece. It has a somewhat different melody. It is also played at a slower pace. It's much longer than any previously recorded version of the song. There's a world weariness in his voice, at age 64, which conveys a recognition of both the beauty and the cost of living in this world. The guitar work also has a somewhat menacing sound. You really feel the "wet pipe" dripping down his neck. The fragility and transience of the images in the song also seems to be enhanced, whereas in the other versions of the song, recorded with full bands, there are a lot of other things for your mind and ear to focus on. This sets a tone for the rest of the CD. It is certainly a more intimate experience than most of his albums recorded after the mid-1970's.

Lovers in a Dangerous Time follows, again looking back 20 something years to another of his iconic 1980's songs. The voice is still strong, but occasionally cracks and is certainly a little lower than it was. The guitar picking is still magnificent. There is a world-weariness in this version that is miles away from the original recording.

This was the first song by Bruce that I ever heard. I was living in Chicago at the time and saw a brief preview of a recent concert appearance in the *Chicago Reader*, though the concert was already past when I read the article. Nevertheless, I was intrigued enough by what the reviewer had to say about his music that I went out to a record store hoping to find some of his music. All I could find was a cassette of

Stealing Fire, so I bought it and listened to it as soon as I got home. I was blown away by the pulsating bass line and the words that followed and have been a fan from the first note. That bass, along with the guitar, drums and keyboards pulls the listener along and the energy carries a certain optimism and buoyancy, stopping only for the palpable anger at having to "kick at the darkness 'til it bleeds daylight." Here, it seems like he has been kicking at the darkness all too often in the intervening decades. He's not about to throw in the towel, but it's taken a significant toll.

One of the great things about this CD is the interspersed stories. Bruce has loosened up over the years and now talks to the audience a great deal more than when I first saw him in 1990. This is especially true when he is playing solo.

The *Mercenary Story* that introduces the song *See You Tomorrow* is one of the more revealing anecdotes that Bruce has certainly ever recorded. He tells us about being offered a "summer" job by an acquaintance who was planning to run guns to Cuba and how he considered it for "about a minute" until he realized what his job really would entail. It shows his human frailty and makes the song that much more poignant.

I first heard *Last Night of the World* live and solo at a concert before it was released on **Breakfast in New Orleans** and I've heard him play the song solo several times, so I'm very comfortable with the solo version. The guitar part on the live and studio versions are pretty close.

This is followed by *How I Spent My Fall Vacation*. I really can't hear all that much difference between this version and the one released seven years earlier from his World Café appearance discussed previously.

Tibetan Side of Town is next. This song brings me back to the first time I saw Bruce play live, about 20 years before this recording was made. The voice is a little lower and raspy with age, but the playing is as great as ever. On a song like this, with an extended guitar solo and no bass or drums to help keep time, you get a good sense of how well Bruce keeps time. I'm sure you'd find the beat drifting a little here and there if you laid a metronome beat over it, but he does remarkably well after all these years. I was already a fan of the song from the studio version and the live band version on **Bruce Cockburn Live** is also great. I've probably also heard at least half a dozen versions in concert, mostly solo or nearly solo. It's a great song and it still sounds great.

He follows this with *Pacing The Cage*. It's a little slower and more deliberate than the studio version. The studio version is very stripped down. It starts off solo and a bass guitar comes in on the second verse and there are also some ethereal keyboards way in the background as the song progresses. The solo is played on bass guitar and overall the bass playing by Rob Wasserman is very expressive and it is very much at the forefront of the arrangement, but it is supportive of the guitar playing and doesn't step over it. If you took the studio recording and stripped off the bass and keyboards it would be almost identical to this live version though just a tick faster.

The *Bearded Folk Singer Story* contains a funny exchange with the audience that I will not reveal here. In any event, Bruce recounts a story from his college days at Berklee where he played a hayride for fraternity and sorority members somewhere in the environs of Boston on a moonlit night.

This is followed by his instrumental song *End of All Rivers*. This song is significantly dependent on the use of electronics, particularly delay and echo, which allows Bruce to play along with himself. Prior to the perfection of that technology it would have been necessary to play this piece with a second guitarist or to overdub a second guitar in the studio. Having seen him play the piece live and having this live recording we can be assured that he indeed can do it. Whether or not one considers it essentially an electronic trick, it certainly requires skill to pull it off and the piece is an interesting instrumental work.

The final track on **Disc One** is *Soul of a Man*, originally recorded for **Nothing But a Burning Light**. The studio version arrangement is minimalist; just Bruce on guitar with a drumbeat and some light percussion. You can make a strong argument that NBBL is one of the best produced of Bruce's CDs, especially his vocals, but all the instruments are nearly perfectly recorded. That said, this is a very strong version and one of the best vocal parts on this entire collection.

Disc Two starts off with *Wait No More* and as on the studio recording, starts out with Bruce playing a Middle Eastern riff on his dobro. The guitar part is pretty much the same as the studio version. This version is very effective, to the extent that at least in the moment, you don't really miss the drums, percussion, backing vocals and most particularly Hugh Marsh's incomparable violin. The violin work on the studio version is what really makes it stand out.

City Is Hungry is the lone previously unrecorded song on the CD. In his intro, he says that this is the first time he's played this song in front of "actual humans, who have paid to be there." By his standards, it is a somewhat slight song, a little slice of life slow blues, which is almost but not quite a traditional 12 bar blues. He's on a city street with his girl and he builds the song out of a few seemingly random observations: the subway, a drunk on a park bench, the concrete and lights illuminating the river in the darkness. At the end his baby starts to dance around. It captures an intimate moment that could easily be forgotten or missed entirely in our busy lives. The couple is either on their way to a night out or returning from a night out, but they stop and just live for a few seconds in that scene. There's an atonal jazz-inflected solo in the middle. It's a nice little recording and it's hard to see how a full band arrangement would enhance the results.

This is followed by his now classic song *Put It In Your Heart*, one of the best 9/11 songs anybody has written. Whether done with a full band, like the original studio recording, or just on 12-string guitar it is a powerful statement. I would give the studio version the nod, because it is so well done, but this version is also very good and filled with passion, and I love hearing him solo without any accompaniment.

As a complete change of pace, to shift the mood from the anguish of 9/11 Bruce tells a story about *Tramps In The Street*, talking about how he meets and chats with the homeless pan handlers in his new (at the time) home in Kingston, Ontario. Near the end of the story, he talks about walking down the street in Toronto one time when a cyclist across the street yelled at him "I hate your music," a comment that he found both disturbing and refreshing.

By now, *Wondering Where The Lions Are* is about as sacred a song as there is in Bruce's catalogue. It reminds me of sitting around a campfire as a child with everyone singing well-worn folk songs. Now, it's almost more about the audience participation. For me, that suggests it has lost a little of its edge and intrinsic beauty, which is truly a shame. This is not to say that he phones this version in or that it isn't good, but hopefully, he can feel free now and in the future to drop the song from the repertoire every now and then to give it and himself a break.

This is followed by a passionate version of *If A Tree Falls*, which makes good use of reverb and delay, particularly on the solo. The guitar sound has lots of bass and the vocal performance is very good. While some of my favorite Cockburn songs are on **Big Circumstance**, I'm not a big fan of the arrangements and production, particularly the keyboard sound, which is a little sharp-edged to my ear and the vocals are sometimes buried in the mix a little too much. The electric guitar part on this song is, to me, a little annoying in places. So, it shouldn't be surprising that I prefer this solo version. As a fan, one thing I'd love is to hear **Big Circumstance** remixed and remastered. But, of course, that's never going to happen.

After that, we have the third released version of *Celestial Horses,* all within a decade, and the second solo acoustic version, so hopefully Bruce feels that he finally got what he wanted to hear for this song on record. This version captures the vibe about as well as the studio version, but to me, so does the version released in 2002 recorded for World Café. On the studio version, Bruce plays electric guitar and there are drums, upright bass, backing vocals and the incomparable Hugh Marsh on violin. Because of the audience and the better recording environment this is probably also slightly better than the World Café version, but not by much to my ears.

If I Had A Rocket Launcher was an encore performance, since he asks the management if it is okay to play a couple more songs. Originally recorded on **Stealing Fire**, this was also recorded for his 1990 **Live** album. The studio version is full band, with a heavy dose of keyboards along with the bass and drums. The 1990 version rocks a little harder with the keyboard part a little less prominent, with Fergus Marsh playing the keyboard fills and the bass part on Chapman Stick and Bruce playing electric guitar. The vocals are exceptional. The solo acoustic version starts out slow with a little intro before he goes into the signature riff. The guitar playing is as good as any he's recorded live and the vocals are both strong and intimate. Listen carefully to the killer solo.

This is followed by *Child Of The Wind,* previously released on **Nothing But a Burning Light**. As I said earlier, this is one of Bruce's best produced albums. Like many of the songs on that album the arrangements are minimalist: just guitar, bass, violin, and some keyboards. There's no percussion or drums on the version of this song and no backing vocals. Take away the other instruments and the two versions would be nearly identical, both excellent performances well recorded.

The actual concert portion of the CD concludes with a version of *Tie Me At The Crossroads*, a fitting closing song which makes light of death and legacy. The studio version is a rocking romp with a raucous chorus utilizing as many voices as they could find. Bruce makes due with solo guitar and his one voice. It's obviously different, but he pulls it off nicely.

At the end of the second disc, this recording includes a few things from one of the sound checks, starting with an improvised instrumental piece, called *String Thing* on the liner notes. This morphs into a fragmentary version of a song by Bill Hawkins called *The Trains Don't Run Here Anymore*. Hawkins was a poet and early mentor of Bruce's during his rock and roll days in the mid-1960's.

This is followed by a straightforward version of *Kit Carson*. This has never been one of my favorite songs – too much editorializing and not enough showing. Compare it to a song like *Indian Wars* and you can hear the difference. But again, this is a no-frills version of the song which is not terribly different from the T Bone Burnett produced studio version.

The CD concludes with a strong version of *Mama Just Wants To Barrelhouse All Night Long* which ends with an atonal jazzy solo, similar to the one he played on *City is Hungry*, though this solo seems to disintegrate at the end rather than resolving.

I'm not sure what the intended purpose was for the sound check materials. It certainly shows a little bit of what Bruce is like without the audience and the bright lights. Obviously, they had about 18 minutes to fill on the CD, but that's not exactly a great reason. There are plenty of songs that he played on the tour that didn't make the cut for one reason or another, including the two songs that he plays in full during this sound check. Perhaps they were happy with the songs they had picked and the order they placed them in and had a hard time making a coherent album when they added in other material. Clearly, these pieces feel different and don't feel like they quite belong with the rest, but here they are.

12 *You Pay Your Money and You Take Your Chance*

We shall not cease from exploration
And the end of all our exploring
Will be to arrive where we started
And know the place for the first time.

T.S. Eliot, *Little Gidding*

What does it all mean? Do Bruce Cockburn's songs add up to a many-faceted picture of a world of wonders?   Certainly they present a varied and honest picture of this world and the human experience, warts and all; perhaps too many warts for some listeners.

The song *World of Wonders* is a beautiful evocation of a moment of peace and transcendence in a troubled world; the "darkness alive with possibilities."   He sees "a rainbow shining in a bead of spittle" and "falling diamonds in rattling rain." He stands "dazzled with my heart in flames." But there is a sense, mostly unspoken, that this "brief arctic bloom" of beauty is teetering on the edge of heartbreak.

The album **World of Wonders** is something of a microcosm of Cockburn's body of work as a whole, if perhaps on the darker side of the scale.   It begins with his rage at the IMF and the bankers who are "modern slavers in drag as champions of freedom."   In *Lily of the*

Midnight Sky, he misses his lover and "the cold of your absence blows from/ the silent TV, the parking lot." He's about to explode from his desire for her. At the end of the song he is reduced to thinking of putting on his "dog mask" to "howl for you."

The song *World of Wonders* follows, giving us a brief glimpse of beauty, hope and peace. But the bloom fades and we are left in the dying days of divided Berlin and the "scratchy acid-bitten transparent winter trees" and "brownish haze" of Germany. Only once does he get to glimpse the "moon over that anal retentive border wall." In *People See Through You* he takes direct aim at American foreign policy, particularly our "primitive cunning/and high tech means" and our "anti-matter language/contrived to conceal," a song that still resonates strongly 30 years after it was released, though it seems now that we don't even care that people see through us. This is followed by the quirky love song, *See How I Miss You,* with its cast of misfits – "the walking graffiti, survivalist bums" and "even the secret police" - who "shout that you're the one." The song is as much or more a commentary on the total dysfunction of our society as it is a love song.

This is followed by the stately and somber *Santiago Dawn,* where he imagines the victims of Pinochet's coup rising out of their graves to come home and meet the dawn after a decade of repression and darkness. *Dancing in Paradise* presents the dichotomy of the tourist "paradise" and natural beauty of Jamaica and it's dark underbelly of poverty, hunger, and police violence where "a naked man, sores on his neck,/lies for days in Washington Blvd. gnawing chicken bones." The album closes with a more hopeful song written in a different island country, where "the hour of darkness is the time to dance" and "lay down your burdens". The "beating of the sea sends a message/to the far starlight" that "'we're doing okay down here tonight.'"

Perhaps the most succinct expression of Bruce's worldview comes from the song *Lovers in a Dangerous Time,* particularly the lines: "one day you're waiting for the sky to fall/then you're dazzled by the beauty of it all." Later in the same song, he tells us that "we're creatures open to the thrust of grace," but it doesn't come easy. Sometimes, we have to "kick at the darkness/till it bleeds daylight." It takes effort and commitment and even courage to realize our angelic nature and overcome the beast within us. In his long, disturbing song *You've Never Seen Everything* he sings that we "ride the ribbon of shadow" and "never feel the light falling all around." The light is always there, but we simply don't see it or feel it most of the time. Too many of us are overwhelmed with the darkness and depravity that smacks us in the face every day when we turn on the TV or the radio or open a newspaper.

I think one of the things that many of us appreciate about Bruce is that he truly sees the darkness, but has the capacity to not let it overwhelm him. Sure, he was beaten down personally and spiritually in the early 1980's. He has had his share of despair or doubt. But he's had the ability to endure and then transcend. And rather than retreat from the darkness, he pushed further. The point of his song *All the Diamonds* is not to get lazy and enjoy the quiet life in the "Harbour Town." It's to take a risk and sail into the unknown; if you are lucky, perhaps to eventually "reach the far shore of enlightenment." Faith is about mystery, not certainty.

Bruce's spiritual journey has had many twists and turns. A voracious reader, he steeped himself in the Beat Poets, Science Fiction, Fantasy, Eastern Religions, the Occult, the Bible, and Sufi mystics, among other things to try and make sense of the world and our place in the universe. In his early work, he was particularly wary of cities and sought out peace and tranquility in the wilderness and in nature. Cities were corrupt places where men were blinded from spirit by greed, ambition, and temptations of the flesh.

When he finally committed himself to Christianity in the mid 70's, his association of Christ with the elemental forces of nature was particularly strong and revealing. There is a certain naiveté and innocence about the early songs. As his horizons broadened through the late 1970's through travel and then personal hardship, his spiritual writing broadened as well. His spiritual journey came to incorporate other people and their dreams and struggles. He found that he could find spirit even when jetlagged on a crowded Tokyo street, or perhaps I should say that spirit always seems to find him. And he found that spirit could be sometimes absent in places like a moonlit beach in the Tropics. He found that even churches could be corrupt in songs like *Lament for the Last Days* and later in *Gospel of Bondage.*

His song *Justice* seems to be a pivotal song in interpreting his evolving view of religion. The teachings of Jesus, Islam, Buddhism and other religions are beautiful and inspiring. What man has done in the name of those teachings has often been violent and troubling. But words still matter. He tells us that we've "got to search the silence of the soul's wild places/For a voice that can cross the spaces," to bridge our differences and get beyond "tribe and state."

Throughout the journey, certain things have remained true. The following are some things that I get from his work, both from the spiritual and the not-so spiritual songs. The universe is inherently divine. Spiritual forces animate the world and there's more to this world than meets the eye. At the same time, even though everything is divine, we usually just get fleeting glimpses of it, as with sunlight shimmering on the waves.

Most people are blinded to that reality most of or all the time, either because they choose not to see, don't make the effort to see, or don't know that there's anything to see. To get beyond these fleeting glimpses requires one to be genuine and committed.

Bruce's religion is not about rules or laws and conventions. It has little to do with slavish adherence to traditions, though he is respectful of traditions. His religion or spirituality is based on experience and practice, more about feeling than thinking. It is about being in the presence of the divine and opening yourself to it. He has a childlike curiosity about the world, about music and how the two play together to create meaning and understanding.

He believes that Christ's message is all about love and freedom. You might call it freedom from the tyranny of rules, but it is also freedom from the limits of the material world. From Buddhism and Taoism or even modern physics, he gets the notion that this world or what we generally perceive to be the world is an illusion, constantly in flux. It is constantly in a state of creation and destruction. When you touch something it is already gone or changed. Finally, God or the divine is boundless, without beginning or end.

Bruce has said repeatedly over the years that "I don't make any of this shit up. People think it's imagination, but it's not. I don't have any imagination, I just report."[1] As Bruce put it in *Child of the Wind*, how you see things, "depends on what you look at obviously/but even more it depends on the way that you see." He makes a similar statement, though perhaps a little less stridently in a 1999 interview about the song *Birmingham Shadows*:

> I try to write out of my own experience. It's not that I feel like I've got all this stuff to teach people. It's just that my life and my quest have gone through these different things, and the songs are a trail. Hopefully, somebody can find something to use in there. I'm trying to describe what I see at each point along the way.

> Most of the songs come out of very particular things, like Birmingham Shadows, or the stuff from Central America, or Get Up Jonah, for that matter. At other times they pull from more than one experience. But the important thing is that the songs *come out of life*. They're not a reproduction of life. They're not an attempt to pin life down. They assume a life of their own.[2]

The songs are excerpts from a diary or dispatches from the "real world." As he says here, he tries "to write out of [his] own experience," the whole truth and nothing but the truth. The songs are non-fiction rather than fiction.

Despite such admonitions, it is clear that there is something different about Bruce's work than simple journalism. Indeed, there is an element in his work that is reminiscent of novelists like Gabriel Garcia Marquez and the so-called "magical realists." In a recent interview with Brian Walsh, Bruce makes a comment on love that elucidates this connection:

> They're gonna find a particle, that's the love particle one of these days, that's so sub-atomic that it just sticks everything together... I really feel that love is a force in the universe as physical as gravity.[3]

Bruce not only sees the universe as alive at a fundamental level, but infused with love. It is a very particle of our being.

Comparisons are always imperfect and often a subject of much controversy. Recently, a number of significant songwriters and performers have died (Glenn Frey, David Bowie, and Prince, in this case) and I thought again about how musicians' careers often seem to be over-hyped or trivialized at the moment of their deaths. How much we grieve and, as fans, project our heroes status in the Musical Firmament is largely dependent on the degree to which we were serious fans of a particular artist and the degree to which their music was a part of the soundtrack of our lives. Do we know everything, or just the hits that got played over and over on the radio? Do we continue to listen, even when radio and TV has moved on to the next big thing? It is difficult, perhaps even impossible to be totally objective about something as subjective as musical taste, especially when it is tied up with fashion and celebrity. How do we separate the artistic value from the celebrity?

Bruce's work doesn't show up on such American-centric lists as the *Rolling Stone* 500 greatest songs or albums of all time, or the 100 greatest guitarists. There won't be a glossy special issue of Rolling Stone to commemorate his passing in, hopefully, some distant future. Clearly, he should be on these lists and it is an oversight of epic proportions that he is not. The following are some comparisons that come to my mind. You can take these musings with a very large grain of salt.

Bruce is one of the most singularly confessional songwriters since late Beatles or post-Beatles John Lennon. Certainly *Imagine* and *Across the Universe* leap immediately to mind because of the spiritual content, but there is also the Lennon of *Help, I'm So Tired, Instant Karma, Watching the Wheels, Starting Over* and *Jealous Guy*. There's an unflinching honesty and emotional nakedness in their work that is unmistakable. Lennon was not a virtuoso guitar player, but as songwriters there's a great similarity in their points of view and method. Bruce lacks Lennon's caustic wit. It would have been very interesting to see where Lennon's work would have taken him over the last thirty-six years since his untimely death.

There was a time when Bruce was referred to as the Canadian Bob Dylan, and there are elements of the comparison that are apt, especially now in retrospect. Both have had amazingly long, varied and productive careers. Both have stretched the language in their songwriting. Both have been musically, artistically and spiritually restless. They have experimented with style. There has been a strong political content to their work. Both have been very private.

Guitar playing and the Nobel Prize aside, the major difference that I see is that Bruce is always Bruce. Dylan is a chameleon, a master of disguises. While obviously all the songs are his, from song to song and album to album it is often difficult to get a sense of the man behind the songs. In that sense, Dylan is more like Shakespeare, ever changing and enigmatic, a master storyteller weaving his songs seemingly out of thin air. Bruce is always much more grounded, though also generally sparing in personal details. The songs are almost always clearly about what he is seeing, thinking and feeling. His life and experiences are the connecting fiber between all the songs. Bruce was troubled enough at his own propensity to wear masks that he called himself out on it in his early song *Man of a 1000 Faces*.

Dylan has also spent the last 50 years mining just about every vein of what we now consider "roots" music or Americana, everything from folk, country, and blues to rockabilly and rock and roll, and now even Sinatra. Bruce has certainly covered some of the same territory, but there is also a much more serious jazz and world music aspect to his playing and composition. And while Dylan has stretched the boundaries of traditional song structure and language, Bruce has been far more experimental in the use of spoken word and non-rhyming lyrics.

Paul Simon is another songwriter that I would compare to Bruce. Again, he's had a long and productive career, and certainly he's been a much more successful pop musician. His work has been more musically varied than Dylan, with his excursions into South African and Brazilian rhythms and instrumentation. He's also dabbled a little bit in Jazz. As is the case with Dylan, he's more of a classic storyteller and songwriter than Bruce is, but when he's talking through his own voice, you tend to know it. He's not nearly as inscrutable as Dylan. His spirituality is clearly evident in his middle and late period works, such as *Graceland*, *Rhythm of the Saints* and *So Beautiful or So What*.

Though older than Bruce by more than a decade, Leonard Cohen's music career got started at about the same time. Prior to that, Cohen had been a published poet and had written a couple of novels. His songs often deal with religion and spiritual concerns, as well as relationships and sexuality. Although a Jew by birth and upbringing, Cohen has had a long interest in and involvement with Zen Buddhism, including spending much of the 1990's in a Zen Monastery.

The basis of any comparison between Bruce and Cohen would be primarily about the lyrics. I'm not sure anyone would call Cohen a virtuoso musician, but he has been an astute musical collaborator throughout his career and has made the most of his limited vocal range. Whether you consider early songs like *Suzanne* or *Bird on a Wire* or later songs like *Halleluiah*, *Everybody Knows* or *The Future* there is a similar breadth of subject matter, a combination of the personal, spiritual and political and a disarming honesty that links the two songwriters.

What about Bruce and Neil Young? Both grew up musically in the same Toronto milieu. They are roughly the same age (Young is actually a little younger). They both started out in folk. Neil has also been incredibly productive and musically restless, careening between the punk and grunge ferocity of his work with Crazy Horse and Pearl Jam and the gentle folk of *Harvest* or his late masterpiece *Prairie Wind*. Young has certainly done his share of political and polemical songs during his career.

His work has often been louder and more ragged than Bruce has ever gotten, though perhaps Neil's fury is what Bruce had in mind when he remarked that he was thinking of making a loud record, but had to settle for the folk of **Small Source of Comfort** because of his nomadic circumstances. Neil has been much less of a perfectionist about his guitar playing and writing. You get the impression of his working very fast to get the thoughts and sounds out into the world, analogous to the way Ginsberg and Kerouac wrote.

As guitarists, Bruce and Richard Thompson are twin sons of different mothers. Both are equally skilled on acoustic and electric guitar. Thompson's electric guitar work leans a little more to the rock and rockabilly side of the sonic spectrum. Both incorporated medieval and Celtic elements into their playing, particularly the acoustic playing. Check out the songs *So Ben Mi Ca Ben Tempo, Beeswing* or *52 Vincent Black Lightning* for examples of Thompson's acoustic versatility and prowess.

Both are extremely passionate performers and great songwriters. And they both have been pretty uncompromising in following their inner musical compass. Richard is more of a chameleon, a shape shifting storyteller like Dylan. He has a great eye for detail, like Bruce. His characters are often working class tough guys, small time crooks and losers, and he tells the stories well, both in first and third person narratives. His music suggests that his movie tastes veer towards Film Noir.

Jackson Browne is another reasonable comparison. His songwriting has the same tension between the political and the personal, but is probably lacking the fully developed spiritual dimension of Cockburn's work. Jackson is probably "better" at keeping those things separate in his songwriting. In terms of guitar virtuosity, it takes both Jackson and his long-time collaborator David Lindley to keep up with Bruce.

Finally, what about the other Bruce? When I wrote the original version of this book, I would not have even thought to make the comparison. After all, Springsteen was and is one of the biggest rock stars on the planet. But he is also a deeply personal storyteller. Recently, I was reading his autobiography and was struck by some strong musical similarities, but also some obvious but telling differences. From **Darkness at the Edge of Town**, through **The River, Born in the USA, The Ghost of Tom Joad** and **The Rising** he has chronicled the travails of working class folks, broken veterans, migrant workers and others left behind in our rustbelt cities and small towns.

One big difference thematically is that spiritual matters are tangential at best in Springsteen's work. One key to his success is that, starting as a bar band performer in a tourist area, he was always keenly aware of the audience and making the audience happy. He was also aware of his friends and not being of the same class as the wealthier folks who would hang out at the beach and yet he took it as his task to use all his energy and skills to give them the best show possible. Cockburn was largely indifferent to his audience in the early days and has been much more reticent.

From the beginning, they were both obsessive about music and getting better. But a couple of other differences emerge from the pages of their respective memoirs. If you take music, the music business, and his musical collaborators out of the book, there is practically nothing left of Springsteen's autobiography. Music, writing and performing are a nearly total obsession for Springsteen. His is a tale filled with concerts, recording sessions, musical triumphs, legal wrangling and failures. His ambition to get to the top of the heap burns brightly through most of the book.

He's travelled the world, but in his memoir he talks mostly about specific concerts from his world tours, barely a word about people he met and places he visited. Though he spends part of the year in California these days, he still lives within shouting distance of where he grew up. Towards the end of his book, he does include more information about his wife (though she sings in the band as well), his kids, and his parents, but that's not really the story he wants to tell. Even with his collaborators, like producer Jon Landau and his band mates, you don't get a sense of them as complete human beings with lives outside their association with him. So, his ego certainly shines through the pages as well. But to give him his due, he is very candid about his flaws and insecurities and the things in himself that he has needed to overcome to be a better human being as well as a megastar.

Most of you can probably think of many more comparisons with songwriters well known and not-so well known. I have mentioned a few in the preceding pages, including collaborators such as Bonnie Raitt, Lucinda Williams, and T Bone Burnett, or acquaintances like Mark Heard. What they all seem to share is a fierce independent streak, and integrity, intensity and passion for their music. They are genuine articles in an increasingly fabricated world.

In response to a question from NPR's Scott Simon on his phrase "alleys where they hide the truth of cities"[4] Bruce had this to say in response:

> Yeah, well, I guess I got on to that idea when I lived in Boston in the sixties, because I was sleepless, as I have been much of my life, or at least disinclined to go to sleep, let's say. And every night before I went to bed I'd go for a long walk, and the alleys were always the most interesting part of the city to walk in at that hour. You know, people's garbage...they don't clean those up the way they do the sidewalks, so you kinda see the other side of things, and I suppose in a way that need to see the other side of things has been one of the driving forces of my entire life.[5]

In addition to his "need to see the other side of things," we can be thankful for Bruce's disinclination to sleep. If you think back, a great many of his songs were written in the middle of the night or just before dawn, when most people would be asleep or tossing and turning in their beds. He's "at home in the darkness, but hungry for dawn."[6]

Some evening you may find yourself standing on a bridge before the cavern of night "trying to catch the scent of what's coming to be..." Imagine Bruce standing with you, whispering in your ear as a trusted guide. And remember that despite the dangers of this world, the "darkness [is] alive with possibility."

James A. Heald

Appendix: Contents of Rumours of Glory

HarperOne, 2014, Hardcover Edition

Unfortunately, Bruce's autobiography does not contain an index, nor is there a table of contents, and the chapters are not titled. This makes it very difficult to go back to any particular incident in the book or review his thoughts surrounding a particular song or period of his life. I have provided a rudimentary index of the 2014 hardcover edition here for your convenience. Of course, my own book has no index either, although chapters and sub-chapters are noted in the table of contents. I hope to create one in the coming months, if resources allow and there is interest in me doing so.

Chapter 15, 299-329

About The Author

Jim Heald is a poet, songwriter, and guitarist. He grew up in the suburbs of New York City. He attended Colby College and Manchester College, Oxford where he studied English Literature and East Asian Studies. He attended graduate school briefly at the University of Pennsylvania, where he studied Oriental languages and history, and received a Masters in Urban Planning from the University of Illinois in Chicago.

Jim picked up the guitar in the mid 70's while hanging around the Old Town School of Folk Music and started turning his poetry into songs. He's played professionally since the late 70's around Chicago, Austin, the Washington DC area, and Sarasota, FL. He has been a two time finalist in the Kerrville Folk Festival New Folk Competition and has three CDs available. He lives with his wife Laura in Sarasota, Florida.

You can follow him on Facebook at JimHealdMusic or at www.JimHealdMusic.com.

Acknowledgments

This book would not have been possible without the hard work and dedication of a number of Bruce's fans. I would like to acknowledge the work that Daniel Keebler has done over many years in collecting reviews and articles about Bruce Cockburn's work and publishing *Gavin's Woodpile (www.brucecockburn.org),* an invaluable resource for any fan or researcher. This is an incredible online resource. Daniel has published his own book on Bruce, a compendium of backstage candid photos that give us a glimpse into the life of a working musician. We are all in his debt. Secondly, I would like to acknowledge the work of the Cockburn Project. All, or nearly all, of Cockburn's lyrics are available online at their site: www.cockburnproject.net. In addition, they have organized comments by Bruce on songs and albums, as well as set lists for concerts and fan commentary.

Both the Cockburn Project and Gavin's Woodpile publish Tour information as soon as it is available. Another invaluable resource has been the Humans Yahoo Group and his Facebook group. I'm not sure that there is a more dedicated and passionate group of fans anywhere on the web. A number of the Humans group graciously read and commented on portions of the original manuscript. Their comments have helped me immensely in the writing process, particularly in separating the wheat from the chaff and focusing on the things that matter. Particular thanks go to Shirley Frieh, Brad Wittington, Larry L. Chaney, Mike Grace, Doug Rintoul, TurquoiseB, Joan Jacobs and Bobbi Wisby for reading early drafts of sections of the book. While I did not take all of your suggestions, I thought about them deeply. The errors and shortcomings that remain are my own. Thanks also to Audrey, who fanatically finds and posts articles, concert reviews, video, interviews, and other Bruce content. We would be at a loss without you. Audrey also violently questioned my right to write this book. Hopefully, the results are worthy of the subject.

I would also like to thank my good friend and college buddy, Ray Mazurek, Professor of American Studies at Penn State. He also read parts of the manuscript and had insightful and thoughtful comments on the section on Imperialism and Human Rights. I remember our late night discussions of poetry and politics as if they were yesterday, including reading Ginsberg, Kenneth Koch (his poem *Sleeping with Women* was always a favorite), Pound, W. C. Williams, Stevens, Yeats and Eliot aloud to each other.

I owe an infinite debt of gratitude to the Old Town School of Folk Music in Chicago. In addition to teaching me how to play the guitar, they significantly expanded my knowledge and understanding of Folk and Acoustic Music. Through their good graces, I got to experience such luminaries as Doc Watson, Odetta, Josh White Jr., Roger McGuinn, Bob Gibson, John Prine, Michael Smith, Tom Dundee, Ed Holstein and a host of others. My teachers and friends, Bill Hanson, Chris Farrell, Chester Kazynski, Terry Shapiro, and Ed McCarthy inspired me and kept me grounded, especially through those first terrifying times on stage. I should also give thanks here to my mother, who gave me my first guitar at age 25, because she had no idea what to get me for Christmas. It was one of the great happy accidents of my life.

I also owe a significant debt to a sadly defunct little coffeehouse and bar in Austin Texas, coincidentally named Chicago House. Peg and Glynda gave me a place to play when I was starting to come into my own as a songwriter and performer. I still remember fondly those heady days in the mid to late 80's when it seemed like anything was possible. I also got to listen firsthand to Texas songwriters like Joe Ely, Butch Hancock, Jimmie Dale Gilmore and personal favorites Jimmy LaFave, Betty Elders, David Rodriguez, and James McMurtry. Thanks also to David Olbermann of KUT radio who always supported my music.

Last, but not least, many thanks to Laura, who has always gone above and beyond to support my music and writing. It is not always easy being a musician's wife. The many hours spent sitting by yourself in near empty clubs, hoping that a few friends or fans will show up is as hard or harder on the wife than it is on the musician. At least I get to close my eyes and sing a song, pretending for a moment or two that I am performing in a packed arena.

Notes

Preface and Introduction

ⁱ Bruce Cockburn. The Gift, Big Circumstance, True North Records, 1988.

ⁱⁱ http://www.folk.org/page/peoplesvoice

ⁱⁱⁱ Transcript of acceptance speech, published on http://cockburnproject.net

^{iv} Craig MacInnes. "In Praise of Bruceness," Ottawa Citizen, March 4, 2001. Reprinted on http://www.brucecockburn.org/woodpile_keebler_2001.pdf

^v Craig MacInnes. "In Praise of Bruceness," Ottawa Citizen, March 4, 2001. Reprinted on http://www.brucecockburn.org/woodpile_keebler_2001.pdf

^{vi} Bob Gersztyn. "Bruce Cockburn Part 2", Folkwax Ezine. November 16, 2006. The Folkwax Website is no longer available. You can find a copy of this interview at http://www.cockburnproject.net in the News Archive.

^{vi} Bruce Cockburn. Hills of Morning. Dancing in the Dragon's Jaw. True North Records, 1979.

Chapter 1: Origins

¹ Cathleen Falsani. Interview with Bruce Cockburn, 2006. http://cathleenfalsani.com/2011/03/22/godstuff-from-the-way-back-machine-the-06-bruce-cockburn-god-factor-interview/

² Bruce Cockburn. "Bruce Cockburn May Change Your Mind: Guitars"

Magnet Magazine, March 23, 2011.
http://www.magnetmagazine.com/?s=Bruce+Cockburn,

[3] Michael Geisterfer. "On the Road with Bruce Cockburn" Gavin's
Woodpile, September 9, 2004.
http://www.brucecockburn.org/media_2004.htm (need permission to
quote)

[4] Dennis Cook. "Bruce Cockburn: Water into Wine", JamBase, 2009.
http://www.jambase.com/Articles/18077/Bruce-Cockburn-Water-Into-
Wine/0

[5] Ibid.

[6] Jeffrey Pepper Rodgers. "Bruce Cockburn Lesson: Your insider tour to
Cockburn's brilliant one-man-band guitar style," Acoustic Guitar
Magazine, July 2009.
http://www.acousticguitar.com/article/default.aspx?articleid=24632

[7] Ibid.

[8] Kevin Ransom. "Bruce Cockburn topical as ever on new live CD," Ann
Arbor News, Ann Arbor, Michigan, April 18, 2009. Reprinted on
http://www.brucecockburn.org/media_2009.htm

[9] Daniel Keebler, Gavin's Woodpile.
http://www.brucecockburn.org/biography_1960s.htm

[10] Mark Small. "Living in the Present Tense with Bruce Cockburn,"
Gavin's Woodpile, Issue #50, April, 2002. Available at
http://www.brucecockburn.org/woodpile_keebler_2002.pdf

[11] Daniel Keebler, Gavin's Woodpile.
http://www.brucecockburn.org/biography_1960s.htm

[12] From World of Wonders Tour Program, circa 1986. posted on
www.thecockburnproject.net

[13] from "Singer Follows 'Morality' to Success" by Salvatore Caputo, The Arizona Republic, 6 October 1995. Posted on www.thecockburnproject.net

[14] For example: Eric Anderson, Joan Baez, Jim Croce, Tim Hardin, Tim Buckley, Tom Rush, Phil Ochs, Country Joe, Arlo Guthrie, Tom Paxton, Mason Williams, Judy Collins, British Groups like Fairport Convention and Pentangle. The list is probably endless.

[15] Alan Niester. "True North's strong spirit," The Globe and Mail, Toronto, March 29, 2006. Posted on http://www.brucecockburn.org/media_2006.htm

[16] Bernie Finkelstein. True North: A Life Inside the Music Business, MClelland & Stewart, 2012. Chapter 8, Kindle Edition.

[17] Mark Small. "Living in the Present Tense with Bruce Cockburn," Gavin's Woodpile, Issue #50, April, 2002. Available at http://www.brucecockburn.org/woodpile_keebler_2002.pdf

[18] Bruce Cockburn and Greg King. Rumours of Glory, HarperOne, 2014, p. 109.

Chapter 2: On The Road

[1] Bruce Cockburn. Going to the Country, Bruce Cockburn, True North Records, 1970.

[2] Adam Levy. "Songwriting Advice from Bruce Cockburn," Acoustic Guitar, July 2012. Available at http://www.acguitar.com/article/default.aspx?articleid=26946

[3] Arthur McGregor, ed. "All the Diamonds: Selected Songs from 1969-1979" (songbook), OFC Publications, Ottawa, 1986, p. 4.

[4] Bruce Cockburn. Silver Wheels, In the Falling Dark, True North Records, 1976.

[5] David Dye. Various Artists: In Their Own Words: a bunch of songwriters sittin' around singing, Vol. 2, The Bottom Line, NY, NY, April 23, 1995. quoted on http://cockburnproject.net/songs&music/sw.html

[6] Arthur McGregor, ed. "All The Diamonds" songbook, OFC Publications, 1986. Quoted on http://www.cockburnproject.net/songs&music/sw.html

[7] Helen Vendler. "Allen Ginsberg Considers His Country and Himself," NY Times, April 15, 1973. http://www.nytimes.com/books/01/04/08/specials/ginsberg-fall.html

[8] Bruce Cockburn. Northern Lights, Dancing in the Dragon's Jaw, True North Records, 1979.

[9] The Song was written in late August, 1978 driving the 300 km from Calgary to Medicine Hat, Alberta. http://www.cockburnproject.net/songs&music/nl.html and google maps.

[10] http://en.wikipedia.org/wiki/Stigmata

[11] Bruce Cockburn. Life Short Call Now, Life Short Call Now, True North Records, 2006.

[12] Bruce Cockburn. The Iris of the World, Small Source of Comfort, True North Records, 2011.

[13] Bruce Cockburn. January in the Halifax Airport, Joy Will Find a Way, True North Records, 1975.

[14] Bruce Cockburn. Night Train, The Charity of Night, True North Records, 1996.

[15] Bruce Cockburn and Greg King. Rumours of Glory, HarperOne, 2014, p. 413.

[16] http://en.wikipedia.org/wiki/Ch%C3%A2teau_d'If

[17] Bruce Cockburn. How I Spent My Fall Vacation, Humans, True North Records, 1980.

[18] RCA "Special Radio Series" LP, Volume Two (1980). Quoted on http://www.cockburnproject.net/songs&music/hismfv.html

[19] Bernie Finkelstein, Bruce's long-time friend, manager and the former owner of True North Records.

[20] Dennis Cook. "Bruce Cockburn: Water into Wine", JamBase, 2009. http://www.jambase.com/Articles/18077/Bruce-Cockburn-Water-Into-Wine/0

[21] Ibid.

[22] Bruce Cockburn. Tokyo, Humans, True North Records, 1980.

[23] Bruce Cockburn. Berlin Tonight, World of Wonders, True North Records, 1986.

[24] Bruce Cockburn. Radium Rain, Big Circumstance, True North Records,1988.

[25] I wonder if Bruce thought of the old Burt Bacharach song, *Raindrops Keep Falling on My Head* after he wrote this line. It makes an interesting contrast.

[26] Bruce Cockburn, Never so Free, "Salt, Sun, and Time," True North Records, 1974.

[27] Arthur MacGregor, ed. "All The Diamonds" songbook, , OFC Publications 1986. Quoted on http://www.cockburnproject.net/songs&music/nsf.html

> "...the rugged, witch-misted coasts of Devon and Cornwall...July days in Britain when the sun actually shone."

[28] Bruce Cockburn. Waiting for the Moon, The Trouble with Normal, True North Records, 1983.

[29] Bruce Cockburn. Dancing in Paradise, World of Wonders, True North Records, 1986.

[30] http://en.wikipedia.org/wiki/Jim_Reeves

[31] Bruce Cockburn. Down Here Tonight, World of Wonders, True North Records, 1986.

[32] Arthur McGregor, ed. "Rumours of Glory 1980-1990" (songbook), OFC Publications, Ottawa, 1990. Quoted on http://www.cockburnproject.net/

[33] Bruce Cockburn. Tibetan Side of Town, Big Circumstance, True North Records, 1988.

[34] Arthur McGregor, ed. "Rumours of Glory 1980-1990" (songbook), OFC Publications, Ottawa, 1990. quoted on http://www.cockburnproject.net/tsot.html

[35] Bruce Cockburn. Dust and Diesel, Stealing Fire, True North Records, 1984.

[36] William Ruhlmann. "Bruce Cockburn - A Burning Light and All the Rest", Goldmine magazine, 3 April 1992. Quoted on http://www.cockburnproject.net/songs&music/dad.html

[37] Bruce Cockburn. The Coming Rains, The Charity of Night, True North Records, 1996.

[38] Bruce Cockburn. The Mines of Mozambique, The Charity of Night, True North Records, 1996.

[39] Kim Bolan. "Mines still threat in Mozambique, Cockburn says: Cross-country tour precedes visit to African country", *The Vancouver Sun*, 26 September 1995. Quoted on

---

http://www.cockburnproject.net/songs&music/tmom.html

[40] Bruce Cockburn. Postcards from Cambodia, You've Never Seen Everything, True North Records, 2003.

[41] http://www.cockburnproject.net/songs&music/pfc.html

[42] Bruce Cockburn and Greg King. Rumours of Glory, HarperOne, 2014, p. 469.

[43] Bruce Cockburn. Santiago Dawn, World of Wonders, True North Records, 1986.

[44] Bruce does not play a traditional Charango. His was made by luthier Linda Manzer, based on the original instrument. It looks like a very small guitar and sounds a little like a mandolin.

[45] Bruce Cockburn. Strange Waters, The Charity of Night, True North Records, 1996.

[45] Bruce Cockburn and Greg King. Rumours of Glory, HarperOne, 2014, p. 267.

Chapter 3: Spirituality in the Early Works

[1] Brian J. Walsh. Kicking at the Darkness: Bruce Cockburn and the Christian Imagination, Brazos Press, 2011, location 354/6658. Kindle Ed.

[2] Ibid.

[3] Bruce Cockburn. Answers to questions asked by the Humans discussion list. July-November 1995. Quoted on http://www.cockburnproject.net.

[4] Wikipedia. Thomas Merton. http://en.wikipedia.org/wiki/Thomas_Merton

[5] Wikipedia. Chogyam Trungpa.
http://en.wikipedia.org/wiki/Ch%C3%B6gyam_Trungpa

[6] http://www.diamond-sutra.com/diamond_sutra_text/page32.html

[7] Bruce Cockburn. To Raise the Morning Star, Stealing Fire, True North Records, 1984.

[8] William Ruhlmann. "Bruce Cockburn - A Burning Light and All the Rest," Goldmine magazine, 3 April 1992. Quoted on http://cockburnproject.net/albums/saltsunandtime.html

[9] Alex Roslin. "Christian soldier finds hope in a fallen world," Prairie Dog News, August 2, 2007.
http://albloggedup.blogspot.com/2007/09/bruce-cockburn.html.
Reprinted on http://www.brucecockburn.org/media_2007.htm

[10] Bruce Cockburn. Nanzen Ji, Further Adventures of, True North Records, 1978.

[11] http://www.yamasa.org/japan/english/destinations/kyoto/nanzenji.html

[12] Arthur McGregor, ed. "All The Diamonds" songbook. OFC Publications, 1986. Quoted on http://www.cockburnproject.net/songs&music/bsky.html

[13] Here are the verses parsed out as the two "stories."

> Geese come rushing on a river of wind
> Wild music ripples like a wake behind
> Go higher, go higher where the wind is all
> Where the bullets get tired and fall
> They fly out of vision taking part of my soul
>
> Well, maybe together we can touch down whole
> I never saw the colours in the northern dark
> But there were all those people floating like Noah's Ark
> And we all rush away on a river of wind
> But if I live I'll be coming back again

14 Jesse James DeConto, "Camp Meeting at the Wild Goose Festival," The Christian Century, July 25, 2011. http://christiancentury.org/article/2011-07/camp-meeting

15 Bruce Cockburn. Mystery, Life Short Call Now, True North Records, 2006.

16 Bob Gersztyn. "Bruce Cockburn Part 2", Folkwax Ezine. November 16, 2006. The Folkwax Website is no longer available.

17 Cathleen Falsani. Interview with Bruce Cockburn, 2006. http://cathleenfalsani.com/2011/03/22/godstuff-from-the-way-back-machine-the-06-bruce-cockburn-god-factor-interview/

18 Bruce Cockburn. Answers to questions asked by the Humans discussion list. July-November 1995. Quoted on http://www.cockburnproject.net.

19 Bruce Cockburn and Greg King. Rumours of Glory, HarperOne, 2014, p. 29.

20 Christine M. Bochen, ed., *Thomas Merton: Essential Writings*, Orbis Books, New York, NY, 2012, p. 55.

21 Bruce Cockburn: Live at Hastings Lake, Alberta, Lutheran Student Movement National Study Conference. Recorded 30 & 31 August 1979. Transcribed by Stephen Larson. Submitted by Nigel Parry. Quoted on http://www.cockburnproject.net/songs&music/atd.html.

22 http://www.diamond-sutra.com/diamond_sutra_text/page13.html

23 Brian J. Walsh. Kicking at the Darkness: Bruce Cockburn and the Christian Imagination, Brazos Press, 2011, Kindle Ed.

24 http://www.jesuswalk.com/christian-symbols/ship.htm

25 Christine M. Bochen, ed., *Thomas Merton: Essential Writings*, Orbis, New York, NY, 2012, p. 61.

[26] Ibid.

[27] Arthur McGregor, ed. "All The Diamonds" songbook, OFC Publications 1986. Quoted on http://www.cockburnproject.net/songs&music/atd.html

[28] World Of Wonders Tour Program, circa 1986. Quoted on http://www.cockburnproject.net/songs&music/atd.html

[29] Bruce Cockburn. Album notes, Night Vision, True North Records, 1973. Quoted on http://www.cockburnproject.net/albums/nightvision.html

[30] Described in more detail in my song, *Waiting for the Bombs to Fall*. Jim Heald. Waiting for the Bombs to Fall, Wings of Time, Missing Link Music, 1997.

[31] Paul Zollo. *Songwriters on Songwriting*. Second Da Capo Press, 2003, p. 546.

> "I have a relative who is involved in one of those kinds of government jobs where they can't say what they do. The part you can say involves monitoring other people's radio transmissions and breaking codes. At that time China and the Soviet Union were almost at war on their mutual border. And both of them had nuclear capabilities. I had dinner with this relative of mine and he said, "We could wake up tomorrow to a nuclear war." Coming from him, it was a serious statement. So I woke up the next morning and it wasn't a nuclear war. [Laughs] It was a real nice day and there was all this good stuff going on and I had a dream that night which is the dream that is referred to in the first verse of the song, where there were lions at the door, but they weren't threatening, it was kind of a peaceful thing. And it reflected a previous dream that was a real nightmare where the lions were threatening."

[32] Quoted on http://www.cockburnproject.net/songs&music/wwtla.html

[33] Charles Williams, *The Place of the Lion*, Mundanus, London, 1931.

Kindle edition. Chapter 1.

[34] Ibid. Chapter 4.

[35] C.S. Lewis. *On Stories: And Other Essays on Literature.* 1982, p. xix & 53. ISBN 0-15-668788-7. *It all Began with a Picture* is reprinted there from the *Radio Times,* 15 July 1960. Quoted on Wikipedia.

[36] Told to Audrey Pearson. Posted 25 November 2002 on http://www.cockburnproject.net/songs&music/wwtla.html

[37] Wikipedia. Charles Williams http://en.wikipedia.org/wiki/Charles_Williams_(British_writer)

[38] J.M.W. Turner (1775-1851). British Landscape Painter. His later work gets very abstract and is filled with color and light, presaging the Impressionists and much Modern Art. Pretty much the only place to see the breadth and depth of his art is in the Tate Gallery in London.

[39] Brian Walsh. Interview with Bruce Cockburn, Calvin College, Part 3, 20 April 2012. http://www.thebrazosblog.com/2012/05/brian-walsh-interviews-bruce-cockburn-parts-3-4/

[40] Bruce Cockburn and Greg King. Rumours of Glory, HarperOne, p. 151.

[41] Reported by Audrey Pearson on Humans, 15 February 2000. Quoted on http://www.cockburnproject.net/songs&music/feastof.html

[42] Bruce Cockburn and Greg King. Rumours of Glory, HarperOne, p. 160.

[43] Brian Walsh. Interview with Bruce Cockburn, Calvin College, Part 2, 20 April 2012. http://www.thebrazosblog.com/2012/05/brian-walsh-interviews-bruce-cockburn-part-2/

[44] Phil Catalfo. Interview with Bruce Cockburn, "Music That Matters" programme, New Dimensions Radio, San Francisco, California,15 July 1986. Quoted on http://www.cockburnproject.net/albums/dancinginthedragonsjaws.html

[45] Charles Williams, *The Place of the Lion*, Mundanus, London, 1931. Kindle edition. Chapter 10.

[46] Arthur McGregor, ed. "All The Diamonds" songbook, OFC Publications 1986. Quoted on http://www.cockburnproject.net/songs&music/cd.html

[47] http://www.britannica.com/EBchecked/topic/141380/Coyote

[48] Ibid.

[49] Genesis 1:2. King James Bible. http://www.kingjamesbible.com/B01C001.htm

[50] Bruce Cockburn. Badlands Flashback, Dancing in the Dragon's Jaw, True North Records, 1979. Translation from http://www.cockburnproject.net/songs&music/bf.html

[51] Arthur McGregor, ed. "All The Diamonds" songbook. OFC Publications 1986. Quoted on http://www.cockburnproject.net/songs&music/ib.html

> "New York, street life under the angular ribbons of sky shaped around the tops of buildings - a book of poems by the Japanese writer Kenji Miyazawa- and an acute awareness of the absence of a work visa for the gig at the Other End."

[52] Brian J. Walsh. Kicking at the Darkness: Bruce Cockburn and the Christian Imagination, Brazos Press, 2011, Chapter 7, location xxx/6658. Kindle Ed.

[53] http://www.holymtn.com/gods/shiva.htm. This information can be obtained from many sources. This was simply the most succinct statement that I could find on the subject.

Chapter 4: Earthly and Spiritual Love

[1] "You touch me like the pressure of the stars on the darkness."

[2] Bruce Cockburn. Love Song, High Winds White Sky, True North Records, 1971.

[3] Bruce Cockburn. High Winds White Sky, High Winds White Sky, True North Records, 1971.

[4] Arthur McGregor, ed. "All The Diamonds" songbook, OFC Publications 1986. Quoted on http://www.cockburnproject.net/songs&music/hwws.html

[5] The song is undated and could have been written before he was married.

[6] Bruce Cockburn. Stained Glass, "Sun, Salt, and Time," True North Records, 1974.

[7] Django Reinhardt, 1910-1953. A Gypsy, born in Belgium. One of the great guitar players of all time. He had an unusual style as a result of getting seriously burned in a fire as a youth and losing the use of two fingers on his left hand. http://en.wikipedia.org/wiki/Django_Reinhardt

[8] Bruce Cockburn and Rik Emmett. Nuages. 1981. http://www.youtube.com/watch?v=E-Y_2iTZNKY

[9] Bruce Cockburn, A Long Time Love Song, Joy Will Find a Way, True North Records, 1975.

[10] Arthur McGregor, ed. "All The Diamonds" songbook, OFC Publications 1986. Quoted on http://www.cockburnproject.net

[11] Bruce Cockburn. Little Seahorse, In the Falling Dark, True North Records, 1976.

[12] Bruce Cockburn. After the Rain, Dancing in the Dragon's Jaw, True North Records, 1979.

[13] Bruce Cockburn. Comments at "Circles In The Stream" concert. 1977. Paraphrased and submitted by Julian Morin. Quoted on http://www.cockburnproject.net/songs&music/atr.html

[14] http://psychcentral.com/lib/2006/the-5-stages-of-loss-and-grief/

[15] Stephen Holden. "Bruce Cockburn's Quiet Optimism", High Fidelity, 1981. Quoted on http://www.cockburnproject.net/albums/humans.html

[16] Bruce Cockburn. More not More, Humans, True North Records, 1980.

[17] Wanda Mallette, Bob Morrison, and Patti Ryan. Looking for Love, Full Moon, 1980.

[18] Bruce Cockburn. You Get Bigger As You go, Humans, True North Records, 1980.

[19] Bruce Cockburn. What About the Bond, Humans, True North Records, 1980.

[20] Bruce Cockburn and Greg King. Rumours of Glory, HarperOne, 2014, p. 186.

[21] Bruce Cockburn. Fascist Architecture, Humans, True North Records, 1980.

[22] Paul Zollo. *Songwriters on Songwriting*. Second Da Capo Press, 2003, p. 547.

[23] Bruce Cockburn and Greg King. Rumours of Glory, HarperOne, 2014, p. 132.

[24] Bruce Cockburn. The Rose Above the Sky, Humans, True North Records, 1980.

[25] Bruce Cockburn. You Pay Your Money and You Take Your Chances, Inner City Front, True North Records, 1981.

[26] Bruce Cockburn. The Strong One, Inner City Front, True North Records, 1981.

[27] Bruce Cockburn. All's Quiet on the Inner City Front, Inner City Front, True North Records, 1981.

[28] Bruce Cockburn. Wanna Go Walking, Inner City Front, True North Records, 1981.

[29] Bernie Finkelstein is referenced in *How I Spent My Fall Vacation*, his wife Kitty in *Laughter,* Tom Kelly in *Tibetan Side of Town* and "Sally" in *Postcards to Cambodia,* apparently one of his traveling companions. This is only an observation. I have no idea how it compares with other songwriters. The Beatles catalog is populated with a seeming cast of thousands, but most of them are obviously fictional or fictionalized. Also keep in mind the old line about the names being changed to protect the innocent. I would suspect that the more personal the song, the less likely it is to name a person.

[30] Bruce Cockburn. And We Dance, Inner City Front, True North Records, 1981.

[31] Arthur McGregor, ed. "Rumours of Glory 1980-1990" (songbook), OFC Publications, Ottawa, 1990. Quoted on http://www.cockburnproject.net/songs&music/awd.html

[32] Bruce Cockburn. Loner, Inner City Front, True North Records, 1981.

[33] Bruce Cockburn. The Coldest Night of the Year, Inner City Front, True North Records, 2002 (reissue).

Chapter 5: Lovers in Dangerous Times

[1] Bruce Cockburn. Going Up Against Chaos, The Trouble With Normal, True North Records, 1983.

[2] Bruce Cockburn. Sahara Gold, Stealing Fire, True North Records, 1984.

[3] http://www.metmuseum.org/toah/hd/gold/hd_gold.htm

[4] Bruce Cockburn. Making Contact, Stealing Fire, True North Records, 1984. The song *Down Here Tonight*, which appears on **World of Wonders,** was also written on the same trip and has a similar feel and complementary message.

[5] Bruce Cockburn. Lily of the Midnight Sky, World of Wonders, True North Records, 1986.

[6] Bruce Cockburn. See How I Miss You, World of Wonders, True North Records, 1986.

[7] Bruce Cockburn. Don't Feel Your Touch, Big Circumstance, True North Records, 1988.

[8] Bruce Cockburn. Pangs of Love, Big Circumstance, True North Records, 1988.

[9] Bruce Cockburn. Great Big Love, Nothing But a Burning Light, Columbia Records, 1992.

[10] Bruce Cockburn and Greg King. Rumours of Glory, HarperOne, 2014, pp. 331-339

[11] Bruce Cockburn. One of the Best Ones, Nothing But a Burning Light, Columbia Records, 1992.

[12] http://en.wikipedia.org/wiki/The_Nine_Billion_Names_of_God

[13] Bruce Cockburn. Somebody Touched Me, Nothing But a Burning Light, Columbia Records, 1992.

[14] Alanna Nash. Stereo Review, December, 1991. Quoted on http://cockburn.douwevanderzwaag.com/

[15] Bruce Cockburn. Listen for the Laugh, Dart to the Heart, Columbia Records, 1994.

[16] Sedge Thompson. "Interview on West Coast Live at the Kate Wolf Memorial Music Festival", 29 June 2002. Quoted on http://www.cockburnproject.net/songs&music/lftl.html

[17] Bruce Cockburn. All the Ways I Want You, Dart to the Heart, Columbia Records, 1994.

[18] Bruce Cockburn. The Coldest Night of the Year, Inner City Front, True North Records, 2002. This was released as a single originally.

[19] Bruce Cockburn. Southland of the Heart, Dart to the Heart, Columbia Records, 1994.

[20] Bruce Cockburn. Live on My Mind, The Charity of Night, True North Records, 1996.

[21] Bruce Cockburn. Mango, "Breakfast in New Orleans, Dinner in Timbuktu," True North Records, 1999.

[22] Album credits and http://en.wikipedia.org/wiki/Kora_(instrument)

[23] Bruce Cockburn. Isn't That What Friends are For, "Breakfast in New Orleans, Dinner in Timbuktu," True North Records, 1999.

[24] Laura Ellen, "Live in the Sty interview/live performance " program, KPIG radio station, Freedom, California, 24 August 1999. Quoted on http://www.cockburnproject.net/songs&music/itwfaf.html

[25] Gerard Vos, translated into English by Arjan El Fassed. "The Rage of Bruce Cockburn", Platenblad, July, 1999. Quoted on http://www.cockburnproject.net/songs&music/lhf.html

[26] Bruce Cockburn. Open, You've Never Seen Everything, True North Records, 2003.

[27] http://www.themystica.com/mystica/articles/k/kundalini.html

[28] Richard Hoare. Interview -"Catching Up With Cockburn," Gavin's Woodpile, #59, Oct 2003. Available at http://www.brucecockburn.org/woodpile_keebler_2003.pdf

[29] Bruce Cockburn. Wait No More, You've Never Seen Everything, True North Records, 2003.

[30] Bruce Cockburn. See You Tomorrow, You've Never Seen Everything, True North Records, 2003.

[31] Bruce Cockburn. The Mercenary (spoken introduction), Slice of Life, True North Records, 2009.

[32] David Rodriguez. Hurricane, The True Cross, Dejadisc Records, 1992. Information available at http://www.davidrodriguez.nl/index.html. David is another artist who was very simpatico with Bruce. He moved to the Netherlands in the 1990's and his music is somewhat difficult to find, Dejadisc having gone out of business. Some of his material is available on Amazon. He died in 2015.

Chapter 6: Imperialism and Human Rights

[1] Bruce Cockburn and Greg King. Rumours of Glory, HarperOne, 2014, p. 206.

[2] Ibid., p. 210.

[3] Bruce Cockburn. Rumours of Glory, HarperOne, 2014, p. 265.

[4] http://en.wikipedia.org/wiki/Carlos_Fonseca_Amador

[5] http://www.orotravel.com/destination_expanded.php?tid=34

[6] http://en.wikipedia.org/wiki/Tom_Mix

[7] http://en.wikipedia.org/wiki/Vlad_III_Dracula

[8] Most of this section is based on materials in

---

http://en.wikipedia.org/wiki/History_of_Nicaragua

[9] Most of this section is based on materials in
http://en.wikipedia.org/wiki/History_of_Guatemala and
http://en.wikipedia.org/wiki/Jacobo_%C3%81rbenz_Guzm%C3%A1n

[10] Brad Buchholz. "A Rising Northern Star: Canadian Bruce Cockburn Wins More U.S. Converts", *Dallas Morning News*, 12 January 1992. Quoted on http://www.cockburnproject.net/songs&music/iiharl.html

[11] William Ruhlmann."Bruce Cockburn - A Burning Light and All the Rest", Goldmine magazine, 3 April 1992. Quoted on http://www.cockburnproject.net/songs&music/iiharl.html

[12] Brad Wheeler. Bruce Cockburn Set for Luminato Honours - 40 Years of songs to Live By. *The Globe and Mail*, June 16, 2010. Quoted on http://www.cockburnproject.net/songs&music/iiharl.html

[13] Arthur McGregor, ed. "Rumours of Glory 1980-1990" (songbook)., OFC Publications, Ottawa, 1990. Quoted on http://www.cockburnproject.net/songs&music/sl.html

[14] Bruce Cockburn. Live performance at Massey Hall, Toronto, Canada, 25 March 2000. Submitted by David Macklin. Quoted on http://www.cockburnproject.net/songs&music/sl.html

[15] Bruce Cockburn. Mighty Trucks of Midnight, Nothing But a Burning Light, True North Records, 1991.

[16] Bruce Cockburn. Trickle Down, You've Never Seen Everything, True North Records, 2003.

[17] Jeffrey Pepper Rodgers. "Traveling Light Bruce Cockburn enlivens his new songs with forays into electronica and modern jazz," Acoustic Guitar, September 2003. Quoted on http://www.cockburnproject.net/songs&music/td.html

Chapter 7: Indian Wars

[1] Arthur McGregor, ed. "Rumours of Glory 1980-1990" (songbook), OFC Publications, Ottawa, 1990.

[2] Bruce Cockburn. Hoop Dancer, The Trouble with Normal, True North Records, 1983.

[3] The Encyclopedia of Saskatchewan,
http://esask.uregina.ca/entry/almighty_voice_1875-97.html

[4] Wikipedia. Ghost of Anna Mae.
http://en.wikipedia.org/wiki/Anna_Mae_Aquash

[5] Lahri Bond."Bruce Cockburn an Update", Dirty Linen (#40), June/July 1992. Quoted on
http://www.cockburnproject.net/songs&music/adlm.html

[6] Bruce Cockburn. Kit Carson, Nothing But a Burning Light, True North Records, 1991.

[7] Lahri Bond. "Bruce Cockburn an Update" Dirty Linen (#40), June/July 1992. Quoted on http://www.cockburnproject.net/songs&music/kc.html

[8] Ibid.

[9] Bruce Cockburn. Indian Wars, Nothing But a Burning Light, True North Records, 1991.

[10] The other two books are *The Magic Journey* and *The Nirvana Blues*. For my money, *The Magic Journey* is the best of the three books and takes a longer term look at the transformation of the landscape and the politics behind it.

[11] Bruce Cockburn. Put Our Hearts Together, The Trouble with Normal, True North Records, 1983.

[12] Bruce Cockburn. To Raise the Morning Star, Stealing Fire, True North Records, 1984.

13 Eunice Amarantides. "Singing in a Dangerous Time", *TheOtherSide*, January/February 1985. Quoted on http://www.cockburnproject.net/songs&music/trtms.html

Chapter 8: Meditations on the Journey

1 Translated by Michael Brase
http://www.japanandstuff.com/page20/page20.html

2 Bruce Cockburn. Lovers in a Dangerous Time, Stealing Fire, True North Records, 1984.

3 Brad Wheeler. "Bruce Cockburn Set for Luminato Honours - 40 Years of songs to Live By", The Globe and Mail. 15 June 2010.

4 Bruce Cockburn. Answers to questions asked by the Humans discussion list. July-November 1995. Quoted on http://www.cockburnproject.net/songs&music/gw.html

5 Bruce Cockburn. Gavin's Woodpile. In the Falling Dark. True North Records, 1976.

6 James McMurtry wrote a whole song on a similar subject. *Terry's Off the Tracks*. Too Long in the Wasteland. Columbia Records. 1989.

> Terry's off the track
> Sent him away and he won't be coming back for a while
> 15 years old, one night he lost control
> Straight shots, staggered out to the parking lot
> Someone called him names, he was in no mood for games
> He was irate, courting fate.
>
> And it all went off in the blink of an eye
> There's no turning back or questioning why
> It was the heat of the moment, a flash in the pan
> Blood on the gravel and a longneck in his hand.

[7] Bruce Cockburn and Greg King. Rumours of Glory, HarperOne, 2014, p. 149.

[8] Stephen Holden. "Bruce Cockburn's Quiet Optimism", High Fidelity, 1981. Quoted on http://www.cockburnproject.net/songs&music/rog.html

[9] Arthur McGregor, ed. "Rumours of Glory 1980-1990" (songbook), OFC Publications, Ottawa, 1990. Quoted on http://www.cockburnproject.net/songs&music/rog.html

[10] Bruce Cockburn. Rumours of Glory, Humans, True North Records, 1981.

[11] Bruce Cockburn and Greg King. Rumours of Glory, HarperOne, 2014, p. 197.
[12] Bruce Cockburn. Child of the Wind, Nothing But a Burning Light, Columbia Records, 1992.

[13] http://www.cockburnproject.net/songs&music/cotw.html

[14] Bruce Cockburn. Planet of the Clowns, The Trouble with Normal, True North Records, 1983.

[15] Eliza Gilkyson. Beautiful World, 2008. Red House Records. http://www.elizagilkyson.com

[16] Paul Zollo. *Songwriters on Songwriting*. Second Da Capo Press, 2003, p. 547.

[17] Bruce Cockburn. Pacing the Cage, The Charity of Night, True North Records, 1996.

[18] Alexander Varty. "Night Reveals Clues, Not Answers - Bruce Cockburn internalizes his angst while looking forward to an awakening", The Georgia Straight, 22-29 May 1997. Quoted on http://www.cockburnproject.net/songs&music/ptc.html

19 http://www.christnotes.org/bible.php?q=Psalm+23

20 Bruce Cockburn and Greg King. Rumours of Glory, HarperOne, 2014, p. 411.

21 Ibid, p 410.

22 Ibid, p. 411.

23 Bruce Cockburn. Understanding Nothing, Big Circumstance, True North Records, 1988.

24 Bruce Cockburn. Closer to the Light, Dart to the Heart, Columbia Records, 1994.

25 Bruce Cockburn. Lord of the Starfields, In the Falling Dark, True North Records,. 1976.

26 Bruce Cockburn. Spoken outro to *Joy Will Find A Way* from the fifth annual 'Christmas With Cockburn' show on the Columbia Radio Hour, Sony Music Studio, New York City, 17 December 1995. Quoted on http://www.cockburnproject.net/songs&music/jwfaw.html

27 "Bruce Cockburn, Breakfast in New Orleans, Dinner in Timbuktu", Ryko press release, undated, circa August 1999. Quoted on http://www.cockburnproject.net/songs&music/umwyc.html

28 Bruce Cockburn and Greg King. Rumours of Glory, HarperOne, 2014, pp. 449-450.

29 Joshua Hammer. The Bad-Ass Librarians of Timbuktu, Simon & Shuster, 2016, p. 168.

30 Bruce Cockburn. Put it in Your Heart, You've Never Seen Everything, True North Records, 2003. Paraphrased.

31 Bruce Cockburn, The Charity of Night, The Charity of Night, True North Records, 1996.

[32] Bruce Cockburn and Greg King, Rumours of Glory, HarperOne, 2014, p. 49.

[33] Ibid, p. 285-289.

[34] Ibid, pp. 270-380 and 420-421.

[35] Mike Boehm. "Bruce Cockburn: Interior Motive", *Los Angeles Times*, 22 November 1994. Quoted on http://www.cockburnproject.net/songs&music/tmatc.html

Chapter 9: World of Wonders: Spirit in the Later Works

[1] Bruce Cockburn and Greg King. Rumours of Glory, HarperOne, 2014, pp. 150-151.

[2] Bruce Cockburn. Lovers in a Dangerous Time, Stealing Fire, True North Records, 1984.

[3] Bruce Cockburn. The Gift, Big Circumstance, True North Records, 1988.

[4] Daniel B. Smith. "What is Art for?" New York Times, Nov 14, 2008. http://www.nytimes.com/2008/11/16/magazine/16hyde-t.html?pagewanted=all

[5] Bruce Cockburn. You've Never Seen Everything, You've Never Seen Everything, True North Records, 2003.

[6] Bruce Cockburn. Broken Wheel, Inner City Front, True North Records, 1981.

[7] Genesis 1:26. http://www.bibleontheweb.com/bible.asp.

[8] Bruce Cockburn. Originally released as a B-side of True North single for "You Pay Your Money and You Take Your Chance" (1981). Notes from http://www.cockburnproject.net/songs&music/tlgof.html

[9] Johnny Walker. Radio Interview, BBC Radio 1, 1990. Transcribed by David Newton. Quoted on
http://www.cockburnproject.net/songs&music/satsd.html

[10] Bruce Cockburn. Conversation after a performance in Indianapolis. 19 June 1997. Reported by Karen Derrick. Quoted on
http://www.cockburnproject.net/songs&music/satsd.html

[11] Yes, Christ was born in the stable. Big Circumstance is just as much his birth as the birth of ordinary people.

[12] Bruce Cockburn and Greg King. Rumours of Glory, HarperOne, 2014, p. 316.
[13] http://www.bartleby.com/108/19/23.html

[14] Liane Hansen. "Bruce Cockburn, Musician, Shares History and Songs of his New CD, Breakfast in New Orleans, Dinner in Timbuktu", Weekend Edition Sunday, National Public Radio, February 6, 2000. Quoted on http://www.cockburnproject.net/songs/lnotw.html.

Sam Phillips was married to T Bone Burnett, though they have subsequently divorced. Bruce told more or less the same story at a performance that I saw at the Birchmere in Alexandria, Virginia in 1998. The story is also repeated in *Rumours of Glory* on page 446-447.

[15] Bruce Cockburn. Closer to the Light, Dart to the Heart, True North Records, 1994.

[16] Bruce Cockburn. Everywhere Dance, You've Never Seen Everything, True North Records, 2003.

[17] Bruce Cockburn. Boundless, Small Source of Comfort, True North Records, 2011.

[18] http://www.biblewheel.com/topics/seven_meaning.asp

[19] Brian Walsh. Interview with Bruce Cockburn, Calvin College, Part 5, 20 April 2012.. Starting at about 1:35. Available at

http://www.thebrazosblog.com/2012/05/brian-walsh-interviews-bruce-cockburn-parts-5-6/. I'm not sure whether he was referring to the 2004 Recall Election or the December 2006 election.

[20] Cathleen Falsani. Interview with Bruce Cockburn, 2006. http://cathleenfalsani.com/2011/03/22/godstuff-from-the-way-back-machine-the-06-bruce-cockburn-god-factor-interview/

[21] Daniel Lumpkin. "Interview: Bruce Cockburn", Christianity Today http://www.christianitytoday.com/ct/music/interviews/2012/brucecockb urn-january24.html?start=1

[22] William Ruhlmann. "Bruce Cockburn - A Burning Light and All the Rest", Goldmine magazine, 3 April 1992. Quoted on http://cockburnproject.net/albums/saltsunandtime.html

[23] Bruce Cockburn. Justice, Inner City Front, True North Records, 1981.

[24] Bruce Cockburn. Gospel of Bondage, Big Circumstance, True North Records, 1988.

[25] Derk Richardson. "Pop Proselytizing: Bruce Cockburn. At Zellerbach Hall, U.C. at Berkeley, Friday, Feb. 27th.", The San Francisco Bay Guardian, 9 March 1988. Quoted on http://www.cockburnproject.net/songs&music/gob.html

[26]Brad Buchholz. "A Rising Northern Star: Canadian Bruce Cockburn Wins More U.S. Converts", *Dallas Morning News*, 12 January 1992. Quoted on http://www.cockburnproject.net/songs&music/gob.html

[27] Bruce Cockburn. Put it in Your Heart, You've Never Seen Everything, True North Records, 2003.

[28] Bruce Cockburn. Justice. Inner City Front. 1981.

[29] Bruce Cockburn and Greg King. Rumours of Glory, HarperOne, 2014, p. 455.

[30] Ibid. p. 455.

[31] Ibid. p. 456.

[32] Bruce Cockburn. Each One Lost, Small Source of Comfort, True North Records, 2011.

Chapter 10: Instrumental Music and Jazz

[1] Shelley Gummeson. "Bruce Cockburn's Restless Spirit," CFBX Radio Program Guide, May 2012. http://www.thex.ca/IndexMay12.pdf

[2] Django Reinhardt, 1910-1953. A Gypsy, born in Belgium. One of the great guitar players of all time. He had an unusual style as a result of getting seriously burned in a fire as a youth and losing the use of two fingers on his left hand. http://en.wikipedia.org/wiki/Django_Reinhardt

[3] Adam Levy. "Songwriting Advice from Bruce Cockburn," Acoustic Guitar, July 2012. Available at http://www.acguitar.com/article/default.aspx?articleid=26946

[4] Bruce Cockburn. Ting/the Cauldron, High Winds White Sky, True North Records, 1971.

[5] Bruce Cockburn. Water into Wine, In the Falling Dark, True North Records, 1976.

[6] Bruce Cockburn, Deep Lake, Breakfast in New Orleans, True North Records, 1998.

[7] Bruce Cockburn, Jerusalem Poker, Life Short Call Now, True North Records, 2003.

[8] Bruce Cockburn. Ancestors, Small Source of Comfort, True North Records, 2011.

[9] Bruce Cockburn. Sunwheel Dance, Sunwheel Dance, True North Records, 1972.

[10] Music by Fox Watson is available on iTunes and he has a Facebook page.

[11] Arthur McGregor, ed. "All the Diamonds: Selected Songs from 1969-1979" (songbook), OFC Publications, Ottawa, 1986. Quoted on http://www.cockburnproject.net/songs&music/sdance.html

[12] Ibid.

[13] Bruce Cockburn. Foxglove, Night Vision, True North Records, 1973.

[14] Obviously, many of Bruce's non-instrumental songs continued in a folk or roots vein. There are also a few other songs based on fiddle tunes, such as *Bright Sky*. Bruce also only recorded a couple of instrumentals in the 1980's that we know of.

[15] Bruce Cockburn. When It's Gone It's Gone, Nothing But a Burning Light, True North Records, 1991.

[16] Bruce Cockburn. Train in the Rain, Dart to the Heart, True North Records, 1994.

[17] Bruce Cockburn. Sunrise on the Mississippi, Dart to the Heart, True North Records, 1994.

[18] Bruce Cockburn. Islands in a Black Sky, Night Vision, True North Records, 1973.

[19] James Jensen. Interview with Bruce Cockburn, Sunset Sound, Los Angeles, circa Spring 1993. Quoted on http://www.cockburnproject.net/songs&music/iiabs.html

[20] Ibid.

[21] Bruce Cockburn. Elegy, Speechless, True North Records, 2005.

[22] Arthur McGregor, ed. "All The Diamonds" songbook, OFC

Publications 1986. Quoted on
http://www.cockburnproject.net/songs&music/ssat.html.

[23] http://en.wikipedia.org/wiki/Loren_Eiseley

[24] Bruce Cockburn. Red Ships Take off in the Distance, Further Adventures Of, True North Records, 1978.

[25] http://www.candyrat.com/artists/DonRoss/

[26] Bruce Cockburn, Peace March, Life Short Call Now, True North Records, 2003.

[27] http://www.andymckee.com/

[28] Bruce Cockburn. Mama Just Wants to Barrelhouse All Night Long, Night Vision, True North Records, 1973. The song is reprised on the live albums Circles in the Stream (1977) and Slice of Life (2009).

[29] Arthur McGregor, ed. "All the Diamonds: Selected Songs from 1969-1979" (songbook), OFC Publications, Ottawa, 1986, p. 26.

[30] Bruce Cockburn. Deja Vu, Night Vision, True North Records, 1973.

[31] Arthur McGregor, ed. "All The Diamonds" songbook, OFC Publications 1986. Quoted on http://www.cockburnproject.net/songs&music/dv.html

[32] Bruce Cockburn. Rise and Fall, Speechless, True North Records, 2005.

[33] Bruce Cockburn. King Kong Goes to Tallahassee, Speechless, True North Records, 2005.

[34] Lynn Saxberg "Interview with Bruce Cockburn," The Ottawa Citizen, 7 September 2005. Quoted on http://www.cockburnproject.net/songs&music/kkgtt.html

[35] Bruce Cockburn, Don't Have to Tell You Why, "Salt, Sun, and Time,"

True North Records, 1974.

[36] Bruce Cockburn, Rouler Sa Bosse, "Salt, Sun, and Time," True North Records, 1974.

[37] Bruce Cockburn. Comments made at his show at the Brock University Centre for the Performing Arts, November 23rd 2005, Speechless Tour, submitted by Joe Orlando. Quoted on http://www.cockburnproject.net/songs&music/rsb.html

[38] Bruce Cockburn. Bohemian 3-Step, Small Source of Comfort, True North Records, 2011.

[39] Bruce Cockburn. Lois on the Autobahn, Small Source of Comfort, True North Records, 2011.

[40] Bruce Cockburn. Comets of Kandahar, Small Source of Comfort, True North Records, 2011.

[41] Press Release- Bruce Cockburn Announces Major North American Tour. 17 January 2011. Quoted on http://www.cockburnproject.net/songs&music/tcok.html

[42] Bruce Cockburn, Nude Descending a Staircase, Life Short Call Now, True North Records, 2003.

[43] Bruce Cockburn. Clocks Don't Bring Tomorrow -- Knives Don't Bring Good News, Night Vision, True North Records, 1973.

[44] Bruce Cockburn, Seeds on the Wind, "Salt, Sun, and Time," True North Records, 1974.

[45] Bruce Cockburn. Cala Luna, The Trouble With Normal, True North Records, 2002.

[46] Bruce Cockburn. The End of All Rivers, Speechless, True North Records, 2005.

[47] Bruce Cockburn. Parnassus and Fog, Small Source of Comfort, True North Records, 2011.

[48] Bruce Cockburn. Giftbearer, In the Falling Dark, True North Records, 1976.

[49] Bruce Cockburn. Radio Shoes, Inner City Front, True North Records, 1981.

[50] Bruce Cockburn, Down to the Delta, Breakfast in New Orleans, True North Records, 1998.

[51] "Bruce Cockburn, Breakfast in New Orleans, Dinner in Timbuktu", Ryko press release, undated, circa August 1999. Quoted on http://www.cockburnproject.net/songs&music/dttd.html

Chapter 11: Live Recordings

[1] https://en.wikipedia.org/wiki/Massey_Hall

[2] http://cockburnproject.net/songs&music/ddrabm.html spoken intro from the fourth annual 'Christmas With Cockburn' show on the Columbia Radio Hour, New York City, 11 December 1994.

[3] http://cockburnproject.net/songs&music/ib.html

[4] http://cockburnproject.net/songs&music/hb.html

[5] http://cockburnproject.net/songs&music/hb.html

[6] http://cockburnproject.net/songs&music/ci.html

[7] http://cockburnproject.net/songs&music/ls.html

[8] http://brucecockburn.org/links/circles-in-the-stream-tour/index.html

[9] Bruce Cockburn and Greg King. Rumours of Glory, HarperOne, 2014, p. 158.

[10] https://en.wikipedia.org/wiki/Ontario_Place_(theme_park)

[11] http://cockburnproject.net/albums/brucecockburnlive.html

[12] https://en.wikipedia.org/wiki/Chapman_Stick

[13] McGregor, Arthur, ed. "Rumours of Glory 1980-1990" (songbook), OFC Publications, Ottawa, 1990. p.85.

[14] Bruce Cockburn, You Pay Your Money and You Take Your Chance. CD Liner Notes, 1997.

[15] http://cockburnproject.net/gigs/1997/may3.html

[16] http://cockburnproject.net/songs&music/aaa.html

Chapter 12: You Pay Your Money and You Take Your Chances

[1] Bob Gersztyn. "Bruce Cockburn Part 2", Folkwax Ezine. November 16, 2006. The Folkwax Website is no longer available.

[2] Susan Adams Kauffman. "Fire in an Open Hand", The Other Side magazine, November/December 1999. Quoted on http://www.cockburnproject.net/songs&music/bs.html

[3] Brian Walsh. Interview with Bruce Cockburn, Calvin College, Part 3, 20 April 2012. http://www.thebrazosblog.com/2012/05/brian-walsh-interviews-bruce-cockburn-parts-3-4/

[4] Bruce Cockburn. Strange Waters, The Charity of Night, True North Records, 1996.

5 Scott Simon. "Weekend Edition", 18 January 1997, National Public Radio. Quoted on http://www.cockburnproject.net/songs&music/strange.html

6 Bruce Cockburn. Birmingham Shadows, The Charity of Night, True North Records, 1996.